Devolution and the Scottish Conservatives

MANCHESTER
1824

Manchester University Press

Devolution and the Scottish Conservatives

Banal activism, electioneering and the politics of irrelevance

Alexander Thomas T. Smith

Manchester University Press
Manchester and New York

Distributed in the United States exclusively
by Palgrave Macmillan

Published by Manchester University Press
Oxford Road, Manchester M13 9NR, UK
and Room 400, 175 Fifth Avenue, New York, NY 10010, USA
www.manchesteruniversitypress.co.uk

Distributed in the United States exclusively by
Palgrave Macmillan, 175 Fifth Avenue,
New York, NY 10010, USA

Distributed in Canada exclusively by
UBC Press, University of British Columbia, 2029 West Mall,
Vancouver, BC, Canada V6T 1Z2

British Library Cataloguing-in-Publication Data is available

Library of Congress Cataloging-in-Publication Data is available

ISBN 978 0 7190 9556 6 *paperback*

First published by Manchester University Press in hardback 2011

This paperback edition first published 2014

Printed by Lightning Source

New Ethnographies

Series editor
Alexander Thomas T. Smith

At its best, ethnography has provided a valuable tool for apprehending a world in flux. A couple of years after the Second World War, Max Gluckman founded the Department of Social Anthropology at the University of Manchester. In the years that followed, he and his colleagues built a programme of ethnographic research that drew eclectically on the work of leading anthropologists, economists and sociologists to explore issues of conflict, reconciliation and social justice 'at home' and abroad. Often placing emphasis on detailed analysis of case studies drawn from small-scale societies and organisations, the famous 'Manchester School' in social anthropology built an enviable reputation for methodological innovation in its attempts to explore the pressing political questions of the second half of the twentieth century. Looking back, that era is often thought to constitute a 'gold standard' for how ethnographers might grapple with new challenges and issues in the contemporary world.

The *New Ethnographies* series aims to build on that ethnographic legacy at Manchester. It will publish the best new ethnographic monographs that promote interdisciplinary debate and methodological innovation in the qualitative social sciences. This includes the growing number of books that seek to apprehend the 'new' ethnographic objects of a seemingly brave new world, some recent examples of which have included auditing, democracy and elections, documents, financial markets, human rights, assisted reproductive technologies and political activism. Analysing such objects has often demanded new skills and techniques from the ethnographer. As a result, this series will give voice to those using ethnographic methods across disciplines to innovate, such as through the application of multi-sited fieldwork and the extended comparative case study method. Such innovations have often challenged more traditional ethnographic approaches. *New Ethnographies* therefore seeks to provide a platform for emerging scholars and their more established counterparts engaging with ethnographic methods in new and imaginative ways.

To Iris,
For her encouragement, faith and inspiration

Rachael and Ciara

In memory of my father,
Thomas George Smith (1948–96)

Contents

Acknowledgements

This book explores how the Scottish Conservatives, who had opposed devolution and the movement for a Scottish Parliament during the 1990s, attempted to mobilise politically following their 'wipe out' at the 1997 general election. Cast to the geographical and institutional margins, senior Tory Party strategists in Dumfries and Galloway, a former stronghold for the Conservative Party in Scotland, worked from the assumption that they had endured their own 'crisis' in representation. The material consequences of this crisis included losses of financial and other resources, legitimacy and local knowledge for Tory activists based locally. This book ethnographically describes the processes, practices and relationships that Tory Party activists enacted during the 2003 Scottish and local government elections. Its central theme is that, having asserted that the difficulties they faced constituted problems of knowledge, local Conservatives became 'banal' activists. Believing themselves to be lacking in the data and information necessary for successful mobilisation during parliamentary elections, local Tory Party strategists attempted to address their knowledge 'crisis' by burying themselves in paperwork and petty bureaucracy. Importantly, such practices have often escaped the attention of anthropologists and other scholars of activism because they appear everyday and mundane and are therefore less noticeable. Bringing them into view analytically has important implications for socio-cultural anthropologists, sociologists and other scholars interested in 'new' ethnographic objects like activism, bureaucracy, democracy, elections and modern knowledge practices.

The ethnographic research on which this book draws was conducted in Dumfries and Galloway between September 2001 and July 2003 while I was studying for my PhD in Social Anthropology at the University of Edinburgh. Financial support for this research was provided through a Pre-Dissertation Fieldwork Grant (no. 6747) from the Wenner-Gren Foundation for Anthropological Research. An Overseas Research Students (ORS) Award coupled with a Social Sciences Overseas Studentship from the University of Edinburgh made pursuing this study financially possible for me, as did a number of small grants from the Newby Trust, the Sir Ernest Cassell Educational Trust and the Sir Richard Stapley Educational Trust. Furthermore, this research began in the context of an MSc degree, which I commenced with the support of a British Chevening scholarship funded by the Foreign and Commonwealth office. I also thank the Arkleton Trust, which, in awarding me the David Moore Memorial Award in 2000, gave both financial support and a welcome vote of confidence in my research during its early stages. I thank all of these funding bodies, organisations and charitable trusts for their support.

I remain indebted to many individuals and organisations – both within and outwith Dumfries and Galloway – that helped me during my fieldwork. As is often the case in ethnographic research, they are too numerous to name here. However, I want to make particular mention of the staff and students at the Crichton Campus of the University of Glasgow who provided me with a warm welcome when I arrived in Dumfries and were important in facilitating my early networking throughout the region. I would also like to acknowledge the help I received from the friendly and approachable staff at the Boundary Commission for Scotland and at Dumfries and Galloway Libraries. Finally, this book would not exist without the cooperation and support of the dozens of activists, staff and volunteers with whom I worked in the two Conservative Party Associations within Dumfries and Galloway: the Dumfries Constituency Conservative Association (DCCA) and the Galloway and Upper Nithsdale Conservative Association (GUNCA).

Parts of this book have been presented at conferences, seminars and workshops in Bristol, Cambridge, Chicago, Edinburgh, Keele, London, Manchester, Montreal, San José, Surrey and Washington DC. I am grateful for the feedback and constructive criticism I have received from colleagues. In addition, an earlier version of Chapter 4 was published in the journal *Political and Legal Anthropology Review* (*PoLAR*) (Smith 2006) after being awarded an Honorable Mention in the 2005 Student Paper Prize Competition run by the Association of Political and Legal Anthropology, and parts of Chapter 6 were published in the *Journal of Legal Anthropology* (Smith 2008). I thank Annelise Riles and Narmala Halstead, both editors of these journals at the time, and several anonymous reviewers for constructively engaging with my research. I also want to thank Natasha Maw and Laurie Taylor from BBC Radio Four's *Thinking Allowed* programme for taking an enthusiastic interest in my work. Their show based on my fieldwork was broadcast on Wednesday 24 August 2005.

I have now held a number of postdoctoral fellowships during which I have been able to set aside time to re-draft my PhD research as a book monograph. These have included: a Postdoctoral Fellowship (PTA-026-27-1102) funded by the Economic and Social Research Council (ESRC), which I held at Edinburgh (2006–7); the Sociological Review Fellowship at Keele University (2007–8); and an Institute for Advanced Studies in the Humanities (IASH) Postdoctoral Fellowship, again at Edinburgh (2008). I also held an Early Career Fellowship funded by the Leverhulme Trust (ECF/2008/0125) in the School of Government and Society at the University of Birmingham (2008–10). I am grateful to all of these funding oranisations for their financial support and to the following individuals in particular, who have assisted me along the way: Caroline Baggaley,

Michaela Benson, Francesca Bray, Sarah Green, John Holmwood, Charles Jedrej, Susanne Langer, Susan Manning, Rolland Monro and Anthea Taylor.

I would like to acknowledge the tireless support of my PhD supervisors, Dr Iris Jean-Klein and Dr Jonathan Hearn. Both were sources of inspiration before and during my fieldwork but especially after my return. I have benefited greatly from the many discussions I had with them and for the help they provided me in bringing this study to fruition. Taking on the supervision of my PhD midway through my fieldwork, Iris played a particularly pivotal role in keeping my research on track. At Manchester University Press, Tony Mason was an enthusiastic advocate for this project right from the start and has been an affable interlocutor ever since. Jennifer Howard also provided valuable assistance, as did Sarah Hunt. I am also indebted to an anonymous reader of my manuscript and to Laura Jeffery, who read it and encouraged me. Their constructive criticism has greatly improved the book, although the usual caveats apply: I alone am responsible for any failings or mistakes within the text.

Carrying out ethnographic research in a sparsely populated region of Scotland proved almost impossible without access to private transportation. This was a formidable challenge for an impoverished PhD student. For helping me to overcome such difficulties, and for providing enormous amounts of moral, logistical and other kinds of support throughout my fieldwork (often at very short notice), I am indebted to my parents-in-law Ted and Andrena Thompson. As Hunter S. Thompson (no relative, of course!) once noted (1994: 13–14), when studying politics one finds 'unexpected friends on both sides' and I would like to particularly acknowledge the many conversations I have had with Ted, usually after dinner on a Sunday night. As a long-time member and supporter of the Labour Party, Ted's perspective on local politics always struck me as insightful and refreshing and I believe this research was greatly improved by his valuable counterperspective on the local Conservative Party. I would also like to acknowledge the support of other members of my family, back home in Australia and here in the United Kingdom: Brian Degenhardt, Georgina Smith, Lachlan Smith and my mother, Jane Smith. Sadly, my father Thomas George Smith (1948–96) did not live long enough to see me complete my education in the United Kingdom let alone write this book. If he is looking down on us now, I hope he is pleased with the results.

Finally, I would like to express my love and deepest gratitude to my wife, Rachael Thompson, for her patience and support, as well as our daughter, Ciara. I never anticipated that two such wonderful people would make my coming to Dumfries so much more worthwhile and ultimately change my life.

Note to international readers

For complex and varied historical reasons, the term 'Tory' is often used to describe members and supporters of the Conservative Party in the United Kingdom. To reduce repetition in the text, I have therefore used the labels 'Conservative' and 'Tory' interchangeably. This was a common practice amongst my informants.

Banal activism

On Saturday 9 June 2001, the *Scotsman* newspaper published a cartoon displaying a country road gridlocked with motorists and caravans. As the procession winds around a bend in the distance, they pass a road sign announcing: 'Welcome to Dumfries and Galloway – Unique Habitat of Scotland's Only Tory MP! Amazing Wonders of Nature!' Published days after the 2001 general election, this cartoon satirised the election of the little-known Scottish Conservative candidate Peter Duncan in the rural southwest of Scotland. Following the 'wipe out' of the Scottish Tories at the 1997 general election, this was an unexpected, indeed surprising, achievement. A number of Tory candidates with higher profiles north of the English border, including the Rt Hon. Malcolm Rifkind QC,[1] failed to win back parliamentary seats in 2001 that the Conservatives had held until 1997. Defeating the Scottish National Party (SNP) by just 74 votes in Galloway and Upper Nithsdale, Mr Duncan was the only successful Scottish Conservative candidate at that election.

With their tongues planted firmly in their cheeks, Murdo MacLeod and Jason Allardyce embellished the political joke in an article entitled 'Return of the lesser-spotted Tory' that was published the following day by the *Scotsman*'s sister newspaper *Scotland on Sunday*. Next to a photograph of a smiling Mr Duncan, the two journalists wrote:

> Unsure of his new habitat, the newly reintroduced species emerges blinking into the sunlight. Physically, he is suited to the new environment – one which is naturally his and which he is expected to re-colonise. But he is alone, and perhaps unsure whether he is ready yet. After a century of releasing once-extinct species back into the wild, Scotland last week went a step further and brought back a beast many thought was gone for good: the Scottish Tory. (*Scotland on Sunday*, 10 June 2001)

Mr Duncan's electoral good fortune in Dumfries and Galloway brought to an end a period of Westminster parliamentary history when Scotland could have been described as a 'Tory free' zone.[2] 'The very reappearance of this species has shocked naturalists and political observers alike, who thought the Scottish Tory was gone and forgotten,' MacLeod and Allardyce wrote, 'a victim of political climate change and a failure on its part to adjust to the new habitat.' Even in rural

Galloway, one could not apparently assume that the 'Tory transplantation' would be successful: 'This is supposed to be a Conservative MP's natural environment – south of Scotland farmland, where Tory voters rail against Labour "townies". Yet in 1997 even its natural richness could not save Ian Lang, the former Scottish secretary' (*Scotland on Sunday*, 10 June 2001).

According to these journalistic accounts, the success of local Conservatives in Dumfries and Galloway marked the return of a political party that had been cast to the geographical and institutional margins of Scottish politics following the defeat of the Thatcher–Major Conservative governments at the 1997 general election. Unpopular in Scotland, Tory rule was brought to a sudden end in 1997 after eighteen years. Losing every single one of the eleven parliamentary constituencies that they had won in 1992, the Scottish Tories were defeated in spectacular political circumstances paralleling the annihilation of Canada's Progressive Conservative government in 1993.[4] This book explores how Conservative activists in Dumfries and Galloway struggled to rebuild politically in the aftermath of that catastrophic electoral failure. Unable to rely on a centralised party organisation for assistance and direction, local Tories had to draw on a much-diminished base of support and scarce resources as they prepared for the 2003 Scottish Parliament and local council elections.

Their efforts to rebuild the local Tory political machine, which their opponents once regarded as formidable, took place in a wider context of dramatic political and constitutional change. Perhaps the most important of these changes was devolution, which the incoming New Labour government led by prime minister Tony Blair supported. In a referendum on devolution held later in 1997, Scots voted overwhelmingly for a Scottish Parliament.[5] On 1 July 1999, the first Scottish Parliament in 292 years – indeed, the first ever to be democratically elected[6] – was opened (Jones 1999: 1; cf Devine 1999, Dewar 1998, Hassan and Lynch 2001, Hassan and Warhurst 2002, Henderson 1999, McCrone 1998). Drawing on ethnographic fieldwork grounded in the anthropological tradition of 'participant observation', I will describe in this book how Tory activists in Dumfries and Galloway responded to these changes by embracing what I will call *banal activism*. This term refers to a set of practices that scholars of Western politics tend to overlook because they more often resemble the mundane activities of paperwork and petty bureaucracy. Put simply, local Conservatives reacted to their traumatic defeat at the 1997 general election by burying themselves in paperwork. However, in their engagement with documents and the discursive instruments constitutive of electioneering, Conservative activists found powerful tools for reworking knowledge about themselves and rebuilding politically in the aftermath of failure.

A stateless nation

Prior to devolution, sociologists and other scholars often described Scotland as a 'stateless nation' (McCrone 1992). That Scotland is a nation has been largely undisputed since the nineteenth century (Alter 1994: 6), particularly by Scottish observers. For example, McCrone (1992: 3) has argued that '[it] is indubitably clear that Scotland survived the Union of 1707 as a separate 'civil society' and as a nation', while Tom Devine published his critically acclaimed history of *The Scottish Nation 1700–2000* in the months immediately following the official opening of the Scottish Parliament. Of course, such inferences might suggest a commitment to nationism (Cohen 1996, 1999) rather than nationhood itself. However, at the very least, Scotland's status as a 'banal' nation (Billig 1995) appears to have been largely taken for granted by many observers.

Assertions of Scotland's historical statelessness made it an interesting case study in the literature on the study of nationalism (e.g. Alter 1985: 99–103, Guibernau 1996: 101, Nairn 1997), especially that concerned with developing a comparative perspective on regionally based nationalist movements throughout Europe (cf Brand 1990, Kellas 1992, Lynch 1996). However, if in a democracy a parliament 'is the principal expression of national identity, power and authority' (McKean 1999: 1), devolution did not necessarily settle the question of who governs Scotland. As Parry (1999: 14) observed in the early years of devolution, the new Parliament competed 'for legitimacy and prominence in a crowded governmental space' with both Westminster and Scottish local government. Furthermore, governing pre-devolution Scotland was already a complex and multilayered affair. For instance, one anthropologist observed a 'spectacle' of agricultural and governmental institutions impinging on the lives of hill sheep farmers in the Scottish borders (Gray 1999: 440, 1996). Prior to commencing my fieldwork, I envisioned a picture of *entangled institutions*. Consider, for example, what at that time was the 'latest inventory' of the 'quango universe': 'three nationalised industries, three public corporations, 36 executive and 30 advisory bodies, three tribunals, 68 NHS bodies, and a penumbra of "local public spending bodies"' (Parry 1999: 12). And these were just the quangos.

The picture potentially gets more complicated if one includes 'civil society', whose claim to being able to 'speak' for Scotland in the absence of a parliament was now open to challenge.[8] Bearing this in mind, the creation of the new Parliament could be said to build on and extend these entanglements, effectively *adding* administrative layers (cf Latour 1993, Riles 2001, Strathern 1999). There might, therefore, have been a recognisable 'change' between the pre- and post-devolution institutional landscape of Scotland, but no recognisable 'rupture'. Given such a crowded governmental space at the time the Scottish Parliament opened, what administrative and organisational forms might be appropriated (cut) in the process of being 'recognised' as (a) distinctly Scottish (state)? These issues potentially presented anthropologists and other social scientists with a unique and innovative opportunity to study the discursive and institutional practices involved in creating a 'new' state in a Western setting.

In Scotland, a state was forming with the benefit of pre-existing (Scottish) political and scholarly traditions as well as a distinctive legal and educational system and a sophisticated archival record. Perhaps a 'nascent state' (Jean-Klein 2000) or what I originally imagined a *state-in-the-making*[9] could have already been located amongst these traditions. But the modern Scottish Parliament and its associated institutions were transforming in the full play of public scrutiny and debate. This involved the new institution mapping itself onto informal organisations and networks that are usually described as part of civil society. Indeed, some scholars highlighted talk of a 'new' politics in Scotland that was derived from the sense that the new institution was a 'civic' parliament whose every action would be 'monitored by committees with roots in civic life' (Paterson 1999: 34). But the Scottish Parliament has also sought to appropriate and work through other existing, formal state structures while paradoxically also cultivating a distinct public space, independent of these structures, in which 'it' can be apprehended. Following the American pragmatist thinker John Dewey (1954 [1927]), I suggest that the emergence of an apparently distinctive Scottish state at the turn of the twenty-first century is best understood as an outcome of the creation of a pro-devolution (Scottish) public in the 1990s.[10] As this state took form, the embers of a discredited, older (Tory) public continued to smoulder in Scotland. How might Conservative activists who had opposed the campaign for the Scottish Parliament throughout the 1990s seek to locate themselves in the new institutional landscape of post-devolution Scotland? I will return to this question towards the end of this chapter.

Devolution has rendered Scotland one of the world's foremost laboratories of constitutional reform and electoral experimentation. It could therefore provide an important resource for the anthropology of activism, democracy and statecraft (e.g. Borneman 1992, 1997, Bourdieu 1998, Ferguson 1990, Greenhouse 1998, Gupta 1995, Navaro-Yashin 2002, Paley 2001, Scott 1998, Taussig 1997, Verdery 1993, West 2005). Given that few ethnographers have focused analytical attention on constitutional and political change in Western liberal democracies, it might seem that these possibilities and practices lie somewhere beyond the purview of social anthropology. For this reason, apprehending the nuances and subtleties of these practices present a particular challenge for the ethnographer. Devolution and an emergent Scottish state might point to other kinds of 'new' ethnographic objects with which anthropologists have grappled in recent decades.

New ethnographic objects

Following the call for 'cultural critique' during the 1980s (Clifford 1988, Clifford and Marcus 1986, Marcus and Fischer 1986) or what has been called the 'postmodern' or 'reflexive' turn in ethnography (Edwards 2000: 21–22), contemporary anthropologists have become increasingly interested in 'knowledge-making practices'. This has inevitably provoked debates about fieldwork methodology and its implications for anthropological theory (e.g. Coleman and Collins 2007, Coleman and von Hellermann 2009, Falzon 2009, Fardon 1990, Gupta and Ferguson 1997a, 1997b). More recently, some have sought to apprehend new ethnographic objects so as to reflect on academic 'knowledge-making practices' in anthropology and the social sciences more generally. Some of the new ethnographic objects that have been studied in recent years include accounting (Maurer 2002), auditing (Strathern 2000), democracy (Paley 2001), documents

(Harper 1997, Riles 2006), elections (Coles 2007), financial markets (Miyazaki 2003), immigration (Coutin 2005), kinship and the new reproductive technologies (Edwards and Strathern 1999; Franklin 1993, 1997; Strathern 1995b, 1999) and political activism (Jean-Klein 2002, Riles 2001).

According to Hiro Miyazaki (2003: 255), much of this anthropological literature is concerned with an old theoretical problem in the social sciences: how to 'access the now'. His interest in 'novel' financial instruments, such as futures, options and currency swaps, is partly an attempt to address this problem by apprehending capitalism as it enters 'a new phase'. Ironically, though, 'in contemplating problems posed by the crisis of the "new" capitalism, social theorists may already be behind, that is, their contemplations may be incongruous with the temporality of the market' (Miyazaki 2003: 255). In other words, as ethnographers attempt to grapple with new analytical objects, they may nonetheless apprehend such objects belatedly. That scholarly interest might be established in new ethnographic objects retrospectively should not be surprising:

> At the heart of social theorists' turn to financial markets and other new research objects is a more general anxiety regarding the incongruity between the temporal orientation of their knowledge and that of the changed or changing world … This anxiety is perhaps intrinsic to all retrospective modes of knowing such as social theory. Yet, for practitioners of such knowledge, the very novelty of their research objects at least temporarily generates its own prospective momentum. (Miyazaki 2003: 255)

Likewise for anthropologists, knowledge is generated retrospectively. What becomes most compelling intellectually is not usually apparent until the anthropologist has immersed him- or herself in the field. In fact, what is really interesting can sometimes only be apprehended after the fact of having carried out ethnographic fieldwork, when the ethnographer returns 'home'. New ethnographic objects therefore present anthropologists with reflexive possibilities for thinking about their own knowledge practices. Indeed, Miyazaki suggests that ethnographers seek research objects that might function as analogues to anthropology so that they can unearth in the practices of others some of the anxieties and incongruities that propel the making of anthropological knowledge. Exploring how both anthropologists and Japanese financial analysts grapple with their own sense of temporal incongruity, Miyazaki is himself trying to overcome a sense of the belated in addressing what is central to current knowledge practices.

In her research on 'illegal' immigration from El Salvador to the USA, Susan Coutin (2005) is similarly concerned with the incongruities that are constitutive of what she calls 'legal fictions' and ethnography. As 'legal and other accounts produce truth', they also generate 'concealed realities' that create a sense of 'territorial integrity' based on exclusion (Coutin 2005: 195). Importantly, such integrity cannot be produced without simultaneously creating 'territorial gaps' that, in Coutin's example, constitute the space occupied by the 'unauthorized' and 'undocumented' immigrant. Coutin talks of these territorial disruptions as a kind of *absenting*, which is 'often partial in that, alongside those who are legally present, unauthorized migrants travel, work, take up residence, shop, and so forth':

> As the unauthorized are both absent and not, this dimension is both totalizing and partial, hidden and visible … [It] is precisely this ambiguity of movement that makes the presence of absented people particularly valuable … Prohibited or hidden practices and persons allow the 'above board' to assume its unmarked status as the dominant version of social reality. (Coutin 2005: 196)

It is worth noting that Coutin draws an analogy between the 'illegal' immigrant in the USA and the anthropologist in the ethnographic monograph, who often writes him- or herself 'out' of the ethnography they produce, while nevertheless remaining as an unseen presence. In Chapter 2, I discuss how the Tory Party similarly continued to exercise a presence in the imaginations of their opponents despite their apparent absence from local and national politics in Scotland after 1997.

Annelise Riles (2001) explores similar questions in her groundbreaking and innovative ethnography of Fijian human rights activists participating in the UN Fourth World Conference on Women in 1995. Focusing on those social practices that are constitutive of international networking, she draws on the work of Marilyn Strathern (1988, 1992, 1996) in particular to refer to 'a set of institutions, knowledge practices, and artefacts … that internally generate the effects of their own reality by reflecting on themselves' (Riles 2001: 3). Trying to gain analytical purchase on this network from the inside out proves especially problematic. However, the ethnographer is potentially caught within the network of his or her informants. How can ethnographers secure a perspective 'from the outside' when the practices being studied are potentially the same as those that they use in their fieldwork? This problem is exacerbated further when many of the ethnographer's informants turn out to be social science graduates, often trained at universities in Western liberal democracies. Such encounters unsettle any distinction between what 'we' do as ethnographers and what engages 'our' informants, out there in the world. The important question here is one of ownership and propriety: when is knowledge named (claimed) as ethnographic, political, sociological or other?

These questions are potentially even more pertinent for those interested in conducting ethnographic fieldwork in the United Kingdom. As Jeanette Edwards (2000: 9–10) has argued, the anthropology of Britain 'has the potential both to add to an understanding of the social milieu it studies and to reveal preoccupations that inform a British tradition of anthropology'. Although carrying out ethnographic research in the United Kingdom might constitute for many an example of conducting anthropology 'at home' (cf Jackson 1987), I rarely considered myself in comfortable or familiar surroundings in Dumfries and Galloway. Having attended universities in my native Australia as well as the United Kingdom, however, I could reasonably be said to have been trained in that 'British' tradition to which Edwards refers. Furthermore, my academic 'home' at the University of Edinburgh was already potentially implicated in my field site in southwest Scotland. As Edwards has noted:

When anthropologists and their informants frame their social worlds in similar ways … it behoves us to reveal how observations that come to be seen as information are generated. In making explicit the process whereby the familiar is construed as such, as well as the way in which the familiar is then garnered to the anthropological enterprise, the process of knowing becomes central to ethnographic description. (Edwards 2000: 13)

Jeanette Edwards and the other scholars mentioned here have not written about British politics or Scotland. However, their interest in new ethnographic objects demonstrates that scholarly practices of making knowledge are implicated in the wider knowledge practices of the people ethnographers have encountered in diverse social contexts. These might include Japanese financial analysts, US immigration lawyers, Fijian human rights activists and, I suggest, Tory Party volunteers in Scotland. Moreover, for all these groups, these practices are capable of producing social effects. This can be particularly true during times of crisis when the instrumental possibilities of such practices can be more fully realised.[11] Conceptually, the anthropological literature on new ethnographic objects described here is important to this book. It informs my argument implicitly even if it does not speak directly to the subject matter of Scottish politics itself.

Banal activism

This book describes a set of knowledge practices that animated the efforts of Conservative activists in Dumfries and Galloway seeking to rebuild politically in the run-up to local government and Scottish Parliament elections held on 1 May 2003. I suggest that these practices, which might be bundled together and described as 'electioneering', constitute a new ethnographic object. Because the practices constitutive of electioneering appear analogous to the mundane activities of petty bureaucracy, anthropologists have tended to overlook them. They are less visible in the ethnographic record of political and social life. However, as Riles (2004) has noted, bureaucracy is geared towards addressing the limits of knowledge. The engagement of Tory activists with these practices is so interesting because it occurred in the aftermath of catastrophic electoral failure that precipitated, amongst other challenges, a knowledge crisis for Scottish Conservatives.

Keeping in mind the literature on new ethnographic objects mentioned above, my central argument is that senior Tory strategists in Dumfries and Galloway worked from the assumption that they had endured their own 'crisis' in representation. The material consequences of this crisis entailed losses of financial and other resources, legitimacy and local knowledge. Unable to rely on support from Scottish Conservative Central Office (SCCO), which now oversaw a fragmented political party, local Tory activists had to improvise from a much-diminished base of support. In the first instance, they did so by embracing practices that were familiar to them from other professional and social contexts: they buried themselves in paperwork. As they mimicked the practices of other knowledge producers, including civil servants, market analysts and social scientists, local Conservatives became preoccupied with the logistical and organisational questions inherent to activist methodology. Put simply, local Conservatives turned to bureaucracy and paperwork to address this crisis and generate new knowledge about themselves and the political landscape in which they found themselves. This served to focus their attention on questions of activist methodology as they sought to build a modern, professional campaign so as to 'catch up' with their opponents, behind whom they felt they had fallen (cf Levine 2004, Miyazaki 2003). Borrowing from Alfred Gell (1992), I therefore approach documents as *technologies* capable of enchanting those who work with them.

Adopting these practices, Tory activists engaged in banal activism.[12] Furthermore, as an ethnographer, I took my cues from my research subjects. This meant focusing analytical attention on the discursive artefacts local Conservatives produced during their campaign for the 2003 elections. Amongst other artefacts, these included canvass and survey materials, leaflets, press releases, spreadsheets and target letters, all of which were treated as instruments capable of generating effects. Party activists invested the majority of their labour and time into the drafting, production and distribution of these materials, even if some of these instruments (such as the survey) might be said to be more effective than others (such as the leaflet). As Polling Day approached, these discursive instruments gripped the imaginations of my informants. In the thick of a sometimes bitterly fought election, the formatting of a survey, the repair of a broken risograph or the visual aesthetic of a leaflet could demand a more dedicated and immediate response, intellectually and physically, from my research subjects than, say, questions of campaign strategy or party policy. Under these circumstances, questions of form and method came to dominate over those of ideology and principle.

Local Tories experienced a kind of narrowing of their horizons, conceptually and physically, as they immersed themselves in banal activism, hunkering down in front of a computer screen, photocopier or stack of envelopes ready for stuffing. Party activists, working to a series of deadlines, engaged with these activities as part of their daily routine (as I outline in Chapter 4). However, they were tackled as small projects so that in the context of the overall campaign, the organisation of a postal survey, for instance, would become a 'critical event' (cf Das 1995) for activists, albeit on a micro-scale. As the election approached, the Tory campaign was punctuated by many such smaller 'events'. These could include meetings of the Core Campaign Team, deadlines for local newspaper copy, occasional altercations with rival activists, and excursions to canvass or leaflet a housing estate or neighbouring village. Taken on their own, the significance of such small-scale events was hardly apparent. Their importance and meaning was amplified, however, in the wider flow of activity that made up the campaign.

This book offers a 'thick description' (Geertz 1973) of such banal forms and practices, which potentially present a 'puzzle of scale' (cf Strathern 1999) for both the activist and the ethnographer. For the Tory volunteer, for instance, much could turn on knowledge that might seem, to an anthropological audience, flimsy, ludicrous, sketchy or 'thin'. However, I will argue in the later chapters that drawing bold conclusions from sketchy data had important consequences for local Conservatives who had invested huge amounts of energy, resources and time in their campaign. Those moments when the scale of the activity I was de-scribing seemed to me most skewed usually concerned the making of the very discursive instruments and other documents that local Tories considered vital to their campaign. These instruments produced one, very important, effect: in gen-erating a paper trail, activists were able to bring the local Conservative campaign into view as a discursive artefact or object itself. Like policy (Shore and Wright 1997, Wright 1994), the Tory campaign in Dumfries and Galloway is best under-stood as having possessed a finite social life that lasted just a handful of months, quickly coming to a quiet end in the dying hours of Polling Day.[13] As an object, the campaign manifested as something other than a 'community' or 'political party', either of which might have warranted ethnographic attention as objects in their own right.[14] In this book, I eschew these objects to focus on the efforts of Tory activists as they brought a 'lesser-spotted' figure into view: a political cam-paign. These efforts and the day-to-day practices they generate are largely absent from the anthropological literature more generally. My book therefore extends the ethnographic record of contemporary Britain.

My focus on the local Tory Party's engagement with banal activism, which demands attentiveness to the instrumental possibilities of paperwork and a commitment to organising at the micro-local level, constitutes an alternative to, rather than a substitute for, the kinds of ethnographic objects that have more traditionally occupied the ethnographic imagination. These might include the symbolic construction of community and identity (e.g. Cohen 1982) or kinship and social relations (e.g. Edwards 2000, Strathern 1988). However, while these longstanding anthropological themes are not the explicit focus of my study, they remain implicit to my argument. In the chapters that follow, I describe how the discursive instruments with which Tory activists worked were often vested with the idea that they were capable of generating positive electoral and social effects for the Conservative Party. As I argue in Chapter 6, for example, an instru-ment like the Local Opinion Survey became a prosthetic tool that enabled Party strategists to 'reach out' and forge relations with their potential supporters. In this way, Tory activists sought to read social relations in order to shape them via such discursive instruments. Importantly, although the bureaucratic practices they employed seemed familiar, local Conservatives did not engage in them as if their campaign was 'business as usual'. Rather, they embraced banal activism as something 'new' and 'different' from how they had attempted to organise in past elections. For politically disenfranchised groups like the Scottish Tories, this was an empowering and reassuring experience.

The forgotten region

The potential for the Scottish Conservatives to embrace banal activism and at-tempt to rebuild politically varied considerably across Scotland. The areas where Tory activists appeared 'strong' in number tended to be those described as their former electoral 'strongholds'. Sometimes, these were located at the geographi-cal periphery of Scotland, which might have further amplified their sense of having been marginalised by recent political events. One such area was Dumfries and Galloway, which in the 1997 referendum had voted against the Scottish Parliament being granted tax-varying powers after only slightly endorsing the creation of the new institution.[15] Indeed, when Lindsay Paterson observed that those who lived outside Scotland's urbanised Central Belt might possess 'a residual mistrust' of the new Parliament (1999: 38–39), he may have had Dumfries and Galloway in mind. That in the rural southwest of Scotland the Conservative Party might rediscover lost electoral support amongst local sceptics of devolution seemed like a plausible hypothesis from which to begin my study.

I arrived in Dumfries to commence my fieldwork on 11 September 2001, the fourth anniversary of the 1997 devolution referendum.[16] With a population of 31,146, Dumfries is the administrative capital and largest town in Dumfries and Galloway, a Scottish Local Authority in southwest Scotland of almost 150,000 residents.[17] Taking in 2,481 square miles, the region is an historic 'borderland' between England, Scotland and Ireland and the site of several battles between England and Scotland during the Scottish Wars of Independence.[18] More recently, foot-and-mouth disease had wreaked havoc on the local economy in 2001. This had been one of the first major policy crises to confront the new Scottish Parliament.[19] The fact that the spread of this epidemic from England was halted in the country's southern borderlands may at the time have reinforced the region's status as both a frontier and a periphery of Scotland.

Politically, the component parts of Dumfries and Galloway were, in fact, separate entities until after the Second World War. Prior to the radical reforms of the Local Government (Scotland) Act 1974, which saw the formation of the Dumfries and Galloway Regional Council (McConnell 2004),[20] the region did not exist as an integrated 'whole' (cf Strathern 1991) in an administrative sense. Instead, there were four district authorities dominated by retired military men – so-called 'colonels' juntas' (McCulloch 2000: 517) – based on the old counties of Dumfries and Galloway: Annandale and Eskdale, Nithsdale, Kirkcudbrightshire (also known as the Stewartry) and Wigtownshire. Furthermore, transportation links remain poor across the region. The A75 remains the most important trunk road linking Dumfries in the east to the many smaller communities of rural Galloway in the west. However, taking in all of the Stewartry and Wigtownshire as well as parts of Nithsdale, Galloway is sometimes described as 'a land apart' (McCulloch 2000: 1) or even 'another country, detached from the rest of Scotland' (Lang 2002: 43). Indeed, the area had been ruled as a separate entity from the rest of Scotland during the High Middle Ages. It had also been the Covenanting stronghold during the eighteenth century and was therefore the focus of constant military incursions. More distant from consumer markets and lacking both the raw materials and 'the means of generating industrial power', the local economy has been based on agriculture, light industry and other ancillary businesses for much of its history (McCulloch 2000: 519).

In the east of the region, Dumfriesshire encompasses all of Annandale and Eskdale and takes in most of Nithsdale. As the main county town, Dumfries is an 800-year-old historic market town that enjoys a somewhat iconic status in the Scottish nationalist imagination because of its association with the famous Scottish poet Robert Burns as well as Robert the Bruce.[21] Despite this, however, it is 'easy to miss Dumfries' as one travels 'north into Scotland from Carlisle' along the M74, 'past the little border village of Gretna, where runaway lovers from the south used to be married at the blacksmith's anvil, and head directly for Lockerbie and the pass of Beattock' (Forrester 2004: xiii). In accordance with ideas about the region being peripheral to, and apart from, the rest of Scotland, many local residents believe that it is often 'forgotten' by others. In a particularly striking example of this kind of thinking, shortly after I concluded my fieldwork in the summer of 2003, one local newspaper published a two-page article entitled, simply, 'The Forgotten Region'. Quoted in this article were a number of local politicians critical of the Scottish Executive[22] for holding back funds that had been earmarked to help the local Tourist Board in the aftermath of foot-and-mouth. 'It doesn't matter who is in power – Labour or Tory – we're always forgotten', one local journalist told me a few days later. 'That's who we are: the Forgotten Region.'[23]

Of course, that local people might access such imagery is not unique to Dumfries and Galloway. In her ethnographic study of a small Lancashire town, Jeanette Edwards (2000) noted that many residents described themselves as living in 'the back of beyond', in 'a backwater' or as being 'cut off' from larger towns and nearby cities. She argues that 'while clearly not all viewpoints are disseminated equally and some voices are louder than others, there is equal access to, and availability of, remoteness as a cultural concept. This concept is mobilised for particular reasons and acts as a means of differentiation' (Edwards 2000: 20). Drawing on the wider ethnographic record of Britain (e.g. Frankenburg 1957, 1966, Macdonald 1997, Rapport 1993, 2002, Strathern 1981), Edwards concludes that there is nothing unique about local people framing themselves as 'distant' from the mainstream. To debate whether or not a locality actually is 'remote' would therefore miss the point. Rather, Edwards suggests that what matters most is that '[the] sense of differentiation ... between communities constantly defines and redefines "insider" and "outsider"':

> [But] who is an insider and who an outsider shifts according to the reason for delineating the distinction in the first place. Categories thus formulated are fluid and contingent, but congealed for particular purposes. From any partisan position, it is possible to concretise one possibility, or to solidify one set of connections. (Edwards 2000: 20–21)

I will discuss Edwards in more detail in Chapter 3. However, if Dumfries and Galloway might have been 'forgotten' politically in post-devolution Scotland, it would also seem that anthropologists, sociologists and other social scientists have overlooked the region. As Nadel-Klein (1997) has observed, much of the ethnography of Scotland has focused on the Highlands and Islands (e.g. Byron 1980, Church 1990, Cohen 1982, 1987, Nadel-Klein 1986, 1995, Parman 1990a, 1990b). Some anthropologists have conducted fieldwork in the Scottish Borders (e.g. Gray 2000, Littlejohn 1963, Neville 1979, 1987) and, more recently, South

Ayrshire (Strathern and Stewart 2001). However, no one has yet conducted long-term ethnographic fieldwork in Dumfries and Galloway. Furthermore, the invisibility of southwest Scotland is reflected in the academic social sciences more generally, although Campbell's (1991) historical analysis of land ownership and rural society in southwest Scotland remains an important exception.[24]

Given the paucity of scholarship on southwest Scotland, ethnographic research in Dumfries and Galloway therefore also contributes to basic social scientific research by focusing on an under-studied region. It also seeks to break new ground for anthropology by exploring a set of discursive and other practices constitutive of a party political campaign. Employing the anthropological approach of participant observation, I became involved in the Conservative campaign for the 2003 local government and Scottish Parliament elections. I attended meetings, branch and fundraising events as well as leafleted and canvassed for local Tory candidates along with countless volunteers. I worked with Party professionals and strategists as they drafted, formatted and produced dozens of the discursive artefacts that I will discuss in forthcoming chapters. I also enjoyed access to meetings of the Core Campaign Team (see Chapter 4), a group of seven individuals that met regularly in Dumfries between January and April 2003 and coordinated the Party's campaign across the region. I also participated in meetings of Alex Fergusson's campaign team in Galloway and Upper Nithsdale and worked closely with the Conservative candidate David Mundell on his campaign for the Dumfries constituency. Throughout what follows, I refer to these candidates, members of their teams and a handful of other Party office-bearers and paid staff as 'senior Conservatives', 'key Party strategists' or 'professionals'. I do this deliberately in order to protect confidences and the identities of those amongst them who shared with me insights about the campaign and information that was sometimes sensitive. Whenever I refer to Conservative activists I make reference to a much larger network of candidates, branch office-bearers and volunteers who assisted with the campaign. Real names have been used for quoted speech and other items of information that have been reported publicly in local newspapers or other media.

Chapter outline

In the chapters that follow, I explore how Conservative activists in Dumfries and Galloway became banal activists to address the crisis of irrelevance they faced following their defeat at the 1997 general election.

Chapter 2 provides an account of the destruction of the Scottish Conservatives at both the national and local levels. It begins with an historical overview of Conservatism in Scotland and, in particular, Tory opposition to devolution and the Scottish Parliament during the 1980s and 1990s. It then explores the impact of the 1997 general election on local politics in Dumfries and Galloway, which continued to be regarded by many activists as 'natural' Tory territory despite the apparent 'absence' of Conservatives from local and national politics. These impressions were strengthened when two Conservatives from the area were elected via the mixed-member proportional (MMP) system through the Regional List to the Scottish Parliament. Ironically, this was achieved despite their both being defeated in their attempts to secure the region's two constituency seats. What is paradoxical here, then, is that the very electoral system and institution that they had opposed now helped Tories north of the border reclaim some of the political ground that they had previously lost, allowing them to return to the proverbial political map. This chapter explores what these contradictions and paradoxes meant for local Conservatives who, despite apparently facing a 'crisis' of irrelevance, nevertheless continued to exercise a 'presence' in the imaginations of their opponents.

Chapter 3 takes up evidence presented to a public inquiry convened in November 2002 during the Fifth Periodic Review of Parliamentary Boundaries. It explores the political struggle between local Tories and their opponents over an apparently banal form: electoral boundaries. Although this inquiry concerned proposals to redraw Westminster constituencies that would otherwise have had little impact (if any) on elections to local government and the Scottish Parliament, it became a major focus for political activists in the months prior to the Scottish Parliament elections. Local Labour activists and their allies, for instance, feared that through the Boundary Commission's strict application of the electoral quota, or by playing 'the numbers game', an identity neatly encapsulated in the name attributed to natives of Dumfries (*Doonhamers*) would be lost. The chapter goes on to ask what activists in the region meant when they described a proposed new parliamentary constituency in southern Scotland as 'a hybrid unit' made up of disparate parts that did not belong to the whole (cf Strathern 1991). To conclude, it observes that what particularly mattered to activists at the inquiry were the ways in which diverse elements and material were linked in the asserting of political claims and the work such linkages were made to do.

Chapter 4 provides an overview of the local Tory Party's planning for the 2003 local government and Scottish Parliamentary elections. It explores how local Conservatives sought to build a political machine through the coordination of (limited) activist labour, Party bureaucracy and paperwork. This machine was 'run' by a Core Campaign Team, which comprised senior Party strategists and a handful of elected representatives. The Core Campaign Team oversaw the deployment of four 'instruments' that were vital to the local Party's discursive armoury: the leaflet, press release, survey and target letter. In particular, activists considered their *In Touch* leaflet both an instrument and a building block of their campaign as they sought to 'catch up' and overtake the superior, 'well-oiled' campaigning machine of the local Labour Party. This chapter argues that what empowered *In Touch* in the eyes of Conservative activists was the leaflet's apparent ability to invoke connections between a person (candidate), place (community or council ward) and political party (Conservatives) in the absence of such connections otherwise being obvious to a sceptical electorate. Furthermore, persuasive force and the ability to convince potential supporters that by voting Conservative one could 'make (a) difference' was thought to reside in the aesthetics and the form of this leaflet. For these reasons, the production and distribution of the *In*

Touch leaflet became a central concern for Tory activists. In focusing on such concerns, local Conservatives embraced the idea that the key to electoral success lay in becoming banal activists and addressing (internal) questions of Party organisation and coordination.

Ironically, by invoking such connections between local Tory candidates and a wider community/constituency, the *In Touch* leaflet betrayed an anxiety many Conservative activists shared. This anxiety was grounded in the assumption that local people considered the Tory Party irrelevant in Scotland and that they were therefore not interested in what they had to say. Chapter 5 focuses on this apparent 'crisis' of irrelevance for the Scottish Conservatives. In particular, it describes the ways in which Tory activists used press releases and letters to local newspapers to campaign on a set of seemingly 'banal' local issues. These included opposition to the closure of a local car park, increases in Council Tax and the removal of a roundabout at a busy intersection in Dumfries. Building on the argument from Chapter 4, this chapter suggests that Conservative activists were often less interested in the content of such issues than they were in problems of form. Local Tories became focused more on logistical and organisational questions – that is, activist methodology in the production of *In Touch* leaflets, press releases and letters to the editor – than on the issues that formed the content of their campaign. These instruments were treated as if they were capable of generating electoral effects. Scottish Conservatives hoped that this would be achieved through the promotion of a 'professional-looking' campaign that would register in the memories of even the most casual and disinterested of observers.

Chapter 6 focuses on another important challenge for senior Party strategists as they sought to address their apparent 'crisis' of irrelevance: how to establish the voting intentions of potential supporters in what is otherwise an election by secret ballot. Working within various legal constraints, Conservative activists developed a variety of strategies to render the Electoral Roll 'transparent' so that the political allegiances of thousands of local voters could be discerned (imagined). Two particular discursive artefacts – the survey and the canvass sheet – are analysed in this chapter as performing a politics of self-knowledge (cf Miyazaki 2004: 50–67) for local Tories. Despite resembling bureaucratic forms of modern knowledge production like the census, these were explicitly designed to identify supporters. They therefore stand in stark contrast to, say, the 'objective' knowledge making practices of quantitative research methods popular in the political and social sciences. Considered here also is the target letter, which was specifically designed to challenge a local political culture that key Party strategists perceived as hostile to them following the 1997 general election. Through the target letter, in particular, senior Conservatives hoped to achieve a positive outcome for local Party candidates in the forthcoming elections. Almost inevitably, however, Tory activists became preoccupied with the banal concerns of designing, producing and distributing these various discursive instruments in addition to the most efficient bureaucratic means of managing the canvass and other data they generated.

Chapter 7 describes some of the methods that local Party strategists devised for assessing their 'progress' on Polling Day and at the election count that followed in order to 'audit' (cf Strathern 2000) their campaign. Senior Tories drew on personal experiences of business and management in the running of their campaign and then mimicked new organisational elites, such as the bureaucrats and civil servants tasked with running the elections locally, as they sought to audit their own campaigning practices. Seeking to assess their campaign in terms of its internal mechanics and its external effects, the challenge of obtaining an 'outside' view of their efforts from a location within the local Party's machinery proved doubly problematic. This was not least because the election results did not conform to the local Party's generally optimistic projections of how they would perform on Polling Day. The various strategies local Conservatives used to 'read' what was happening around them produced some surprising – and potentially unsettling – results. This was partly because they were unable to predict the outcome of the elections in the light of all sorts of diverse factors, such as the weather. Furthermore, Polling Day was also marked by a sense that their rivals had built and achieved momentum in their respective campaigns. This reinforced to Tory activists the unnerving possibility that the election promised other potential outcomes, including defeat. The methodological failure of senior Tory Party strategists to anticipate and effectively account for their electoral failure in turn reinforced their marginal status by rendering redundant their attempts to generate knowledge about themselves and a local political culture they deemed hostile to Conservatism.

Briefly sketching some of the incidents that took place in the aftermath of the 2003 elections, Chapter 8 considers whether local Conservatives had successfully addressed their crisis of irrelevance. The grounds on which activists made judgments about their own knowledge of local politics remained sketchy and uncertain. Senior Tories had to work hard at making political 'change' appear, locally and nationally. The chapter then notes how the Tory Party continues to face challenges in post-devolution Scotland, which at the time of writing is run by a minority SNP administration that has to rely on the Scottish Conservatives – their old Unionist foes – for tacit support to remain in power. Although their voices are often absent from national politics, the Scottish Conservatives continue to exercise a powerful presence in the political imagination of Scotland. The predicament with which the lesser-spotted Tory continues to be confronted therefore confounds straightforward portrayals of contemporary Scottish politics.

Notes

1 Malcolm Rifkind had held Cabinet posts in the Thatcher–Major governments. He recontested Edinburgh Pentlands in the 2001 general election, losing it narrowly to the Labour incumbent who had beaten him in 1997 with 43% of the vote. For more on the 2001 general election, see Butler and Kavanagh (2001).
2 This expression was in occasional use by my ethnographic subjects and was sometimes shortened to an acronym: TFS.
3 It could, however, be argued that the Scottish Tories had never really left but, rather, had

been 'left behind' (cf Levine 2004, Miyazaki 2003).

4   In that election, the Progressive Conservatives held on to only two of the 151 parlia-
    mentary seats they had won at the previous election, losing over 50% of their vote from
    1988.

5   The referendum was passed with 74.3% of the vote (Taylor 1999: 138).

6   The Scottish Parliament is usually regarded as a 'new' institution. However, the 'old'
    medieval Parliament had been suspended in 1707 following the Act of Union with
    England, which meant that it was 're-convened' in 1999 after a recess lasting almost
    three centuries (Hearn 2000, Paterson 1994).

7   The acronym 'quango' means 'quasi non-governmental organisation', a 'democratic
    form that keeps important services out of local government and gives central govern-
    ment rights of intervention without day-to-day responsibility' (Parry 1999: 27).

8   In the struggle 'to define and dispose' the interest of Scotland (Cohen 1997: 98), some
    civic leaders might challenge the legitimacy of the Scottish Parliament by re-fixing the
    terms of Scotland's statelessness (Edwards 1998). For more on anthropological ap-
    proaches to civil society, see Benthall (2000), Comaroff and Comaroff (1999), Coombe
    (1997) and Hann and Dunn (1996).

9   I am thinking of Latour's suggestion (1987: 2–3) that accounting for scientific inven-
    tions is akin to opening a 'black box' or 'set of commands' for which only 'input and
    output count'. He proposes 'opening up' scientific controversies by exploring *science-in-
    the-making* (Latour 1987: 4).

10 To some, this idea might appear to resonate with Tim Mitchell's Foucault-inspired
    argument that the state is a structural *effect* produced through the detailed organisa-
    tion of space, time, function, supervision and surveillance (1990: 95). However, Dewey
    (1954[1927]: 18) critiqued theories of the state that mistakenly attribute to it author-
    ship, offering the corrective that all 'acts are performed by somebody, and all arrange-
    ments and plans are made by somebody in the most concrete sense of "somebody"'. I
    am strongly sympathetic to his emphasis on grounding theories of both the public and
    the state in practice and social relations.

11 Here I am paraphrasing the anthropologist Michael Jackson (1989: 149), who has
    argued that in times of crisis the 'instrumental possibilities' of metaphor and language
    are realised.

12 This term first came up during a conversation I had with Dr Iris Jean-Klein at the
    University of Edinburgh. Famously, Arendt (2007) described how a commitment
    to bureaucratic practice could render evil banal, an argument that informs Michael
    Billig's concept (1995) of 'banal nationalism.' My analysis points to other possibilities
    for the banal in helping order social life and achieving, through routine, a sense of
    organisation.

13 Or as Richard Rorty has said: 'By "campaign," I mean something finite, something that
    can be recognized to have succeeded or to have, so far, failed' (1997: 114).

14 For ethnographic studies of political parties in Western liberal democracies, see Aronoff
    (1977) and Kertzer (1988, 1996). Other recent anthropological studies of British poli-
    tics include Crewe (2005), Faucher-King (2005) and Graham (2005). Most of these
    studies focus on the ritual dimensions of political practice (see also Abeles 1988) rather
    than the bureaucratic and other routine practices discussed in this book.

15 In Dumfries and Galloway, a narrow majority voted for the Parliament while only
    48.8% of local electors supported the idea that the Scottish Parliament should have tax
    varying powers. Out of Scotland's thirty-two local authority areas, the only other region
    to register opposition to the Parliament possessing powers over tax was the Orkney

Islands, which could hardly be described as a former Tory stronghold in Scotland (Hearn 2000: 73).

16 Of course, 11 September is now charged with other meanings since the terrorist attacks that took place in the USA that day.

17 According to the 2001 Census for Scotland, the population of Dumfries and Galloway was 147,765 out of a Scottish total of 5,062,011 (General Register Office for Scotland 2003).

18 For more on borders and borderlands, see Darian-Smith (1999) and Green (2005).

19 For more on the foot-and-mouth crisis in Scotland, see Bell *et al.* (2002) and the Royal Society of Edinburgh (2002).

20 Furthermore, the Act allowed for the setting up of local community councils. Although these did not have any formal powers, they 'were designed to act as conduits between the people living in their area and the relevant district and regional councils' (McCulloch 2000: 517). Community councils constitute important sites of activism, as will be seen in my discussion in Chapter 3 of the Boundary Commission public inquiry held in Dumfries in November 2002 (see also Smith 2006).

21 Robert Burns lived in Dumfries from 1791 to 1796 and is buried at St Michael's church. At Greyfriars Monastery, which used to stand on the site of the Greyfriars church in the town centre, Robert the Bruce assassinated his rival John 'the Red' Comyn before claiming the Scottish throne in 1306 (Fortune and McMillan 2005: 6–7).

22 The Scottish Executive referred then to the Labour–Liberal Democrat coalition government in Scotland. Following the election of an SNP administration in 2007, the Executive was renamed the Scottish Government.

23 These views often contrasted Dumfries and Galloway (and the south of Scotland more generally) with the Highlands and Islands. According to the Southern Uplands Partnership (SUP), for instance, 'the south of Scotland is becoming forgotten by those in authority and invisible to those planning to visit Scotland – left behind socially, economically and environmentally compared to other rural areas, especially the Highlands and Islands' (*SUP News* 2004: 4).

24 In addition, a sociological study of identity constructions amongst the landed elite (Bechhofer *et al.* 1999; McCrone *et al.* 1998) draws heavily on Dumfries and Galloway, no doubt because the area is home to some of Scotland's most powerful landowners. Scotland's largest private landowner is the Duke of Buccleuch, who owns more land north of the border than any other individual or organisation apart from the Forestry Commission. His estate centres on Drumlanrig Castle in Nithsdale but he owns huge tracts of land in Annandale and Eskdale. One Tory activist explained to me that the Duke's enduring influence might partly account for the Party's continued 'strength' in rural Dumfriesshire.

2

A Tory-free Scotland

Pierre Bourdieu once described parliamentary democracy as a struggle in which the most important agents – political parties – are engaged 'in a sublimated form of civil war' (1991: 181). Taking up this metaphor, I would suggest that when I began my fieldwork in September 2001, Dumfries and Galloway resembled a political battlefield which the Conservative Party could be said to have vacated. What eventually made the Scottish Conservatives of potential ethnographic interest to me was exactly this apparent absence: the fact that the Scottish Tory was, so to speak, 'lesser spotted'. During the first few months of my fieldwork, it sometimes seemed as though there was not a Tory in sight. Of course, this was not strictly the case as I attended local meetings dedicated to economic recovery following foot-and-mouth.[1] Conservative representatives, including Alex Fergusson MSP and Peter Duncan MP, were usually vocal participants at these meetings. However, they often sat together in the corner, sometimes seeming like lone individuals without any (visible) backing. Moreover, non-Tory political activists tended to talk about them as if they were not there. It was easy to identify activists from other political parties through the Dumfries-based Crichton University Campus, where I had an office during my fieldwork and a number of students were engaged with local and national political debate. Invitations from various students I met during the first year of my fieldwork took me to several meetings and functions organised by the local Liberal Democrats; a Burns Supper hosted by the local Labour Party; two SNP meetings; and several seminars on Afghanistan, Iraq and the so-called 'war on terror', all of which were convened by the newly formed local branch of the Scottish Socialist Party. At all of these meetings, Conservatives were the subject of much discussion, especially the legacy of Margaret Thatcher and the unpopular Poll Tax. They were, of course, absent from such meetings and therefore unable to speak for themselves during the discussions. And while many non-Tory activists at the Crichton University Campus openly declared their political affiliations, students who supported the local Tories tended to keep their views to themselves.

I was conscious that some students were potential Conservative activists and supporters. Rumours circulated regarding the political views of one mature student who lived in a (rural) council ward represented by a popular, local Tory councillor with whom he shared the same hyphenated surname. But this affable student never expressed his political views in conversations with fellow students. When, much later in my fieldwork, I finally quizzed him, he explained that 'while a few people' knew he was a Conservative, he tried to keep quiet about such things at university: 'you know what students can be like.'[2] Furthermore, when I asked others whether they knew any Tories to whom they might introduce me, it seemed like they too encountered difficulty when trying to discern such political allegiances. One well-placed informant was baffled by my question and exclaimed that he did not know any Conservatives. After thinking it over for a few minutes, he mentioned the name of one prominent landowner that he knew well locally and said: 'I guess he might be a Tory – but then I've never asked him!'[3]

When I introduced myself to local activists and other observers of local politics, I encountered many individuals who were keen to share their knowledge and experiences of living in Dumfries and Galloway with me. As far as informally identifying local Conservatives was concerned, this was perhaps part of the problem: those who engaged with me most enthusiastically early in my fieldwork tended to draw me into networks that inevitably precluded me from meeting local Tories. Within such networks, a common caricature of the predicament facing local Conservatives was that they had retreated to their '*big hooses*' [big houses] outside of Dumfries following the destruction of their once-insurmountable electoral base in the constituency. Their supporters allegedly numbering only a handful of prominent farmers and landowners – the so-called 'county set' – one Labour Party activist told me, 'only the "squire-archy" vote Tory these days.' On another occasion, an SNP activist declared: 'No one votes Conservative anymore, except the Colonel from Carsphairn!' According to my non-Tory informants, even some members of the county set were no longer supporting the Conservatives. The wife of one local landowner, who told me that they both voted Liberal Democrat, explained that the local Conservative Party had selected a candidate in the 2001 general election who fit a negative 'county' stereotype only too well. This was a retired lieutenant colonel whose family had owned land in Dumfriesshire for several centuries, and 'even some of his friends didn't vote for him', she claimed.[4]

Such dismissive, humorous asides about the Scottish Tories appeared to underscore their irrelevance in the new political landscape of post-devolution Scotland. However, the Conservative Party nevertheless seemed to constitute for some of its opponents a tangible electoral threat locally. 'There is still a lot of support for the Conservatives in this town,' said one Labour Party activist over a pint of ale, explaining that it was not in the nature of Conservatives to wear their politics on their sleeves or to be vocal about their opinions, 'but don't underestimate the depth of support that still exists for them in Dumfries.' These statements resonated with journalistic impressions, as noted in Chapter 1, of Dumfries and Galloway as 'natural' Tory territory in a country (Scotland) that remained hostile to Conservatism. Indeed, the Scottish Conservatives had held the two parliamentary seats contained within the region's boundaries until the 1997 general election. The popular Sir (then Lord) Hector Monro had represented the Dumfries constituency since 1964, when he narrowly won it in a by-election against the Labour Party. This seat had been considered the second safest for the Scottish Tories during the 1990s.[5] Not only was there a lot of affection for Lord Monro amongst activists of all political affiliation; many still described Dumfries as a *'wee Tory toon'*.[6] Meanwhile, in neighbouring Galloway and Upper Nithsdale, the anti-devolution Secretary of State for Scotland Rt Hon. Ian Lang had represented the seat since the 1979 general election. He had won it 'back' for the Conservatives from the SNP, which had held the constituency for only one five-year parliamentary term.[7]

Despite their apparent absence from local politics, then, local Conservatives exercised a *presence* in the imaginations of their opponents. Moreover, I suggest that local Tories were defined, in part, by their exclusion from popular narratives in Scotland that equated political 'progress' with the successful campaign for a Scottish Parliament (cf Hearn 2000, 2002), a campaign to which the Thatcher–Major Conservative governments had remained stubbornly opposed. However, most of my non-Tory activists held strong views about the Conservative Party locally and nationally.[8] For many people, the Scottish Conservatives constituted the 'villains' of Scottish politics, not least because of their historic hostility to the Scottish Parliament.[9] As I later learned, senior Conservatives were often aware of the ways in which their opponents portrayed them locally. This chapter explores this paradoxical relationship between the Conservative Party and a region of Scotland that many considered 'natural Tory turf' from which the Scottish Conservatives had nevertheless been recently expunged. Towards the end of this chapter, I introduce the struggle over Boundary Commission proposals to redraw electoral boundaries in the region to demonstrate how anti-Tory activists in general, and Labour supporters in particular, worked to enforce and perpetuate this absence. I begin with a brief account of the decline of Conservatism north of the border and the destruction of the Scottish Tories at both the local and national levels at the 1997 general election, when Scotland became 'Tory-free'.

A Tory-free Scotland

The so-called 'wipe-out' of the Scottish Conservatives at the 1997 general election came after years of decline that some scholars (e.g. Seawright 1996, 1998, 2002) have traced back to the 1950s. Indeed, the Conservative Party in Scotland won over 50% of the popular vote and over half the parliamentary seats north of the border at the 1955 general election. This was the only time in Scottish electoral history that a single political party had commanded a majority of both seats and votes (Hutchison 2001: Chapter 3). By the 1987 and 1992 general elections, however, less than a quarter of Scots supported the Conservative Party. Although popular backing for the party had been falling steadily for years, certain decades, such as the 1970s, saw significant and sudden drops in support. Then, after eighteen years in government, the party imploded in the run-up to the 1997 general election in circumstances that David Seawright (1999: 1) has described as 'nothing short of dramatic'.

Scholars and other observers of politics in Scotland have offered several reasons for the destruction of the Scottish Conservatives in the late 1990s. However, the causes of Tory disintegration remain the subject of much debate and, according to Seawright (1999: 195), amount to a 'lacuna in our academic knowledge'.[10] Indeed, the 'received wisdom' on the decline of Conservatism north of the border is often less persuasive than it might initially seem. For instance, some have speculated that Scotland retains a more general 'left of centre' political disposition that led many Scots to treat Thatcherism with suspicion.[11] According to this view, the Scottish Conservatives became increasingly associated with a hostile, Anglo-centric Other during the 1980s and 1990s. Coupled with the introduction of the Poll Tax north of the border in the late 1980s, which contributed to the alienation of the Protestant, working-class Tory vote, this association proved politically disastrous for Conservatives in Scotland. Yet, Seawright's research suggests that the Scottish Conservatives lost no more support amongst their working-class supporters than any other section of the population during the 1980s and 1990s. Moreover, despite provoking much discontent in Scotland at the time,[12] the Poll Tax appears to have had little impact on the 1992 general election when the Scottish Conservatives increased their parliamentary representation from nine to eleven seats. Similarly, Seawright finds other theories of Tory decline in Scotland unconvincing. These include the electoral impact of internal conflict between the Thatcherite and 'One Nation' wings of the Party, led by Lord Forsyth and the Rt Hon. Malcolm Rifkind respectively, and the Conservative Party's opposition to devolution.[13]

Seawright (1998, 1999) suggests that the decline of Conservatism in Scotland can be traced back to developments in the 1960s when the Party introduced a number of internal reforms to centralise its administration and structure. When the Scottish Unionist Party changed its name to the Conservatives in 1965,[14] a process began by which a series of constitutional reforms centralised the Party's internal administration in Edinburgh and, later, London. This process involved dismantling the Party's dual structure, whereby it had maintained an east and west division in Scotland. Cutting local and regional networks, a 'reinforcing alienation' took place: 'as the party increasingly "centralised" it lost the important local activists ... who could assuage feelings of alienation at the local level' (Seawright 1998: 70). Furthermore, the renaming of the Party had its own impact on this process:

> Crucially, the changing developments in party organisation and identity in the sixties are the link between the moderate slippage in support then and the start of the dramatic fall in the seventies. The desire of the party elite to rid itself of a putative sectarian image led to what may be termed, the throwing out of the baby with the bathwater. A crucial aspect of Unionism was an ability to appeal to powerful symbols in Scottish culture which gave the party a Scottish identity irrespective of its stance on devolution. This the Conservative *boo-word* could not do. And subsequently this was the crucial ingredient the party lost in the sixties. (Seawright 1999: 200–201)

The cumulative effects of this alienation resulted in the Scottish Conservatives, now isolated as the only political party opposed to Scottish 'Home Rule', failing to retain any House of Commons seats at the 1997 general election.

The defeat of the Scottish Conservatives was a particularly traumatic event in the minds of the many Tory activists whom I got to know during my fieldwork. Most had expected that their party would perform badly at the 1997 general election and that the Major government would be defeated. When one activist introduced herself to me as a former local councillor who had retired at the 1995 local government elections, she explained that it had become clear that 'the rot was setting in' by then. This was not a remarkable or unusual observation for many of my informants. It may not have strictly been a coincidence that the popular Conservative MP for Dumfries, Hector Monro, decided to retire at that election.[15] Several party professionals did the same, including the long-serving Election Agent for Galloway and Upper Nithsdale. However, few Conservatives anticipated that their party would lose every parliamentary seat it held in Scotland. A popular and well-known Labour councillor from Annan, Russell Brown, comfortably defeated the Scottish Conservative candidate Struan Stevenson in the Dumfries constituency.[16] Meanwhile, the SNP candidate Alasdair Morgan won Galloway and Upper Nithsdale, beating the Tory incumbent by almost six thousand votes. These losses produced a 'Tory-free Scotland' in terms of both European Parliament and Westminster representation. In Dumfries and Galloway, official representation for the local Tories was reduced to just two local councillors out of a total of seventy. The impact of this electoral catastrophe on the Conservative Party in Scotland cannot be overstated.

Dark days

According to local Conservatives, this election resembled an apocalyptic experience followed by 'dark days'. A young Conservative from Stranraer bitterly described how at the Election Count a triumphant SNP activist leapt onto the stage with a Scottish Saltire in his hands following the declaration of the result in Galloway and Upper Nithsdale. Another Tory activist from Dumfries told me that she had found canvassing during the 1997 general election very stressful because of the hostility she had encountered on the doorstep. Claiming that she had been spat on by a number of people, she had been only one of a small handful of Conservative activists prepared to canvass for the Party at that time.[17] More seriously, stories circulated of a senior Conservative who allegedly attempted suicide during the final weeks of the campaign. Such emotions and tensions spilled over into the count that followed Polling Day that year. A local Tory councillor alleged that a well-known Labour activist had assaulted her husband just prior to the declaration of the Dumfries result in 1997. Such tales resonated with many local Conservatives. In their view, the local Labour Party was an aggressive, even ruthless, organisation. Some Labour strategists were said deliberately to cultivate a 'thuggish' persona. A middle-aged Tory activist explained to me that one senior Labour activist was one to 'never work alone'. Labour Party activists 'hunt in packs,' he said. 'Our people do not like getting involved in local politics because they find it intimidating. There aren't many of us and those of us who try to get on to things have to fight on our own.' Another Conservative activist regularly referred to this same Labour activist as 'the Prince of Darkness', noting that he would stage dramatic public entrances 'as if he was Darth Vader or something' with a couple of his colleagues. 'Don't get me wrong,' he would later tell me, 'they cultivate this image. Just watch how they enter the building: they dress in black, sweep into the room and act like they run the place.'

Some of my informants gave the Scottish Conservative candidate for Dumfries Struan Stevenson credit for almost single-handedly holding his campaign to-gether while the local Party Association 'went into meltdown' around him. During this period, the Party's local infrastructure disintegrated and record-keeping fell into disarray. Most Conservatives agreed that there was virtually nothing left locally in the aftermath of defeat. No one could tell me for certain how many people were paid-up Party members in either constituency or whether many of these individuals could be called upon to assist with campaigns and other political activities.[18] Local office-bearers and staff estimated that Conservative Party membership ranged between 400 and 700 in the Dumfries constituency and numbered 700–900 in Galloway and Upper Nithsdale. Senior Conservatives remained concerned about the Party's cash flow problems and the high level of staff turnover in the Associations' offices in Dumfries and Castle Douglas.[19] Beyond each Association's respective Executive and Management Committees, an overwhelming majority of branches – roughly twenty in each constituency – had ceased to organise regular activities. Some branches appeared to contain just one or two members and amounted to little more than names on paper. Only the Dumfries Conservative Ladies Lunch Club, the subject of much mythology within local Conservative Party circles, kept going during these difficult times.[20]

As traumatic as the 1997 general election was for many local Conservatives, it rarely formed the subject of much discussion. My ethnographic subjects tended to treat the decline of the Scottish Tories as something of a mystery that defied rational explanation. A few occasions when the events of 1997 were discussed in casual conversation came about as the result of direct questioning from me. However, most Conservative activists seemed reluctant to revisit these painful memories. I once witnessed an exchange between the former Election Agent for the Dumfries constituency Molly Wilson and a key Party strategist. Sitting at a large table in the Conservative Party office in Castle Street, Dumfries, Ms Wilson was opening envelopes containing survey responses when she said to the two or three other activists present:

> You know, I just don't understand it. Why did Dumfries go Labour [in 1997]? I mean, even in the 1970s, when Galloway went Scottish Nationalist, we kept hold of Dumfries. It's always been Conservative. But why did it go Labour in 1997? I just don't understand it.

The Party strategist who responded was clearly exasperated by her musings: 'We lost Dumfries because everyone hated us in 1997! Nobody could stand us anymore!' But the elderly Tory activist would not (or could not) entertain this possibility: 'Don't be ridiculous: you're talking absolute nonsense. I have never heard such rubbish.' Their conversation ended abruptly and awkwardly.

Exchanges like this one were rare. When such questions were posed, however, they often seemed rhetorical, more often designed to register feelings of despair. For instance, during the count that took place at Easterbook Hall following the 2003 elections (see Chapter 7), I encountered a handful of younger Tory activists drinking in a nearby pub. While all of them appeared stressed and a little emotional, one young man in particular seemed hysterical. Chris had leafleted a couple of rural hamlets just beyond the boundaries of Dumfries Burgh for the Party. 'Why does everyone hate us?' he wailed, his head in his hands. 'Why don't people vote for us anymore? What have we done?' Bemused, another young Conservative glanced over to me and frowned. 'Who is this guy?' he mouthed. 'Why can't we win?' cried Chris: 'What have we done to make people hate us so much?' Following the anthropologists Hiro Miyazaki and Annelise Riles (2003), I suggest that questions such as these constituted end-points for discussion, precluding further analysis. In their *refusal to know* why the electorate turned on the Thatcher–Major Conservative governments, activists like Ms Wilson and the young man described above spoke of the party's electoral annihilation in 1997 as if voters, unprovoked, had visited suffering upon them.[21]

Guerrilla warfare

For local Conservatives, 1997 brought an end to a Golden Age[22] in Tory electoral representation. Following their annihilation at the ballot box, most activists did not just consider the political present 'qualitatively poorer than the past' (Edwards 2000: 170; cf Cohen 1987, MacDonald 1997) but also quantitatively poorer. In the aftermath of defeat, local Conservatives felt that they had been reduced to a much-diminished base of support with significantly depleted financial and other resources, legitimacy and, with the departure of long-serving MPs and key political activists, local knowledge. In Chapter 4, I will explore how Party activists sought to address their own 'crisis' in representation at the 2003 local government and Scottish Parliament elections.

As is clear from the above discussion, the traumatic events of 1997 possessed an afterlife[23] in the memories of local Conservatives. I now suggest that this was particularly hurtful because of the way in which their voices were excluded from popular narratives of Scottish nationhood that equated political progress with the successful campaign for a new parliament. According to the sociologist Jonathan Hearn (2002: 745), national identity 'inevitably relies on the creation and use of narratives ... that imbue nations and nationalist projects with coherence and purpose'. In Scotland, the movement for constitutional change grew over three decades, 'stimulated in the 1960s by rising economic expectations, in the 1970s by the vision of underwriting an independent Scotland with revenues from newly discovered North Sea oil, and in the 1980s and 1990s by a rejection of Thatcherism' (Hearn 2002: 745–746). Opposition to the neo-liberal policies of the Thatcher–Major Conservative governments was crucial to consolidating public opinion in Scotland behind a devolved parliament. Moreover, support for the SNP and the Labour Party, which decided in the 1980s to back devolution, flourished at the expense of the Scottish Conservatives. Supporters of Home Rule for Scotland flocked to a 'complex array of campaigning groups' (Hearn 2002: 746), including the Campaign for a Scottish Parliament, Common Cause, Democracy for Scotland and the Scottish Constitutional Convention.

Such narratives of national and political progress rendered the anti-devolution Scottish Tories absent in time and space by using their opposition to devolution to associate them with a hostile, Anglo-centric Other. Several Tory activists and (former) representatives were uncomfortable with the idea that they might be regarded 'throwbacks'[24] to a Scotland that some might have described as politically 'pre-modern' (cf Fabian 1983). At the launch of his autobiography in October 2002 at the Wigtown Book Festival in rural Galloway, Rt Hon. Ian Lang described devolution as 'a catalyst for all political opposition' that particularly 'rankled' when his opponents alleged that because of his opposition to a Scottish Parliament he and his colleagues 'did not love or care for Scotland and its historic destiny'. This, he said, was a 'low blow' that he 'always found hurtful' before declaring: 'I defer to no man in my love of Scotland – my own, my native land' (Lang 2002: 199–200).[25]

The destruction of the Scottish Conservatives in 1997 effectively broke the back of potential opposition to devolution in the referendum the New Labour government planned to hold later that year. Conservative strategists struggled to agree how best to respond to the changed political realities they now faced in Scotland. According to Mitchell *et al.* (1998), the Scottish Tories were ill-equipped to campaign against devolution in the months immediately following their 'wipe-out':

> The Conservatives initially decided not to run a campaign but to work under the Think Twice umbrella. This was in recognition of the harm to the campaign if it was identified with the Conservatives. The official Conservative position was to oppose both the Parliament and the tax-varying powers. Having lost all their seats in Scotland at the general election, morale was very low, credibility was damaged, internal recriminations and bitter feuding were taking their toll. Party members were not in the mood for another potentially bruising encounter with the electorate. But it would be impossible for the Conservatives to say nothing. (Mitchell *et al.* 1998: 177)

Tory opposition to a Scottish Parliament failed to register much of an impact in the 1997 referendum on devolution, which passed with an overwhelming majority. However, as noted in the previous chapter, the outcome of the referendum in Dumfries and Galloway was of potential interest to senior Conservative strategists who hoped that the sceptical result registered locally might signal the potential for a Tory revival in the region.

Nonetheless, the electoral prospects of the local Conservatives did not quickly improve. At the first elections for the new Scottish Parliament, held on 1 July 1999, local Tories nominated David Mundell, a BT executive who grew up in Annandale and went to school at Lockerbie Academy, to contest the Dumfries constituency. Alex Fergusson, a South Ayrshire farmer who had been born in the small Galloway town of Portpatrick, ran as the Conservative candidate in Galloway and Upper Nithsdale. Like the Westminster seats with which they shared their boundaries at that time, these two Scottish Parliamentary constituencies were elected on the first-past-the-post electoral system. Neither candidate succeeded in winning 'back' either of these two seats for the Scottish Tories. The Labour Party's Dr Elaine Murray won Dumfries while the then MP for Galloway and Upper Nithsdale, Alasdair Morgan, secured the Scottish Parliament seat of the same name for the SNP. However, this election saw the two unsuccessful Tory candidates winning seats in the Scottish Parliament through the multimember South of Scotland Regional List, which is elected via Proportional Representation (PR).[26] Paradoxically, the very electoral system and institution to which the Conservatives had been opposed now helped them to reclaim some of the political ground they had lost.[27]

Following these elections, the local Conservative Party offices in Dumfries and Castle Douglas received a small injection of funds and administrative support. Amongst other items of equipment, new computers and photocopiers were purchased. In local elections also held that year, the number of Tory councillors quadrupled from two to eight at a time when the total number of councillors was reduced to just forty-seven across the region. An unexpected by-election victory in 2001 against a divided Labour Party in the Solway Border ward gave local Conservatives a further boost, strengthening their base of local representation on Dumfries and Galloway Council. Despite these various improvements, senior Party strategists tended to believe that Tory candidates struggled locally due to disorganisation and poor campaign planning. On the rare occasion when local Conservatives won a ward or a parliamentary constituency, their success was often attributed to chance, apathy amongst non-Tory voters translating into a low turnout at the Poll, the vagaries of PR or the incompetence of their opponents. Rephrasing Pierre Bourdieu from the beginning of this chapter, local Conservatives could be described as engaged in a sublimated form of *guerrilla warfare*, snatching victories from those who opposed them when the latter were caught off guard. This kind of metaphor seemed particularly useful in accounting for the election of Peter Duncan as, then, Scotland's only Tory MP at the 2001 general election. This electoral achievement was by far the most important for the Scottish Conservatives at the time of my fieldwork. Mr Duncan beat a young, inexperienced SNP candidate by just 74 votes in Galloway and Upper Nithsdale following Alasdair Morgan's decision to retire from Westminster and concentrate on his career in the Scottish Parliament.[28] In the aftermath of the foot-and-mouth epidemic, some more-hopeful Conservatives described Mr Duncan's victory as a 'breakthrough' or 'turning point' in local politics. However, the fact that the Labour MP for Dumfries, Russell Brown, defeated the Scottish Conservative candidate Lt Col. John Charteris by roughly 10,000 votes that year potentially undermined such optimism, highlighting Mr Duncan's good fortune in rural Galloway.

I suggest that the mixed electoral success of the Conservative Party in

Dumfries and Galloway served to highlight their marginal status in both local and national politics. Within days of the 1999 local government elections, for instance, Tory councillors were the only political group excluded from negotiations that led to the formation of a coalition administration composed of Independent, Labour, Liberal Democrat and SNP members. Local Conservatives bitterly named this anti-Tory administration the 'Rainbow Alliance', the existence of which appeared to further marginalise the Tory Party in local politics. Moreover, those Conservatives who were elected to the Scottish Parliament through the South of Scotland Regional List were often parodied by their political opponents for having 'got in through the back door' after being defeated in first-past-the-post ballots. This immediately de-legitimised any claim they might make to speak for a 'local' constituency.[29] However, it also resonated with a wider theme, particularly in Labour Party campaign literature, that local voters needed to be vigilant to prevent the Tory Party 'coming back' from the political wilderness, from which they threatened 'taking us back' to a politically pre-modern Scotland.[30]

Contesting boundaries

I now want to build on the above discussion by briefly exploring local newspaper coverage of Boundary Commission proposals to redraw parliamentary constituencies for Westminster elections. These proposals, which I discuss in more detail in Chapter 3, were announced in February 2002 and met with considerable local opposition in Dumfries and Galloway. In the remainder of this chapter, I want to demonstrate how Labour activists and others engaged with this issue and succeeded in reinforcing the marginal status of their Conservative opponents in local politics.[31] Here, I will outline media coverage of these unpopular proposals to show how local Tories were discursively framed by their opponents as antagonists to the aspirations of a local community: Dumfries. By joining forces with other activist groups and local newspapers, Labour strategists claimed to speak on behalf of that community as part of a non-political campaign to prevent the 'heart being torn out of Dumfries'. In contrast, the Conservative Party supported the Boundary Commission proposals. As a result, Labour activists sought through the letters pages of local newspapers to redirect community opposition to the Boundary Commission towards Tory representatives across the region. This served to dissociate local Conservatives from a community (Dumfries) to which they might have otherwise wanted to belong (claim) and which, at the 2003 elections, they would aspire to represent. As Edwards and Strathern (1999: 151) have observed, this 'divisive side' of the making of community is 'often missing' from academic discourse. After all, the idea of 'community' remains attractive because of its apparent 'inclusiveness', yet it also excludes: '[The] excluded are excluded by virtue of their failure to be part of something. Of course, the excluded may also be identified by virtue of their own power or other characteristics (class, accent, lifestyle), which set them 'off' from others' (Edwards and Strathern 1999: 153). By using this issue to discursively sideline local Conservative representatives, Labour activists succeeded in evoking Dumfries as a community that was also 'Tory-free', making their own (political) claim to the Town (in opposition to the County) as their turf.

On Wednesday, 6 February 2002, *Dumfries and Galloway Standard* ran a front-page news story in which the Labour MP for Dumfries, Russell Brown, launched a pre-emptive attack on the Boundary Commission proposals, to be published the next day. These proposals had been formulated during the Fifth Periodic Review of Parliamentary Constituencies in Scotland, which sought to reduce the number of Scottish MPs from 72 to 59. This was in line with the 1998 Scotland Act, the passing of which had led to the opening of Scotland's new Parliament. Proposing to merge most of Dumfries with the bulk of the Galloway and Upper Nithsdale constituency, the Boundary Commission sought to forge a new Parliamentary seat called Dumfries and Galloway. The rest of Dumfriesshire, including two council wards on the edge of Dumfries called Heathhall and Lochar, would become part of a new constituency called Peebles, Clydesdale and Annandale (PCA). This new constituency stretched from the English border almost all the way to Edinburgh. Predicting 'widespread opposition' to these proposals, Mr Brown said:

> The Boundary Commission has simply taken Dumfries constituency and torn it into three, scattering the parts throughout the south of Scotland and displaying utter contempt for the people of the area. I came into politics to represent a community. You only have to look at the names of these new constituencies to see that they have no common community. The idea that people in one part of Dumfries town should be represented by the MP for Stranraer and the other part of the town should be represented by an MP who covers South Lanarkshire and the Borders is a complete nonsense. (*Dumfries and Galloway Standard*, 6 February 2002)

The editorial in that day's *Standard* sided with Mr Brown. Describing the proposals as amongst 'the daftest' the Boundary Commission had ever devised, the newspaper argued:

> There must be some sort of logic behind Boundary Commission proposals which would throw Gretna, Annan, Locharbriggs and Sanquhar into a new constituency along with Peebles and Biggar! It's just difficult the fathom. The numbers game is important given that Scottish Westminster constituencies have to be cut. But that can surely only play a small part in the deliberations. What about the sense of community, the common bond that holds people together [?] (*Dumfries and Galloway Standard*, 6 February 2002)

The proposal to create the new PCA constituency quickly became the main focus of criticism. In an article entitled 'Border grievers',[32] the well-known *Standard* journalist Doug Archibald asserted that the proposals 'would wipe the Dumfries constituency off the political map' while the free weekly *Dumfries Courier* described the Boundary Commission's plans to 'float off Heathhall and Locharbriggs into a vast new Peebles, Clydesdale and Annandale constituency' as 'bizarre':

There has been an immediate backlash to the plan ... Locharbriggs councillor Beth Gordon is collecting the necessary 100 signatures to lodge a formal objection and Dumfries and Galloway Council members are expected to support a similar move next week. (*Dumfries Courier*, 8 February 2002)

According to this story, Russell Brown MP opposed the Boundary Commission proposals 'because of the damage that would be caused to local identity and democracy'. He warned: 'Whoever is elected as the MPs for the proposed new seats would not be representing natural community-based constituencies.' The *Dumfries Courier*, owned by Dumfriesshire Newspapers,[33] also supported Mr Brown in their editorial:

In defence of the Boundary Commission they had a remit to produce constituencies of an average 70,000 voters. That, however, in our view is simply all that can be said in favour of their plans. We share the view ... that as presently proposed the plans will lead to resentment and confusion amongst voters. As the MP [Russell Brown] points out in a strongly worded statement the changes show a complete disregard for historical, administrative and geographical links. Indeed we are sure that to many the proposals will simply appear absurd. (*Dumfries Courier*, 8 February 2002)

'There may be a temptation for some to calculate possible political advantage from the proposals,' the editorial then warned. 'We would hope rather what is being put forward by the Boundary Commission is judged on its relevance for the electorate in this area.'

On Friday 15 February 2002, the *Standard* devoted two pages to the Commission's proposals under the headline 'Boundary Backlash'. Across the centrefold appeared a full-colour map of southern Scotland outlining the proposed new Parliamentary constituencies. In the bottom left-hand corner appeared an article entitled 'Councillors fear divided loyalty if plans proceed'. Next to a photograph of Dumfries Provost and Heathhall councillor Ken Cameron with Lochar councillor Beth Gordon, the angry Provost was quoted as saying:

I have never seen anything quite like this. To split Dumfries ... We are a Royal Burgh. We grew from the Vennel through the High Street, expanded out to Kingholm, Heathhall and Locharbriggs. We have a population of 40,000 and we are a community. Now they want to split us up. We have to fight this all the way. (*Dumfries and Galloway Standard*, 15 February 2002)

In 'Battle lines drawn in political protest', which appeared above this story in the top right-hand corner of the page, the leader of the Conservative councillors, Allan Wright, pointed out that 64% of the residents living within the proposed new PCA constituency would, in fact, be living in Dumfriesshire. He therefore argued that a 'more suitable' name should be sought for this constituency in an early indication that local Tories would support key aspects of the Boundary Commission's proposals.

Echoing this coverage, the *Courier* printed an article entitled 'Opposition mounts to boundary changes', which reported that the deadline for lodging objections to the proposals was to be Wednesday 6 March 2002. Opponents scheduled a meeting in the Locharbriggs Community Centre for 7pm on Monday 18 February. Four individuals jointly chaired the meeting: the two Independent councillors for Heathhall and Lochar – Provost Cameron and Councillor Gordon respectively – as well as Russell Brown MP and the Labour MSP for Dumfries, Dr Elaine Murray. According to Mr Brown: 'This is a non-political campaign and I know that some residents have been angered by politicians who have commented that the plans are fine because they are good for their own political party' (*Dumfries Courier*, 8 February 2002). Approximately 250 people attended this meeting, the first of several that the newly formed Heathhall and Lochar Working Group held to campaign against the proposals right up to a few days before the Commission's public inquiry on 14–15 November 2002. Around the same time, Dumfries and Galloway Council decided formally to object to the proposed boundary changes and set up their own working group on the issue 'despite objections from the Tory group' of councillors (*Dumfries and Galloway Standard*, 20 February 2002).

Following the establishment of the Heathhall and Lochar Working Group, opposition to the Commission's proposals quickly gathered pace as a petition circulated in Dumfries attracted several hundred signatures. Dumfriesshire Newspapers decided to launch their own campaign to oppose the new electoral boundaries and 'Keep our identity!' With the council lodging a formal objection, it was now inevitable that the Boundary Commission would hold a public inquiry into its proposals for Dumfries and Galloway. However, the *Courier* actively encouraged its readers to object to the changes, inviting them to cut out and complete a coupon in the bottom right-hand corner of the page before returning it to their newspaper office in Annan. 'The big fear is that the lack of community identity in both constituencies would lead to apathy at future Westminster elections,' the *Courier* argued, 'a weakening of the region's identity and local democracy' (*Dumfries Courier*, 22 February 2002). A week later, the *Courier* reported that their campaign had generated a 'massive response' from 'around 1100 people.' The article also reported that Mr Brown had called upon community councils throughout the region to make their own submissions 'to let the Commission know community views.'

Anti-politics

Drawing on the support of a variety of political and other community groups in Dumfries, opponents of the proposed boundary changes were able to present themselves as 'non-political' advocates for the community. As a result, some involved in this campaign were able to argue that the Scottish Conservatives, who had decided to support the Boundary Commission's proposals, were motivated solely by electoral self-interest. I now suggest that casting the motives of the Tory Party in Scotland in this way performed a kind of *anti-politics* in which the partisan, political interests of some are identified and named while others are disguised.[34] This can be clearly seen in the letters pages of local newspapers.

In addition to the press coverage described above, several letters to the editor

were published on this issue. As most of them were 'written' by Labour activists and councillors as well as their Conservative opponents, the letters pages of
local newspapers effectively became a discursive battleground for rival activists.[35]
The first was published under the name of a local tradesman who was one of
the Dumfries Labour Party's then most effective fundraisers. Entitled 'Proposed
boundaries shake-up is farcical', it quickly honed on another political target:

> It is difficult to imagine that anybody sensible could find these proposals to be
> fair or acceptable – which is probably why local Tory Politicians have given them
> their full backing. Whilst it will be of little surprise to many people that the Tories
> have taken a 'What's in it for me?' attitude to the proposals, I wonder if the people
> of Locharbriggs and Heathhall are aware that Tory List MSP David Mundell,
> the Tories' candidate at the last General Election John Charteris, and the Tory
> Councillors on Dumfries and Galloway Council have actually given their full
> backing to the bizarre plans and described the decision to dump Locharbriggs
> and Heathhall out of Dumfries as 'good news for the Conservative Party'?
> (*Dumfries Courier*, 27 February 2002)

This was the first of several letters that accused local Tory representatives of
supporting the boundary changes for reasons of political expediency. In a letter
entitled 'Constituency split makes no sense', another Labour activist congratulated Dumfriesshire Newspapers for organising their campaign to 'Keep our
identity!' He then went on to attack the stance of the South of Scotland MSP
David Mundell, addressing both local electors in Northeast Dumfries at the same
time as the aspiring Conservative candidate himself:

> We expect our local politicians to support us, so I have a very clear message to
> Mr Mundell. He has said that he will be standing for the Conservative Party in
> Dumfries Constituency at the Scottish Parliament election next year and no doubt
> he will be looking for the votes of the people of Locharbriggs and Heathhall.
> However, unless he is willing to back our community against the Boundary
> Commission's plans to boot Heathhall and Locharbirggs out of Dumfries
> Constituency, then I am sure I will not be the only resident who will have no hesi-
> tation in booting out Mr Mundell's plans to represent Dumfries Constituency.
> (*Dumfries Courier*, 1 March 2002)

The long-serving Labour councillor Tom McAughtrie also set his sights on Mr
Mundell. 'It is not often that David Mundell MSP is right and true to form he is
wrong again,' he quipped:

> Mr Mundell and his Conservative cohorts are obviously driven by their cynical
> desire to manipulate boundaries their advantage, rather than listening to the view
> of the people. No, I am afraid that Mr Mundell is suffering from a classic example
> of foot-in-the-mouth disease and the sooner he is humanely democratically
> culled the better for everyone. (*Dumfries and Galloway Standard*, 8 March 2002)

In response to these letters, the Tory MP for Galloway and Upper Nithsdale,
Peter Duncan, argued that the proposed changes were inevitable because of the
Scotland Act 1998, which the Blair government had introduced. In 'Status quo
not an option', he wrote:

[If] you believe that the new constituencies will be too large geographically, then your argument is not with the Boundary Commission, it is with those MPs who voted for the Scotland Act in 1998. That legislation created the Scottish Parliament and stipulated that the average constituency size for Westminster would have to increase to 70,000. It is, frankly, ridiculous now to renege on that part of the deal, as is being attempted by Russell Brown MP and Dumfries and Galloway Council. (*Dumfries and Galloway Standard*, 8 March 2002)

Furthermore, Mr Duncan suggested that there were other reasons why the local Labour Party opposed the proposals:

The Labour Party has spent most of the last four weeks dedicated to designing a constituency that suits them politically. The MP and MSP for Dumfries have each spent a huge amount of time on press comments, press releases, public meetings, postcard campaigns and party political planning. The people of Dumfries deserve full-time representation on the issues that matter; not misinformation and distortion from those spending all their time on gerrymandering. (*Dumfries and Galloway Standard*, 8 March 2002)

Prominent amongst the other Conservative letter-writers was Lt Col. John Charteris, the unsuccessful candidate for the Dumfries constituency in the 2001 general election. In a letter entitled 'Boundary Commission proposals', he argued that Mr Brown had his own 'deeper' reasons for opposing the boundary changes:

What is very good news is that Russell Brown will lose his seat [if the Boundary Commission proposals are implemented] and the new constituency will almost certainly have a built-in Conservative majority. Russell Brown voted for the reduced number of Westminster constituencies in Scotland and we all know what happens to the turkey who votes for Christmas. (*Dumfries Courier*, 8 March 2002)

Of course, to assert that the new PCA constituency contained a 'built-in Conservative majority' appeared to articulate an explicit reason why the local Tory Party might possess an interest in supporting the changes. This was probably not Lt Col. Charteris' intention. However, some Party strategists explained to me later that his intervention in the debate about the Boundary Commission proposals had been 'unhelpful' to their wider campaign. But they also felt that the local Labour Party had equally strong electoral reasons for wanting to preserve the status quo. Furthermore, they found Mr Brown's assertion that the campaign against the boundary changes was 'non-political' disingenuous. As one Tory activist argued in a letter to the *Dumfries Courier* on 8 March 2002: 'In your previous issue, you published a photograph of ten adults and one child marking the [Keep our identity!] campaign's launch. Of that number, eight adults are known Labour supporters – including a Labour MP and a Labour MSP – scarcely an apolitical group!'

This did not, however, stop local Labour activists from charging that the Scottish Conservatives were trying to 'manipulate' the Boundary Commission proposals to their own electoral advantage. As Councillor McAughtrie responded:

John Charteris seems to believe one of the seats will have a built-in Tory majority, I say to him, don't count your chickens before they hatch. After all, the electorate gave him a red face and a bloody nose at the last election. The Tories would do well to heed the people rather than trying to manipulate matters to their own advantage. (*Dumfries Courier*, 15 March 2002)

In the next chapter, I explore the struggle over the Boundary Commission proposals in more detail, focusing particularly on testimony presented to a public inquiry held on this issue in Dumfries on 14–15 November 2002. For now, I want to note that letters from Labour activists like those described above sought to portray local Tory support for the Boundary Commission proposals as motivated by political self-interest and a desire to maximise the Party's future electoral chances. Such attacks were empowered locally because Labour activists were able to identify themselves as supporters of a 'non-political' campaign to oppose the boundary changes. The Labour MP Russell Brown and his supporters could therefore disguise their own political interest in seeking to preserve the electoral status quo at the same time as politicising that of the local Tory Party, which they claimed was playing politics by selfishly asking 'What's in it for me?' rather than seeking to 'speak out' for the community. Politics, according to this argument, is practised in opposition to community; it is peddled from somewhere else. Indeed, the idea of 'community' can be 'mobilized to designate an inclusive set of people and to exclude others; who belongs to it shifts according to the reasons for formulating it' (Edwards 2000: 248). Asserting the right to name certain arguments and positions 'political' became itself a powerful tool in the hands of local Labour activists. On this occasion, they succeeded in casting Conservative representatives to the margins of local politics by discursively situating them in opposition to the community. Nevertheless, from this marginal location, local Tories continued to exercise a compelling presence in the imaginations of their opponents, as the above press coverage demonstrates.

Notes

1 Those that were better attended included annual meetings of local and regional civic organisations like the Solway Firth Partnership and the Southern Uplands Partnership, both of which attracted over 100 participants.
2 I tutored an introductory course at the Crichton University Campus and this individual had been one of my students. In December 2002, I attended my first official Conservative Party event: Christmas drinks at a *big hoose* near Lockerbie. A Conservative MSP introduced me to the property owner and Chairman of the local branch, the very student about whom I had had my suspicions! My surprise was later replaced by embarrassment when I won the evening's (non-alcoholic) raffle prize.
3 I later learnt that this individual was an important financial donor to the local Conservative Party.
4 For more on Lt Col. John Charteris, see Chapter 5.
5 The 'safest' seat was Eastwood, just outside Glasgow. Very few Scottish Conservatives had anticipated defeat in these two constituencies before the 1997 general election.

6 This description was used on the menu at the Labour Party Burns Supper I attended in January 2002. Almost 200 people attended this event, including many important local opinion-formers. It was held in memory of a recently deceased Labour activist who had been prominent in the community and had been the candidate Lord Monro defeated when he was first elected in 1964.

7 According to the Rt Hon. Lang, he won the 1979 general election because local Tories regarded rural Galloway as 'a natural Tory seat that had gone wrong' for which they demonstrated 'massive determination to win … back' (Lang 2002: 43).

8 These ranged from humorous stories about Lord Monro, which were told with considerable affection, to bitter accounts of Thatcherism, which one woman I met blamed for the destruction of her husband's small business in the 1980s.

9 Some Conservatives, including members of the Scottish Tory Reform Group (STRG), supported devolution (cf Hearn 2000). One STRG supporter who lived near Dumfries told me about her disillusionment with her party on this issue. She remembered campaigning for a Scottish Parliament in the 1970s with many leading Tories, including Sir Malcolm Rifkind MP. A proud 'One Nation' Tory and passionate about human rights, she had partly attributed the dramatic deterioration in the Party's electoral fortunes north of the border to the death of the pro-devolution Conservative MP Alick Buchanan-Smith in the early 1990s.

10 As Hutchison (2001: 176) notes, very little scholarship exists on the Scottish Conservatives, unlike the Scottish Labour Party and the SNP (but not, interestingly, the Liberal Democrats).

11 Although for a recent reappraisal of Margaret Thatcher's legacy in Scotland, see Torrance (2009).

12 The Poll Tax was introduced in Scotland several months before England. This contributed to a sense that Scotland was being penalised and treated differently.

13 Ironically, the UK Conservatives were the first political Party to embrace devolution, under Ted Heath's leadership in the late 1960s (cf Lang 2002). This policy was reversed under the leadership of Margaret Thatcher in the 1970s, which prompted Alick Buchanan-Smith MP to resign as Shadow Secretary of State for Scotland.

14 Lord Monro had been Chairman and Vice-President of the Dumfries Unionist Party before his first election as MP. During this period, it was common for Scottish Tories to run as Unionist candidates in elections, partly to appeal to anti-Labour Liberal voters who found themselves disenfranchised following the collapse of their party during the inter-war period (cf Hutchison 2001). According to the minutes of the Kirkcudbright branch of the Labour Party, which are archived in the Stewartry Museum, local Labour activists had debated in September 1959 whether they should support a Liberal candidate 'so that the Tories might be defeated' at the next general election. However, this idea was rejected when it was pointed out that 'so far as we are concerned Liberals and Tories are one and [the] same'.

15 Several activists speculated that if Lord Monro had not retired in 1997, he might have held Dumfries as Scotland's only surviving Tory MP on a much-reduced margin.

16 Struan Stevenson was a farmer from South Ayrshire who was later elected a Conservative MEP in the 1999 European elections. On a low voter turnout, this election was an unexpected success for the Scottish Conservatives, who won two of seven available seats in the European Parliament.

17 This memory remained painful for her. In 2003, she refused to canvass on her own and seemed reluctant to do so even when in the company of other volunteers.

18 At that time, the Scottish Conservative and Unionist Party was divided into

'Associations' that covered most of Scotland's 72 parliamentary constituencies. Two of the largest were the Dumfries Conservative Constituency Association and Galloway and Upper Nithsdale. The branch returns kept by the local Party Associations often contained the names and addresses of former members who had not paid their subscriptions ('subs') in many years. These individuals were usually treated as if they were still party members.

19 The local Associations usually paid the salaries of staff that worked for them by cheque in monthly arrears. Given the uncertainties surrounding the Party's cash flow, these professionals were often paid late. This was perceived to be one of the contributing factors to the high turnover of Conservative Party staff in Dumfries and Galloway.

20 The Dumfries Conservative Ladies Lunch Club held a series of well-attended lunches with guest speakers throughout the year. It continued to organise meetings even when the local Party's network of branches and grassroots activists collapsed around it, thus setting a positive example for other activists to follow.

21 Without seeking to equate the political humiliation of the Scottish Tories in the late 1990s with the physical suffering of her ethnographic subjects, I borrow this notion from the anthropologist Veena Das (1995: 20).

22 'Remembering' a better age marked by past glories is vital for motivating activists, as Richard Handler (1988: 50–51) has argued in relation to the nationalist imagination.

23 Borrowing from Malkki (1997: 92–93), I suggest that the 'trauma' of being displaced institutionally left emotional 'traces and afterlives' on local Party activists.

24 When she learned that I was writing an ethnography of Scottish Tories, a Liberal Democrat supporter laughed, retorting: 'I can see the newspaper headline already: Anthropologist Discovers Neanderthal Man Alive and Well and Voting Tory in Dumfries and Galloway!' Her humour would appear to reveal as much about her understanding of social anthropology as it might about Scottish Conservatism.

25 A staunch anti-devolutionist, the Rt Hon. Lang was often caricatured by Scottish Nationalists in the region as the public face of Thatcherism in Scotland in the early 1990s. Residing instead in neighbouring South Ayrshire, the fact that he did not live in his constituency formed the basis of a local SNP campaign to portray him as 'an absentee landlord' who spent all his time in London.

26 For more on the differences between FPTP and PR elections, see Lundberg 2007.

27 Seventeen Conservatives were elected to the Scottish Parliament via PR. In the Ayr by-election held a few months later, the Conservative Party won its first FPTP seat in the Scottish Parliament, bringing their total number to eighteen MSPs.

28 For more on that election, see Butler and Kavanagh (2002).

29 Scottish Parliament rules prevented List MSPs from identifying themselves with geographical units smaller than the Region through which they were elected. This was intended to avoid confusion and duplication of representation between 'Constituency' and 'List' Members of the Scottish Parliament. South of Scotland Tory MSPs attempted to sidestep this rule by describing themselves as 'local' so that David Mundell, for example, became the 'local' South of Scotland MSP with an office in Castle Street, Dumfries. A practice adopted by other parties elsewhere in Scotland, this was widely resented by Constituency MSPs who accused List MSPs of 'shadowing' them in their parliamentary work.

30 In their leaflet entitled *Dumfries Constituency Rose* distributed in April 2003, for example, the local Labour Party declared: 'Don't let the Tories take us back with cuts to schools and hospitals.' I discuss this leaflet in Chapter 5.

31 For more on local newspapers in Dumfries and Galloway, see Chapter 5.

32 This was a pun on border 'reivers', bandits who attacked travellers in the borderlands of southern Scotland and northern England during the Middle Ages (Neville 1998; see also Gray 1999, 2000).

33 See Chapter 5 for more on this newspaper group.

34 I borrow this notion of anti-politics from the anthropologist James Ferguson (1990), although he uses the term somewhat differently to explore the unacknowledged outcomes of a failed and misguided development project in Lesotho.

35 I have no reason to doubt that those who claimed public authorship of such letters actually wrote them. However, I later learnt that many 'political' letters to the editor were, in fact, 'ghost written' by senior activists and party professionals. This is discussed further in Chapter 5.

3

Dispelling Doonhamers: naming and the numbers game

> We are talking about percentages, the mileages between A and B, what percentage of what constituency is going to be in what. We are talking about people – that's what the Boundary Commission should be about and there are exceptions ... where the Boundary Commission can deviate from the quota of 70,000 and these are the reasons being put forward by the Dumfries and Galloway Council. (*Labour councillor John Forteath during the Boundary Commission public inquiry*)

In accordance with the 1998 Scotland Act, one consequence of Scottish devolution saw the number of Scottish MPs at Westminster cut from 72 to 59.[1] This reduction was designed to 'correct' an imbalance that had grown over a long electoral history in which parliamentary constituencies in Scotland had been made smaller than those in England in order to 'protect' Scottish interests at Westminster (cf Bogdanor 1999). With the advent of the Scottish Parliament, the Boundary Commission for Scotland was charged with the task of cutting the number of MPs north of the border during the Fifth Periodic Review of Parliamentary Constituencies in Scotland. It sought to achieve this goal by applying, for the first time, the electoral quota for English constituencies, which stood at 69,934 electors, to Scotland. On 7 February 2002, the Boundary Commission published provisional recommendations to abolish the Dumfries constituency represented by the Labour MP Russell Brown. As discussed at the end of the previous chapter, these proposals met fierce resistance from local activists in Dumfries and Galloway. Fearing a loss of identity neatly encapsulated in the name attributed to natives of Dumfries (Doonhamers), activists from the Heathhall and Lochar Working Group and their local Labour Party allies rallied against the proposed PCA constituency. The new parliamentary seat was variously described in local newspapers as 'a hybrid unit', 'leftovers', 'a thing of rags and patches', 'a faceless, rural conglomeration' and 'an incredible area with no identity'.[2] All of these descriptions evoked an idea that the new PCA constituency was made of disparate parts that did not belong to the whole (cf Strathern 1992a). In this chapter, then, I analyse what activists meant when they described a parliamentary constituency as a hybrid. Given that electoral boundaries have attracted very little inter-est from social scientists, let alone anthropologists, this might seem a somewhat banal issue on which to focus ethnographic attention. Yet, as Richard Ford (2001: 216) has argued, territorial jurisdiction is not a 'neutral slate on which a pre-existing and authentic identity can be inscribed'. To explore a debate around the making of parliamentary constituencies in rural Scotland, I borrow from Jeanette Edwards (2000: 31) the idea that the material described in this chapter provides 'an ethnographic window' for discerning 'notions of what constitutes relatedness, which usually remain implicit'.[3]

The Boundary Commission held a public inquiry in Dumfries on 14–15 November 2002 in the council's offices on English Street, Dumfries. Many acti-vists viewed this inquiry as an opportunity to persuade the Commission to abandon its proposals to abolish the Dumfries constituency on the grounds that this would break 'local ties' between communities. However, they faced two dif-ficult hurdles. First, local Conservatives had mobilised a campaign to support the Boundary Commission proposals. Second, and possibly more importantly, it was not clear what evidence or criteria the Boundary Commission might consider relevant in determining whether or not to heed local opposition to its proposals. Indeed, in their history of electoral boundaries in Britain, Rossiter *et al.* (1999) argue that the so-called 'British compromise', which seeks to reconcile conflict-ing interests within the electoral system, remains ambiguous:

> It expresses two of the main requirements – equal representation of people and separate representation of communities – in its redistricting rules which … are ambiguous and unclear with regard to the relative priority of the various criteria. With regard to the third – the representation of party interests – it allows the parties to seek influence over the redistricting procedures, within the context of the other, ambiguous, criteria. (Rossiter et al. 1999: 16)

Confronted with such ambiguity, activists presented evidence to the two-day in-quiry in terms with which they were familiar (cf Edwards 2000: 23). As a result, it was not always clear where the argument was going or whether it would 'make a difference'. An Assistant Commissioner appointed by the Boundary Commission presided at the public inquiry. Next to him sat a stenographer, whose transcript of the two days would later appear on the Boundary Commission's web site (www.bcomm-scotland.gov.uk). To his left was a chair from which 'witnesses' would 'give evidence'. Sitting at tables immediately in front of him were representatives of the local Labour Party as well as the Scottish Conservatives. An audience of up to 100 people sat beyond them. The ethnographic material presented here has been reconstructed from observations I made as a member of that audience as well as the transcript of the inquiry itself.

This two-day event adopted many quasi-legal forms. For instance, witnesses were subjected to 'cross-examination' from other witnesses. Roger Pratt, a profes-sional Election Agent employed by the Scottish Conservative and Unionist Party, led the questioning of opponents to the Boundary Commission's proposals. Likewise, John Denning, a solicitor working for the local Labour Party, headed the interrogation of (mainly Conservative Party) supporters of the proposals. However, in some important areas, the inquiry did not conform to the legal conventions one might expect of other inquiries, tribunals and commissions (e.g. Dominy 2001: 207–232, Wilson 2001) or even a parliamentary debate. Unlike the experience of Mashpee Indians asserting a land claim on Cape Cod (Clifford 1988), for instance, there was very little discussion about the rules of evidence (cf Ginzburg 1990, 1999), although it was not very clear why this should have been the case. Witnesses presented copious amounts of information without necessarily establishing their sources, drawing on diverse genres of knowledge production (Miyazaki 2004: 71). For some, it seemed as if the sheer strength of public feeling, which highlighted the need to put 'local ties' between people and 'communities' before 'a numbers game', combined with the weight of words themselves, would be enough to persuade the Boundary Commission to preserve the status quo. Furthermore, despite the best efforts of the Assistant Commissioner to keep proceedings running smoothly, the formalities of the inquiry were under constant negotiation. When one person was refused permission to cross-examine a witness on the grounds that he was not prepared to 'give evidence' himself, he promptly volunteered to 'come forward as a witness' and the questioning recommenced. On another occasion, when a witness concluded his testimony with a few lines from the hymn 'Abide With Me', a puzzled Assistant Commissioner asked a much-amused audience: 'Well, who wishes to follow that?'

From these observations, it would be tempting to focus the following analysis on the ways in which knowledge is linked to performance and social enactment or to refer to social relations, status and institutions as well as to specific communities of interpretation. It would also be interesting to foreground the apparent disjuncture between the knowledge and experience of local people in a community like Dumfries and that framed by formal and abstract entities like 'constituencies' through which social actors are believed to achieve political and legal representation. While these themes remain implicit in my analysis, I want to remain firmly focused on another question: what did activists mean when they described a parliamentary constituency as a hybrid? I suggest that what particularly matters here are the ways in which diverse elements and material are linked in the making of political claims rather than the individual elements themselves. In 'connecting up', so to speak, these linkages are made to do work, 'ideas trigger other ideas' (Edwards 1993: 46) and claims travel. Such work, a kind of 'joining up the dots' and making of connections that can proceed at a sometimes-frenetic pace, is central to banal activism.

Hybrid knowledge

I begin with Edwards' (2000: 67) suggestion that by harnessing diverse sources and involving (mixing) what might appear contradictory practices, knowledge itself is a 'hybrid'. Indeed, a bewildering array of statistics and information was cited during the inquiry to highlight the proximity or distance between different communities. Arguments raged over the significance of postcodes, the mileage between towns and villages, bus timetables, labour-force statistics, census and electoral data, and the importance of local knowledge. There was also lengthy historical analysis of Dumfries and surrounding towns, drawing on the work of popular local historians and testimony presented during previous Boundary Commission reviews.

The idea that knowledge is a hybrid, a complex interplay of diverse (heterogeneous) elements, is consistent with a view of modern knowledge as 'infinitely complex' (Riles 2001: 18). This view is available equally to the ethnographer and the would-be political activist alike. For instance, the former Tory MP for Dumfries Lord Monro underscored this idea of knowledge-as-complexity when he observed that Conservative Party submissions to the Commission had covered 'employment, history, local festivals, sport, recreation, tourism, agriculture and forestry', while 'the interests of the elderly and the young have not been overlooked'. Linking diverse materials also featured strongly in the potted (auto) biographies of activists as they gave 'evidence' as 'witnesses'. For example, the Provost of Dumfries, Ken Cameron, highlighted his long involvement with local government as well as his 'pride' in Dumfries:

> I am the Provost of Dumfries – a councillor for 36 years and [I have] seen many changes – twice Provost – and I don't think that anybody [has done] any more for the people than myself. I go about the communities of Dumfries and our town and round about and I know the views and this has really upset me – the Boundary Commission suggestions of splitting our town of Dumfries – the beautiful town of Dumfries.

If the Provost could speak of the connections between the constituent parts of Dumfries, a Conservative Party witness introduced himself as being able to detail the 'strong links' between Dumfries and rural Galloway:

> Sir, my name is David Steel and I'd like to speak on Galloway's strong links with Dumfries. I am the Chairman of Galloway and Upper Nithsdale Conservative Association. All my life, my home has been Gatehouse of Fleet. I am a member of the local development initiative, a member of the Children's Panel in Dumfries and Galloway, and I am also involved in a number of historical research projects. I would like to make a short statement drawing on my experience of historical research.

Here, Mr Steel refers to his 'experience of historical research' as well as his position as a spokesman for the local Conservative Party Association. Similarly, a Labour Party activist from Annan placed emphasis on his involvement with several 'nonpolitical organisations', including a number of groups dedicated to local history:

> My name is John Clyde and I have lived in ... Annan for the past five years. I am an active member of the Royal Burgh of Annan Community Council and a member of the following nonpolitical organisations: Annan Initiative for the regeneration of Annan Town, the Solway Heritage Society, the Heritage Society, the Solway Burns Club, and I am also an active member of the local Church of Scotland Parish Church.

These introductions foreground a sense of being connected and belonging to a wider community (Cohen 1982, Lovell 1998). Some witnesses also claimed to possess knowledge of their (local) communities through other forms and instruments with which scholars of political activism would be familiar. For instance, one Labour activist from Lockerbie arrived armed with a petition signed by 122 people. However, while activists drew on diverse biographical details in their testimony, many – such as Robin Wishart from the Labour Party – spoke on the basis of possessing professional 'expertise':

> My name is Robin Wishart and I live in the town of Dumfries. I am in practice as
> a Chartered Accountant in a local firm. I have also had experience as a Member
> of the Nithsdale District [Council] … I have also served six years [with] Scottish
> Enterprise Dumfries and Galloway … and presently am Secretary of Loreburn
> Community Council and [have] recently been appointed Chairman of the
> Dumfries Town Centre Partnership.

Mr Wishart asserted a level of professional expertise that allowed him to use and interpret 'recent' employment data to discredit Conservative Party claims that most of the local workforce was engaged in agriculture and other primary industries (see below). Immersing one in, or making links with, community councils and other local democratic forms led to a competition over 'representative-ness'[4] between activists eager to persuade the Assistant Commissioner of the efficacy of local knowledge in general and that to which they could individually speak in particular. Perhaps with a hint of cynicism, one Conservative Party activist described himself as 'Chairman for the second time of Langholm, Ewes and Westerkirk Community Council; a Board Member of the Langholm Community Initiative; a Board Member of the Eskdale Foundation, et cetera, et cetera.'

Other witnesses, however, did not speak as professional experts. Rather, being 'born and bred' (Edwards 2000) in the area allowed them to speak with authority about the local community. Such an idea was often made explicit. For instance, one Tory councillor introduced himself as someone who had been 'born and brought up' in Dumfriesshire while another activist said he was 'born and bred' in nearby Annan. As the Lord Lieutenant of Dumfries explained when he gave evidence: 'I have been in Dumfriesshire – I have lived in Dumfriesshire for over 70 years – and my family before me a long time longer. So I know this county fairly well, I think.'

Following Edwards (2000), then, I suggest that activists made claims to indigenous 'expertise' based on two alternative kinds of experience: that gained through living in the local area or that derived from study, typified here through the establishment of specific forms of professional expertise. However:

> Rather than seeing these as alternative forms of acquiring knowledge (as differ-
> ent epistemologies), it is more useful … to see them as aspects of each other. A
> notion that knowledge is acquired through study requires a counterpoint, in this
> case, that one can know through experience (and vice versa). (Edwards 2000: 65)

As a result, 'knowing shifts between these two possibilities', which 'are each implicated in the other' (Edwards 2000: 67). The point is that one form of knowledge is 'screened out' at the moment the other is brought into view, but that the two forms necessarily rely on and sustain each other. However, time spent and experience gained through living in a community as well as studying it is not, in itself, adequate. Respect and affection for the local community is also vital (Edwards 2000: 65–66). But if knowledge is a hybrid derived from two alternate, albeit mutually constitutive, epistemologies, does it point to anything about the kind of hybrid that local activists thought the proposed new PCA constituency represented? I return to this question shortly.

Dispelling Doonhamers

Vital for many witnesses' assertions of 'born and bred' status was being able to make a claim to a name. Arguments over names and naming featured strongly at the public inquiry, as they have more generally in political anthropology (e.g. Hansen 2001, Kertzer 1996). I focus here on one particular name – *Doonhamer* – which one resident of Dumfries, Alan Rogerson, defined for the benefit of the Assistant Commissioner:

> A Doonhamer is a person born and bred in Dumfries and really has lived there all their life … I am led to believe it comes from when people who used to stay up in the Strathclyde area but traditionally came from Dumfries during the war time, and they would always say at the end of the week after working in the factories, 'I'm going *doon hame*' [down home]. So the people from the Glasgow area started calling them the Doonhamers, and I believe that's the history behind it.

Arguing against the Commission's proposals, Mr Rogerson declared:

> [First] and foremost I am a Doonhamer. Now that, maybe, doesn't mean a lot to the people across the way here [referring to Conservative Party activists sitting in the audience] but to me that means a Hell of a lot. I have lived in Dumfries all of my life and [am] an integral part of the community and I want to remain part of that community … What I would also like to say, Sir … the Nith – that is the river running right through the heart of Dumfries – Nithsdale. I want to remain part of Dumfries. The Provost earlier spoke about the history, the Royal Burgh—800 years plus! I live in that Burgh – the heart of that Burgh. It isn't by chance that my postcode is DG1 – that means I live in the centre of Dumfries.

Mr Rogerson marshals (links) diverse elements to demonstrate the relationship between a name (Doonhamer) and the object named (Dumfries). These include a river running 'right through the heart of Dumfries', 800 years of history and a postcode. These disparate elements are brought together to give some definition, a sense of place (cf Feld and Basso 1996), to Dumfries. Each of these elements perhaps lacks significance on its own but through being brought (tied) together they are able to amplify one another (cf Gray 1999, 2000) so that the overall claim becomes more than the sum of its parts. In addition, these elements are connected 'without making assumptions about level and hierarchy' (Strathern 1996: 522).

Furthermore, by also referring to testimony that the Provost presented earlier,

Mr Rogerson is able to draw on even more elements, including the town's literary history[5] and historical data surrounding schools, churches, and war memorials. In his evidence, which Mr Rogerson in effect appropriates, the Provost spoke about questions of geography and demographic spread as well before claiming the DG1 postcode as 'our stamp' and citing *Guid Nychburries* (Good Neighbors), an annual local festival in which the Provost plays a central role.[6] Connecting some of these elements, even if only partially (Strathern 1991), might seem 'absurd' or even 'surreal'. However, all of them (and more) made sense to local opponents of the proposals who expressed pride in '*oor toon*' (our town).

I suggest that naming functions to locate (differentiate) a town and its people in both time and space, by bringing together (aggregating) a range of kin-based and associative connections. The role naming plays in making persons seems relevant here:

> Naming acts, on the one hand, to differentiate – it gives voice to variability – while on the other, it aggregates – making the connections between people conspicuous … Above all, they attach persons to specific others … It is those attachments that also give persons their unique characteristics. (Edwards 1993: 58)

Similarly, naming a town and its people foregrounds certain kinds of associations while screening out others. Making a claim to a name enables activists to assert a 'proprietorial identity … over a large range of animate, inanimate, and quasi-animate entities', such as 'one's own past, the place where one lives, inheritance, family names and so forth' (Edwards and Strathern 1999: 149). In this way, naming is closely allied to a concept of belonging, which 'has such an embracing (inclusive) effect … that it can encompass any form of association, including … appropriations which draw any manner of human or non-human elements towards one: "my colleague", "my illness", "my house", "my cat", "my way"' (Edwards and Strathern 1999: 150). To this list might be added another 'element' that a name can appropriate: 'my' or 'our MP'. Arguments about the disparate communities of PCA were often framed in terms of how difficult it would be for local people in one part of the constituency to access their Member of Parliament if he or she was based in another, distant ('alien') part. As a Labour activist from Lockerbie put it:

> In any democracy, it is important that the electorate are [sic] properly represented and if they are to wholeheartedly embrace and use their democratic rights, it is important that they identify with the people who they are being asked to elect. In an area as diverse and as geographically spread as the Commission's proposed constituency, it is inevitable that at least one of the different communities would have a Member of Parliament who they will have little in common with and who will have a limited knowledge of their locality. If this proposal is not overturned, then the resultant socially irrelevant constituency will only serve to contribute to voter apathy and to a further disillusionment by the electorate of our-hard-fought-for parliamentary democracy.

This activist, Ted Brown, argued under 'cross-examination' that the issue was one of identity 'and of identifying with the electoral system'. What mattered from his perspective was whether or not local residents viewed the Labour MP for Dumfries Russell Brown as 'our MP', a man who would always 'put Dumfries first'. According to Mr Brown, people living in Lockerbie 'have no connection' with the town of Peebles, which is located in the Scottish Borders near Edinburgh but would become part of the new parliamentary constituency. As a result, local people would not identify with (claim) an MP based in the Scottish Borders.

Roger Pratt from the Conservative Party confronted him on this question of 'distance':

MR PRATT: Why would anyone from Lockerbie travel to Peebles?
MR BROWN: That's a very good question.
MR PRATT: They wouldn't have to, would they, apart from the Member of Parliament?
MR BROWN: You are suggesting that the people of Lockerbie wouldn't have to travel to Peebles. I haven't suggested that they would, but I think what you are doing is reinforcing the point that there is no cultural, historical link or no common ties between Lockerbie and Peebles, whereas I think [an] enormous amount of evidence suggests that the people of Lockerbie have a lot of cultural and historical ties with Dumfries, which they regard as their county town.

On the one hand, Mr Pratt conceded that there were no 'links' to draw residents of Lockerbie to Peebles. This was in contrast to Dumfries, which they could claim as 'their county town'. On the other, it could be said that the absence of such links meant that it was not necessary for them to be asserted in the first place. Only a Member of Parliament would have to contrive to make them. In an inversion of my earlier contention that local people might make a claim to 'our MP', this point demanded that an MP should make a proprietorial claim to the new seat: 'my constituency'.

Should the Boundary Commission implement its proposals, one of the few certain outcomes would be that the parliamentary seat of Dumfries would cease to exist. No one would therefore be able to represent (claim) that constituency beyond the 2005 general election. In contrast, it seemed very unlikely that Mr Rogerson's postcode would change as a result of the proposals.[7] Meanwhile, Conservative activists argued that the Boundary Commission changes would not 'tear the heart out of Dumfries' and that residents from Northeast Dumfries would still be able to call themselves 'Doonhamers'. Following Mr Rogerson's testimony, Mr Pratt from the Conservative Party declared: 'I'm sure whatever parliamentary constituency [in which you end up living] you will always be a proud Doonhamer.' This remark, conveyed with an air of condescension, provoked an angry murmur from the audience, but other Conservative activists were not deterred. Citing the experience of the Scottish Tories at the 1997 general election, the Conservative MSP David Mundell stated:

I know many Conservatives thought that if they woke up on the ... 1st of May 1997, and Hector Monro wasn't their MP that the world would stop. But in fact it didn't; it just carried on. So it [the Boundary Commission proposals] is not the earth shattering change. People will still be Doonhamers – will still all come together, I'm sure – in the way that we do to fight for Dumfries and to campaign for the area.

These points may have resonated with the Assistant Commissioner. They certainly echoed with some of my own personal scepticism about the occasionally melodramatic claims made in defence of the status quo. This is not to deny, however, the strength of feeling locally about the proposed changes. As I have already stated, in an inquiry where it was unclear how the Boundary Commission might be persuaded to abandon its recommendations, activists argued with passion from what they knew.

A good mix

I have already noted the assertion of one Labour activist that residents of Lockerbie could make a claim to Dumfries as their county town:

> Lockerbie is only some 13 miles from Dumfries and can be regarded as a dormitory town for Dumfries … I can categorically state that many people in Lockerbie are wholeheartedly against the Boundary Commission proposals and have absolutely no desire to be split away from Dumfries, or any wish to be forced into an alien and irrelevant connection with parts of Lanarkshire and the Scottish Borders.

The Labour MP Russell Brown agreed:

> Thousands of people, every day, travel to Dumfries from Annandale and Eskdale for work, social pursuits or education, and they have as much of a stake in the town's development as residents who actually live in Dumfries. The links … are so profound that it would be impossible for an MP for Dumfries constituency to put one area ahead of the other because each relies so much on the other.

From this perspective, the component parts of Dumfriesshire are thought to belong to the whole (constituency). Those living in communities throughout the county are just as entitled to make a claim to Dumfries as Doonhamers themselves. Indeed, while everyone has a stake in the development of Dumfries, the importance of one area cannot be made a priority over another, as all of Dumfriesshire's 'parts' appear mutually constitutive of each other as well as the whole. At the same time, a relationship is implied here between Town and Country (cf Williams 1975). As the Labour MSP for Dumfries Dr Elaine Murray put it:

> There are no historic community ties which link all the disparate towns and villages in the proposed Peebles, Clydesdale, and Annandale seat. Yet, it would be formed by breaking the historic link between rural Dumfriesshire and its county town of Dumfries. Dumfriesshire was forged over many centuries of common history and shared experience; it was not drawn on a map by bureaucrats.

Not only are the 'ties' that bind 'fellow Doonhamers' together at stake, then; so are the 'common history and shared experience' that link the communities of 'rural Dumfriesshire' with their county town. Two heterogeneous elements – the urban and the rural – are connected here. According to Russell Brown MP, to break this link is to flirt with (economic) catastrophe:

> I reject completely any suggestion that the rural nature of some parts of the district make it more appropriate to be lumped in with some communities in completely different regions simply because they too include some rural areas ... Such a move could have a serious economic impact, if it was proposed to centre a large percentage of the economic activity solely around agriculture.

Either curious or sceptical that new parliamentary boundaries could have 'a serious economic impact' on local communities, the Assistant Commissioner asked Russell Brown MP to clarify this point. He responded:

> I believe it works well here in Dumfries constituency, where we do have a fair amount of agriculture and we also have [a] manufacturing sector, and tourism. There is a good mix there ... I think it is good to have a mix and diversification of industrial sectors operating.

Mixing urban and rural industries and interests – of linking heterogeneous elements together within the same constituency – can be viewed as a version of another kind of hybrid in which town and country have been substituted for, say, human and nonhuman elements (cf Latour 1993) or nature and culture/nurture (Edwards 2000). Indeed, what a lot of Conservative activists found attractive about the proposed PCA constituency was its allegedly 'rural' characteristics. Diane Stavely, a non-Tory Party supporter of the Boundary Commission proposals who lived near Langholm, said:

> At the moment, Dumfries constituency to me is Dumfries town dominated, and it means we have an urban MP who naturally has to concentrate on [the] majority of his electors. Agriculture and tourism and its allied industries must be freed from the ever changing of goalposts ... I know our local MP is accessible. It is just that I believe that there are horses for courses and what I need is a rural MP.

Ivor Hyslop, a Conservative councillor, put it this way:

> The idea of a rural constituency to allow rural voices to be heard cannot be seen as an unreasonable proposal. The current Dumfries constituency – because of Dumfries town – has a predominantly urban agenda and any proposal that would allow rural issues to be highlighted by their MP would be of great advantage for the area.

One irony of rendering the Dumfries constituency 'a good mix' of urban and rural elements, in which the town dominates, is that it perhaps better resembles 'a hybrid unit' than the new PCA constituency, which the Boundary Commission had inadvertently distilled of its heterogeneous elements to render essentially 'rural'. Bruno Latour (1993: 10–11) has described 'two sets of practices': one of translation and one of purification, that work together in tandem to produce, in the case of translation, 'mixtures' between different 'types of beings' or, as a result of purification, two 'distinct ontological zones'.[8] These practices are entangled with one another. The denial of the former by the latter 'allows the expanded proliferation of the hybrids whose existence, whose very possibility, it denies' (Latour 1993: 34, original italics).[9] I suggest that these two sets of contradictory yet related practices provide a useful means of thinking about the ways in which rival activists argued over varied combinations or distillations of urban and rural elements during this public inquiry.

Nevertheless, local Labour activists challenged their opponents to explain how certain 'elements' made PCA a 'rural' constituency. Under cross-examination, Ms Stavely had some difficulty identifying whether the textile industry in the small town of Langholm was an 'urban' or 'rural' element, despite insisting that it could be found in 'sparsely populated rural areas'. Meanwhile, Mr Denning from the Labour Party quizzed Councillor Hyslop over his assertion that the Dumfries MP Russell Brown promoted 'an urban agenda'. Revealing that agriculture was the issue on which Mr Brown had spoken most in the House of Commons, Mr Denning declared that this demonstrated that 'rural voices' were 'being heard'. Another Labour activist continued to cross-examine Councillor Hyslop:

MR CLYDE: Right … we heard earlier only 9 percent of the people actually work in rural pursuits. So would the people of that constituency be best served with an MP looking after 9 percent of people that live in it or the 91 percent of people who are not involved in the rural pursuits? … But you still think an MP looking after the rural pursuits would be best to serve that area?

CLR HYSLOP: I think what we said was 9 percent worked in agriculture, not rural pursuits. The rural pursuits are tourism, forestry and the textile industry is also based on the – you know – they need wool and stuff in agriculture. So I think there is more than just 9 percent there – of the population – obviously working [in] rural activities.

There is a fascinating contradiction here. On the one hand, the Dumfries constituency is 'a good mix' of urban and rural elements in which the main town (Dumfries) dominates the smaller communities of the county (Dumfriesshire). These elements are linked in an unequal yet mutually constitutive relationship. On the other, the proposed PCA constituency is 'a hybrid unit' even though it appears predominantly rural, mostly distilled of its urban elements. It is a hybrid not because it links heterogeneous elements. Rather, it is composed of homogenous (rural) 'leftovers' that allegedly cannot be connected even in the most obvious of senses, such as driving from one place to another. Urban and rural elements may be opposed but they nevertheless mediate each other.

The numbers game

During the second day of the public inquiry, the Conservative MSP David Mundell succinctly summed up the central problem with which defenders of the status quo were confronted: could the Boundary Commission justify retaining two parliamentary constituencies in southwest Scotland if it meant deviating from its electoral quota by as much as 15,000 voters per parliamentary seat? He said:

> You have to make the argument to the Commission, which is independent; it isn't influenced by the local press here; it isn't influenced by emotional consideration. You have to make the argument that Galloway and Upper Nithsdale [constituency] can retain 54,000 people. I agree, Dumfries is a sustainable constituency at 63,000 … but you have to be able to make the argument that Galloway and Upper Nithsdale can be sustained at 54,000.

If the Galloway and Upper Nithsdale constituency was too small for the Boundary Commission to retain, then to where would it have to be extended to make up the numbers? The local Conservative MP for Galloway and Upper Nithsdale Peter Duncan offered an answer. Based on his view that communities in Dumfries and Galloway looked 'progressively eastwards' for work, leisure and services, he claimed that 'residents of Kirkcudbright would shop in Dumfries in the same way as residents of Annan would often do the same in Carlisle'. Importantly, the logic of 'looking toward', or linking, towns and villages in such a direction meant that communities in Galloway could make an equal, perhaps stronger, claim to Dumfries as those to its east in Dumfriesshire. It was not just that rural Dumfriesshire could claim Dumfries as its main county town. As the administrative centre for the entire region, Dumfries was also *ensnared* by potentially stronger 'ties' to rural Galloway. Furthermore, the idea that places can be linked as they 'look progressively eastwards' evokes a sense of movement (but not necessarily momentum). When activists made connections between different places, they then spoke about them as if the places themselves moved.[10] This metaphor was especially seductive for the Boundary Commission's opponents, as the following exchange between the Labour councillor John Forteath and Ian Livingston, a 'witness' from the Conservative Party, suggests:

CLR FORTEATH: Mr Livingston, you realise by … taking this Ward out of Dumfries that you are moving Dumfries hospital, Dumfries maternity home, the Crichton campus, and Dumfries Castle into Peeblesshire?

MR LIVINGSTON: And Caerlaverock Castle as well. It all goes into the Westminster constituency. It doesn't physically move.

CLR FORTEATH: Do you also realise that the split up St Michaels Street – looking South, looking towards Glencaple – that this proposal takes the properties on the right hand side of St Michaels Street – the old folks home, the Ship Inn (God forbid) and the area down to the Dock Park – that area jumps over the other side of the street into Peebles?

MR LIVINGSTON: Yes.

CLR FORTEATH: And then the houses on the other side of St Michaels Street go into the Dumfries and Galloway [constituency]? It seems completely illogical.

Many found it difficult to resist the idea that once the connections had been made, claims extend their reach to (other) places, which are then moved (pulled).

Indeed, places 'move', 'jump', or 'go into' different constituencies. Some activists may have found this talk unsettling. When one starts 'playing the numbers game' – or, as one starts to connect disparate parts to form whole new parliamentary constituencies – some towns risk being drawn in all sorts of different directions. Entangled with other communities in distant places, some no longer resemble 'Dumfries and Galloway looking towns' at all, as Peter Duncan MP said of those in Upper Nithsdale:

> It is the case that these ... do differ from those further down the Nith Valley in that their heritage is very much linked to the coal mining industry and as a result retain many of their historic links with the other coalfield communities of Ayrshire and Lanarkshire. The local residents will certainly consider a shopping or leisure trip to Ayr, Kilmarnock, or Lanark before they consider the journey to Dumfries. The local junior football team play in the Ayrshire league ... There is a genuine crossover here.

Strathern and Edwards (1999: 152) have suggested that people 'take pleasure in making links of logic or narrative' and that linkages can 'appear exciting, especially when they cross apparent boundaries'. For opponents of the Commission's proposals, however, the connections local Conservative activists made generated a sense of despair that in some cases bordered on disgust. As if conceding defeat during the inquiry itself, Labour MSP Dr Elaine Murray suggested that the Boundary Commission might have been persuaded to retain the Dumfries constituency if 'everybody had sung from the same hymn sheet'. For some, that local Tories had 'broken ranks' was analogous to an act of treachery. During the cross-examination of one Conservative MSP, a resident of Dumfries exclaimed:

> I would say to you, Sir, do you feel guilty? Because, you are guilty – why, guilty by association! ... Sir, so don't sling it at other people! You are guilty in law by association!

As baffling as this outburst seemed, it nevertheless pointed to the ways in which Tory activists were themselves entangled in various local associations. Indeed, those opposed to the Commission's proposals could even make a claim over Conservative activists (and vice versa), many of which were connected with their political opponents through community councils and 'nonpolitical groups' devoted to historical research as well as other activities. Local Tories could not deny these linkages, or the (local) knowledge that others possessed of them as a result. An ethnographer might share with the would-be activist a view that there is 'something productive and generative in making connections', but in this example it did not always seem that 'connective terms' carried 'positive overtones' (Strathern and Edwards 1999: 152).

It would not be until after the Scottish Parliament elections held six months later on 1 May 2003 that the Boundary Commission published its revised recommendations (see Chapter 8). While plans to abolish the old Dumfries constituency would remain largely unchanged, the 'new' proposals indicated that at least some of the evidence presented at the two-day public inquiry had produced an effect. Importantly, the revised recommendations would include the addition of two 'urban' council wards, Heathhall and Lochar, to the Dumfries and Galloway constituency so that they remained 'linked' with the rest of the town. 'Playing the numbers game', however, the Commission planned to compensate for this move by switching two predominantly 'rural' council wards, Caerlaverock and Nithsdale East, to the proposed new 'hybrid' (PCA) constituency, despite the fact that they contained smaller, 'urban' segments of Dumfries. Interestingly, the substitution of one set of council wards on the edge of Dumfries for another several months later would not appear to provoke anything comparable to the earlier reaction of local people. This might be indicative of a realisation on behalf of many of my informants that much of what was presented to the public inquiry ultimately turned out to be irrelevant to the Boundary Commission's decision-making. From this perspective, it might be better to view the debates that consumed the public inquiry as a performance of a politics of self-knowledge (cf Miyazaki 2004: 50–67) insofar as rival activists competed to enact their respective claims about Dumfries and its surrounding communities. No wonder putting a name (Doonhamer) to a place (Dumfries) mattered so much. To do so meant invoking a set of connections (a hybrid) that differentiated as well as aggregated persons, places and – in the example of arguing over the making of parliamentary constituencies – democratic institutions. These themes inform my exploration of banal activism in the chapters to follow.

Notes

1   Originally, the intention had been to reduce the number of Scottish MPs to 57. However, an exception was made to 'protect' two smaller parliamentary seats for the remote islands of Scotland: (a) the Western Isles and (b) the Orkney and Shetland Islands. Each of these constituencies numbered significantly fewer voters than the electoral quota the Boundary Commission was applying on the mainland.

2   These comments were repeated on numerous occasions in both the *Dumfries Courier* and the *Dumfries and Galloway Standard* during their coverage of the proposals.

3   Jeanette Edwards (2000) treats new reproductive technologies as an 'ethnographic window' through which one can explicate wider ideas about kinship and relatedness in a small Lancashire town (see also Edwards 1993: 43).

4   I borrow this term from Verdery (1993) who has written about the politics of 'representative-ness' in post-socialist Romania.

5   In addition to the poet Robert Burns, the town can claim a connection to the author of *Peter Pan*, J. M. Barrie, who attended high school at Dumfries Academy.

6   Guid Nychburries culminates in the Riding of the Marches (see Neville 1998), an annual ritual concerned with marking the boundaries between Town and Country (cf Williams 1975). Similar rituals include the Beating of the Bounds in Kent (Darian-Smith 1999, 2002) and the Common Ridings in the Scottish Borders (Neville 1979, 1987).

7   Indeed, few local people to whom I spoke thought the changes would make any difference to their lives. One Liberal Democrat activist explained to me after a meeting of the Heathhall and Lochar Working Group that she wondered 'what all the fuss was about' since 'nothing was really going to change' as a result of the proposals.

8   According to Latour (1993: 143), this is a condition of 'the modern critical stance,'

which demands 'an immediate world, emptied of its mediators'.

9   Of course, 'the very concept of the hybrid lends itself to endless narratives of (about, containing) mixture' (Strathern 1996: 522) and can conjoin 'entities' of any kind: 'science, technology, texts, and the contents of activities' (Latour 1993: 5–6).

10   Anthropologists have noted how places might sometimes appear to move in a literal sense, in terms of the apparent impact of erosion and subsidence on physical geography, although one's informants might interpret such movement as a sign that the landscape remains fundamentally unchanged (cf Green 2005: 24–29). Alternatively, Susan Coutin (2005: 202) has argued that 'territories can move or be reconfigured' through migrants 'who exist in multiple places [and] become conduits'.

4

Making (a) difference:
building the political machine

If things seem under control, you're just not going fast enough. (*Mario Andretti, quoted on a sheet of paper pinned to a noticeboard in the local Tory Party office in Castle Street, Dumfries*)

Following the destruction of the Scottish Conservative and Unionist Party at the 1997 general election, local Tories were unable to rely on a centralised Party organisation for direction and support in their preparations for the 2003 Scottish Parliament and local council elections. Drawing on a much-diminished base of support, local Party activists were forced to improvise from scarce resources as they organised their campaign. This chapter provides an overview of the local Tory Party's election planning, exploring how local Conservatives sought to build a 'political machine' through the co-ordination of (limited) activist labour, Party bureaucracy and paperwork. This machine was 'run' by a Core Campaign Team comprising senior Party strategists and a handful of elected representatives, which oversaw the deployment of four 'instruments' that were vital to the local Conservative Party's discursive armoury. These instruments – the survey, the leaflet, the press release and the target letter – will be explored in this and subsequent chapters. Furthermore, considered central to their wider attempts to 'catch up' with and overtake the superior, 'well-oiled' campaigning machine of the local Labour Party, activists viewed the leaflet, which was called *In Touch*, as both an instrument and a building block of the local Conservative Party campaign. This chapter argues that what empowered *In Touch* in the eyes of Tory activists was the leaflet's ability to apparently invoke a set of connections/substitutions between a person (the candidate), a place (the community/council ward) and a political party (the Conservatives) in the absence of such connections otherwise being apparent to a sceptical electorate. Furthermore, persuasive force and the ability to convince potential supporters that by voting Conservative one could 'make (a) difference' was thought to reside in the aesthetic(s) and the form(s) of this leaflet – that is, in its 'look'. For these reasons, the publication, production and distribution of *In Touch* leaflets became a central concern for banal activists like the Scottish Tories. This chapter, then, argues that in focusing on such activity local Conservatives embraced the idea that their chances of electoral success would be improved primarily by addressing questions of internal Party organisation and coordination. By demonstrating how working with documents served to animate and empower Tory efforts to get organised in the run-up to the 2003 elections, my argument complements that of Abigail Sellen and Richard Harper (2003), who have explored how the material properties of paper afford uses to documents that help to render them vital to office life.

This chapter focuses on a discursive artefact that is often overlooked by scholars of British elections, a piece of paper that is pivotal to the making of a political campaign: the leaflet. I will observe that political leaflets stuffed through letterboxes during parliamentary elections retain power for party political activists in an age when anthropologists have increasingly come to foreground the electronic mediation of 'visibility' at the expense of paper. What made leafleting so attractive to Conservative activists during this election was the fact that throughout Dumfries and Galloway, the communications infrastructure that was needed to support broadband and internet connections was very poor at this time. Broadband services were non-existent in many parts of the region and difficult to access in larger towns like Dumfries and Stranraer. This meant that local Party offices had to access the Internet through slow dial-up services that discouraged and frustrated activists. As a result, the *In Touch* leaflet enabled Party activists to extend the reach of their campaign to a wider (rural) electorate that was not 'wired up' to Internet communications in ways that many now take for granted. Furthermore, activists would often describe these leaflets to me as if persuasive force resided in the aesthetics of *In Touch*. This was not surprising given that these aesthetics appeared instrumental to the process of giving shape and rendering legible a Party political campaign.

Conservative activists had made semi-regular use of *In Touch* leaflets before 2003. During their campaign for the elections held on Thursday, 1 May 2003, they dramatically increased the number of leaflets distributed across the region several-fold. Through *In Touch*, they sought to literally render their candidates as being 'in touch' with the communities and council wards they aspired to represent. Following their annihilation at the 1997 general election, there were many obvious reasons why Scottish Tories were anxious to assert their links to local communities across Dumfries and Galloway. At both local and national levels, Party strategists generally believed that the Scottish Conservatives were engaged in a struggle for electoral survival in the 'new' political landscape of post-devolution Scotland. The purpose of *In Touch* could be said to have been to 'embed' a moribund Conservative Party in the local communities from which senior Tories hoped to solicit electoral support. However, even in constituencies that were often described as 'Tory turf', senior Conservatives worried that they could not rely on the electoral support of the communities amongst which they considered their 'natural' supporters to reside. Put simply, it could no longer be assumed that Dumfries was a 'wee Tory toon' (if it ever was) despite talk and warnings to the contrary from anti-Tory activists. Party strategists therefore had to contend with a doubly alienating effect, which reduced local Tories to what might be called the 'marginal margins' (cf Green 2005: 1–39) at both the local and national levels. As I demonstrated in Chapter 2, local media coverage of unpopular Boundary Commission proposals to redraw parliamentary constituencies in 2002 provided an opportunity for anti-Tory activists to discursively situate local Conservatives as antagonists to the interests of local (non-political) communities. The *In Touch* leaflet gave local Conservatives a means to 'speak' for rural communities to which they had been rendered politically marginal but which, in turn, were themselves peripheral to Scotland.

However, an important assumption informed the production of Conservative Party leaflets and other discursive instruments: local people were not interested in what the local Tories had to say. A belief that much of their 'target' audience remained disinterested in political issues contributed to the emphasis key Party strategists placed on questions of form over expectations of a critical reading from those who received their 'literature'. Indeed, senior Conservatives often speculated that local voters would spend less than twenty seconds reading their leaflets, 'as they carry them from the doorstep to the rubbish bin,' as one of my informants told me. As a result, they anticipated that *In Touch* would be read briefly and casually.[1] Through the repetition of language and the reproduction of recognisable forms (cf Riles 2001), they hoped that these instruments would register some form of recognition in the minds of disinterested potential voters. As Edwards (2000: 69) might put it, such forms constituted 'visual reminders' capable of triggering 'connections' in the minds of 'readers' who might otherwise just glance at these instruments in passing. But local Conservatives viewed even fleetingly achieving such recognition as a difficult challenge. Local Tories shared many anecdotes about local voters who never 'read' political leaflets, which seemed to confirm this view. On Polling Day itself, I witnessed an exchange between one local supporter and a senior Party strategist in Georgetown, Dumfries. After asserting that all his neighbours were potential Conservatives, the supporter declared that the Party never kept in touch with them. 'Why haven't you been leafleting us?' he had asked. The Party strategist to whom the question had been directed later told me of his frustration with such individuals who, in his view, had clearly ignored the many dozens of leaflets local Conservatives had 'shoved' through his letterbox. Unsettlingly for local Tories, stories like this one served to underscore the instability of the *In Touch* leaflet, which could easily be (and frequently was) disposed by the householder to whom it had been sent.

In addition, local Conservatives were unable to rely on much support from Party authorities at Scottish Conservative Central Office in Edinburgh. This was greeted with mixed feelings by key local Tories, who felt compelled to improvise in their political activism (cf Levine 2004) and then relieved that 'national' Conservatives were unable to 'interfere' with their campaign. This left them to borrow ideas for their leaflets from a wide range of sources. Unsurprisingly, one influence was the local Labour Party, which had been more successful than them in recent elections and which they sought to emulate in the professionalism of their campaign leaflets. More importantly, key local strategists, including the three elected Tory parliamentary representatives for the region, all possessed

close links to the South Ayrshire Conservatives. As a result, they plundered campaign ideas and material from the local Conservative Party in South Ayrshire,
which was widely considered the only Tory Association in Scotland that had
retained some semblance of political organisation and professionalism following
the 1997 'wipe out'. Moreover, from further afield, one Conservative activist had
picked up a Liberal Democrat leaflet from a relative's house in Balerno, which
inspired a so-called 'hand written' target letter delivered to potential voters in
key council wards during the campaign's final days (see Chapter 6).

In this chapter, then, I argue that the invocation and weaving together of
people, place and political party in the making of *In Touch* leaflets appealed to
an aesthetic that, at the very least, could be said to have caught the imaginations
of local Tory Party activists (if no one else). Devoting many hours to the writing,
publishing, mass production and distribution of such leaflets, local Conservatives
increasingly invested *In Touch* with additional significance as they came to see it
as a vital 'cog' in the making and mobilisation of a successful political machine.
Viewed in this way as both an instrument and a building block of the local
Conservative Party campaign – as both an 'object' and 'operation' designed to
'produce social effects' (cf Strathern 1996: 522) – activists considered this leaflet
vital to their wider attempts to 'catch up' and overtake the better-organised local
Labour Party. Despite its disposability, the *In Touch* leaflet provided tangible
evidence of another object that was both intangible and otherwise eluded them:
a functioning political organisation. As a result, senior Tories became seduced
by problems of form, concentrating less on matters of content, issues and 'substance' and more on logistical and organisational questions – that is, *activist
methodology* – in the production of *In Touch*. Put simply, key Party strategists
tried to address the electoral challenges that confronted them primarily in terms
of overcoming the difficulties of building a political campaign that would be seen
as 'modern' and 'professional-looking' (cf Jean-Klein 2002: 47). Persuasive force
and the ability to convince potential supporters that by voting Conservative one
could 'make a difference' was thought to reside in producing a professional 'look'
through *In Touch* and other leaflets. The connections invoked by the *In Touch*
leaflet were put to work externally – to persuade 'local people' to support the
Scottish Conservatives – and internally, to build a 'professional-looking' campaign. Conservative activists hoped that the sheer scale of the production and
distribution of this leaflet throughout Dumfries and Galloway would produce
positive electoral effects.

Catching up

As I have previously noted, local Tories felt that they were working from a
much-diminished base of support with significantly depleted financial and other
resources, legitimacy and, with the departure of long-serving MPs and key activists in the immediate aftermath of the 1997 general election, local knowledge.
How would senior Party strategists in Dumfries and Galloway seek to address
their 'crisis' in representation? At that time, many of the Conservative activists

I met despaired that their past campaigns had been built on the ad-hoc efforts of the political amateur rather than the strategic planning of the Party professional. With further coordination and an injection of 'professionalism' into their campaign planning, many believed their chances of winning 'back' the region's two parliamentary constituencies at the 2003 Scottish elections would be significantly increased. Given that elections to Dumfries and Galloway Council were being held on the same day, it is perhaps unsurprising that senior Party strategists viewed their potential success in one election as dependent on their performance in the other. Getting organised for both meant attempting to coordinate their efforts across the region so that local Tories could maximise their chances of 'catching up' (cf Miyazaki 2004) with what many considered the superior campaign organisation of their principal political opposition: the Dumfries Labour Party. In the first instance, senior Tory strategists believed that 'catching up' meant 'getting organised'. To this end, key Conservatives formed a 'Core Campaign Team' which would seek to coordinate the Scottish Parliament campaign in the two local constituencies alongside that for the Dumfries and Galloway Council elections in a 'joined up' way.[2] This Core Campaign Team met at 8.30am every Monday morning, from 6 January until Polling Day on 1 May 2003, in the local Conservative Party's office in Castle Street, Dumfries. During April 2003, the Core Campaign Team met twice a week in order to 'keep up' with the demands of the campaign as the pace of activity 'quickened', so to speak. In addition, Alex Fergusson had his own Campaign Team in Galloway and Upper Nithsdale, also with weekly meetings, to which I enjoyed access. These meetings were usually held later on a Monday morning following those of the Core Campaign Team. Meanwhile, David Mundell directed his own campaign with the assistance of his Election Agent, Alan MacLeod. In light of all this potential activity and management, the Core Campaign Team sought to minimise 'duplication' between these different campaigns as well as harness the Party's resources across the region to maximise 'exposure' for local candidates in the upcoming council elections.

As the Party's only Westminster representative in Scotland, Peter Duncan MP chaired the Core Campaign Team. Also included were the two Members of the Scottish Parliament running for the Dumfries constituency as well as Galloway and Upper Nithsdale: David Mundell and Alex Fergusson respectively. The leader of the Conservative council group in Dumfries and Galloway, Allan Wright, was also part of the Core Campaign Team, as were two Election Agents – Alan MacLeod and Hazel Deane. The input of the two Election Agents that the Party employed in the region was crucial as they were charged with the administration and management of the local Conservative Party Associations and the political campaigns they organise. Finally, I was invited to meetings of this small group of key Tory strategists, partly (from their perspective) in the hope that I might bring something 'new' to these discussions. A metaphor that seemed appropriate for describing my location during this phase in my fieldwork was one of being 'embedded', much like the CNN reporters who travelled with US troops in the early months of the Iraq war (cf Agger 2005). Focusing on the efforts of the Core

Campaign Team, I sought to analyse the making of the Conservative Party campaign from the inside out (cf Riles 2001).

In addition to recruiting candidates, developing media strategies and gathering intelligence on local political developments, the Core Campaign Team sought to coordinate the mass production and distribution of campaigning materials, amongst other activities. The Core Campaign Team discussed a wide range of issues relating to the Conservative Party's campaign across the region. These discussions focused on three discursive artefacts that constituted, for organisational purposes, the essential components of the campaign that was in the making. The first of these was a standard agenda, the items of which structured the meeting. This agenda broke the campaign down to those component parts that key Tory strategists deemed essential and which were therefore considered to require some discussion on a weekly basis. The main items on the agenda – Candidates and Council Group; Media and Message; Literature and Leaflets – provided the Core Campaign Team with mental 'cues' to remind them of their ongoing priorities. Members tasked with initiatives and projects under each of these headings would therefore report on their progress to colleagues at these meetings. Along with the two spreadsheets discussed below, these discursive artefacts 'stood' for the Tory Party campaign.

Importantly, these documents were considered confidential and were designed solely for circulation amongst members of the Core Campaign Team. Very rarely were they made available to the Tory Party membership or a wider public and certainly then not in full. However, these (internal) documents anticipated the production of the (external) *In Touch* leaflets I discuss later. I therefore imagined a *chain of documents*, originating from (within) an emergent (emerging) Tory campaign. I will now outline the two spreadsheets Conservative Party strategists used in order to lay out the building blocks with which they would construct the 'whole': a political campaign. The first of these spreadsheets, entitled 'Dumfries and Galloway Council Campaign – Campaign Plan', was produced during the first couple of weeks of January 2003. Providing a breakdown of what items of 'literature' were to be distributed on which days of the campaign, the Campaign Plan enabled members of the Core Campaign Team to anticipate what and when certain discursive objects would need to be deployed. As a result, key Tory strategists could project their campaign into the coming weeks and months. As the clock ticked down towards Polling Day, so to speak, which was marked in a column on the left-hand side numbering 'D –' however many days were left in the campaign, they could build a sense of prospective momentum. This was achieved by combining two contradictory temporal orientations: the first driven by anticipation of the work that had been planned and the second from an anxiety that time was running 'out' to complete that work. By bringing one temporal orientation to the foreground at the expense of the other, with which it otherwise remains incongruous and must therefore be relegated to the background, prospective momentum is generated (cf Miyazaki 2003: 256, cf Edwards 2000: 248).

Furthermore, these two orientations created a sense of temporal incongruity that I suggest proved productive for senior Conservative Party activists trying to address a theoretical problem with which, as I noted in Chapter 1, anthropologists and other social scientists are also confronted: 'how to access the now' (Miyazaki 2003: 255). If Party strategists felt that they had 'fallen behind' the local Labour Party, then building prospective momentum by imaginatively projecting their campaign into the future became an exercise in 'catching up' *to the present*. Viewed in this way, temporal incongruity is constitutive of a spreadsheet like the Campaign Plan, which was a discursive tool to which key Party activists felt local Tories had embraced belatedly. In addition, the sense that activists were running 'out of time' as they approached Polling Day grew especially acute given the fact that the workload detailed within the Campaign Plan was very demanding. Tory activists found 'delivering' on this Plan extremely burdensome. They nevertheless worked hard to outperform the local Labour Party and produce what they hoped would be 'seen' by potential supporters as a modern, professional political campaign. After all, the use of spreadsheets to plan a campaign in this way was considered by many local activists to be 'novel' and 'innovative' compared with the allegedly ad-hoc fashion in which they had previously organised.

The Campaign Plan, then, worked to create a sense of temporal incongruity that enabled Conservative Party activists to build prospective momentum to 'catch up' with the local Labour Party. However, another important spreadsheet, entitled 'Council Candidates', provided them with another means of assessing the progress of their campaign by locating their electoral base spatially. This spreadsheet became important once key Party strategists decided to nominate a Tory candidate in every one of the 47 council wards across Dumfries and Galloway. This objective, a feat that local Conservatives had never attempted in the past, became central to local Tory Party campaign strategy. There were several reasons behind this decision, but two in particular were considered very important.

First, local Party strategists thought it was vital to present their supporters with the 'choice' of voting Tory, regardless of whether or not they lived in a ward that was considered winnable. Presenting local people with such a choice seemed particularly important given that the local Conservatives were the only political group that remained outside of and potentially opposed to the council administration. Furthermore, senior Conservatives hoped that many local people would vote for them if their hunch that the council administration was very unpopular across the region proved correct, as will be discussed in forthcoming chapters.

Second, much like the Boundary Commission for Scotland, which used council wards as 'building blocks' for new parliamentary constituencies as discussed in Chapter 3, local Conservative strategists approached the identification and selection of council candidates as an exercise in building the Tory campaign across the region. In doing so, the Core Campaign Team hoped to achieve a kind of economy of scale when it came to financing their campaign. This was because they sought to share the costs of the campaign across the maximum number of candidates that they could run for both the local council and the Scottish Parliament. After all, there were stringent limits on how much money an individual candidate could spend on their own campaign. For council, this amount was £250 per candidate. The best way of maximising the finances a political Party could spend in the election was therefore to maximise the number of candidates standing for that Party. For the first time in local history, local Tories succeeded in finding 47 candidates to nominate in every council ward across Dumfries and Galloway in the months prior to 1 May 2003. This meant that the costs of campaigning for both the local council and the Scottish Parliament could be spread across dozens of candidates as, for example, candidates 'doubled up' or were photographed together on the same leaflets. It also helped to streamline their fundraising effort so that in letters soliciting monies from wealthy donors to the Party they could suggest a tidy-sounding sum – £250 per council ward, which several were willing to give. Senior Party strategists also hoped that, by nominating as many candidates as they possibly could across the region, they would succeed in motivating their activists and supporters on Polling Day. On the back of a fully mobilised council campaign, they hoped that the two Scottish Parliamentary constituencies would be won as well.

Recruiting dozens of candidates for this purpose proved an exhausting exercise for senior Conservatives. As they plundered their activist network for potential candidates, discussions of the Core Campaign Team often focused on identifying prospective candidates in particular wards under the agenda item 'Candidates and Council Group'. These discussions usually constituted a kind of *para*-ethnography (cf Marcus 2002), where senior Tories sometimes speculated about the political allegiances of leading, local opinion-formers, usually in terms of their family background or occupational connections, which they then might attempt to recruit as council candidates. The spreadsheet would be consulted during these discussions in order to identify 'gaps' that needed to be filled with a local Tory candidate. Once a person had agreed to stand for a particular ward and a name had been substituted for a blank space on the spreadsheet, key Tory strategists spoke as if another building block of the campaign had been success-fully put in its correct place. As these gaps were progressively 'plugged', activists cast their eyes across this spreadsheet and the Conservative Party campaign would appear to come in and out of focus 'like a picture with a low resolution' (cf Coutin 2005: 201). This work continued until that picture became bold and clear, with all the gaps filled, just a few days before the close of nominations in April 2003. In sum, the two spreadsheets described here, when taken together, allowed senior Conservative Party strategists to imagine their campaign working *as if* it was a machine whose parts had started to function, like clockwork across time and space.[3] In the very act of working with these discursive instruments, the Core Campaign Team generated a sense that it was building a political machine.

In Touch

Of the external documents and paperwork all this internal activity was designed to coordinate and generate, one of the most important was the *In Touch* leaf-let. At least one Party strategist estimated that, in the four months before the

2003 Scottish Parliament and local government elections, over 500,000 copies of this leaflet were distributed across Dumfries and Galloway. As Polling Day approached, members of the Core Campaign Team took comfort from the idea that several dozen Tory Party activists were each delivering hundreds of copies of *In Touch* to households across Dumfries and Galloway on an almost daily basis. Candidates for the local council were also involved in this activity, often using the leaflet as a prop when canvassing local electors on the doorstep. As one senior Tory put it to me, candidates 'needed' something to give potential supporters when they visited them at their homes. Serving to highlight the material significance of the paper-based leaflet and not just its discursive functions, this observation struck me as interesting given that most activists believed the leaflet itself would attract little interest from a potential supporter and was very unlikely to be 'read' by most people.

In Touch was viewed as the main instrument for promoting local candidates in specific communities across the region. The Core Campaign Team planned several versions of this leaflet. The dates on which they would be distributed were identified in the Campaign Plan, along with additional information as to which would be posted via Royal Mail and which would be hand-delivered by Party volunteers. The quality of different versions varied as well. The introductory *In Touch* was a glossy, A4-sized leaflet that was professionally produced at a local printing firm, while the second one was mass-produced in blue and black on a risograph in the local Conservative Party office in Castle Street, Dumfries.[5] The layout of the second *In Touch* was crafted, in part, to resolve a number of logistical problems inherent to the mass-production of the glossy, introductory leaflet. Although retaining the name and the 'swoosh' in the header from the original *In Touch*, this leaflet appeared to senior Tories 'amateur' in its design. One senior Conservative explained to me that this second leaflet would complement the introductory *In Touch* by evoking a sense that local Tories were engaged in grassroots activism on behalf of the community, describing the simplified *In Touch* as possessing 'folk appeal'. He also hoped that the second leaflet would counter potential claims from anti-Tory activists that the Party was outspending its opponents and wasting money on multicoloured campaign literature. Several subsequent versions of *In Touch* were also produced in this way, rehashing information from the first two.

I want to now focus on the first, introductory *In Touch* as it tended to be the version a candidate would seek to distribute the most widely and, in small, rural council wards composed of fewer than 2,500 electors, it was sometimes the only version of the leaflet a candidate might produce. For example, the introductory *In Touch* for the Moffat ward showed the local Conservative candidate for Moffat, Safa Ash-Kuri, who was selected late in the campaign, just a few weeks before Polling Day itself, shaking hands with the Scottish Conservative MSP David Mundell in a black-and-white photograph. The lead story on the leaflet was devoted to an important local issue, in this case uncertainty surrounding the future of the local primary school in Beattock, a small village within the council ward. However, a text box at the bottom of the first page detailed biographical information about the candidate, including the fact that he lives in Moffat with his wife and is 'looking forward' to the birth of their first grandchild: 'Safa is active in many local organisations including the Wildlife Club, Probus, the Badminton Club, Golf Club and is a member of the parish council of St Luke's Church. He is a keen computer user and is campaigning to bring broadband to Moffat.' Such brief 'biographical statements', as the Core Campaign Team referred to them, were common to all leaflets distributed in council wards where local Tories thought they could win.

As candidates were selected, an introductory *In Touch* would be produced detailing such information. In his version of the leaflet, the local Tory candidate for Caerlaverock ward, Christopher Carruthers, was described as 'a retired schoolmaster, having spent most of his career teaching classics':

> However, his passion is cricket, and Chris is currently the President of Scottish Cricket (the governing body of the sport in Scotland) after being Chairman for six years in the 1990s. Christopher is also the Secretary of the Dalton and Carrutherstown Community Council.

Following this summary of Mr Carruthers' interests, his contact details, including residential address and home telephone number, were listed in case any potential supporter should wish to ask him a question. Similarly, personal information and contact details were listed for incumbent Tory councillors like Andrew Bell-Irving in Hoddom and Kinmount ward. '[Attending] community council and other local meetings, holding regular surgeries and dealing with local people's problems personally', Councillor Bell-Irving was described as having 'worked tirelessly for his ward over [the] past 4 years'. Furthermore:

> Andrew lives at Kettleholm with his wife Fiona and their two daughters. He was born and brought up locally and is a passionate advocate for the area. Andrew is well known as a countryside campaigner and is now a part-time farmer, having been badly affected by the foot and mouth outbreak. He is a country sports enthusiast, particularly enjoying shooting and fishing.

Such biographical statements are similar to the potted (auto) biographies with which 'witnesses' introduced themselves to the Boundary Commission public inquiry described in Chapter 3, which had been held less than three months before many of these first *In Touch* leaflets were distributed throughout Dumfries and Galloway. The important point I want to note, however, is that by its very name the *In Touch* leaflet sought to render the connection(s) between a political candidate and the community and constituency they aspired to represent a literal one. Of course, it is not uncommon for people to enjoy making such connections (cf Edwards 1999: 152) or to claim that such connections are unique to a person and a place (e.g. Edwards 2000: 248). As an instrument, however, *In Touch* was designed to mediate (link) a person with a place and then, in turn, *a political party* as well. For local Conservatives, the need to assert such connections was considered vital as a means of grounding a political party that many had thought had 'lost touch' with those it had formerly represented. Understood in this way,

Tory activists and strategists involved in the composition of such leaflets were not so much trying to link up 'the textual formation ... with social relations and a larger cultural system' (cf Hanks 1989: 102). Rather, local Conservatives tried to invoke the existence of such links in the absence of such relations being apparent. Precisely because these links remained weak and unstable, these connections had to be invoked literally and materially via paperwork so as to register in the minds of the 'casual' readers and disinterested voters whose support local Tories sought to solicit. Politically marginal in post-devolution Scotland, senior Conservatives hoped that the *In Touch* leaflet would help to connect and then entrench their candidates in communities from which they felt the Party had been excluded, therefore producing social – and electoral – effects.

Making (a) difference

Of course, whether the *In Touch* leaflet generated such effects – whether, in fact, it 'made a difference', as my informants would have put it – is another question entirely. As I will discuss in later chapters, potential answers to this question were not obvious to Party activists, particularly once the results of the election were known. However, the point worth restating is that key Tory strategists worked from the assumption that these leaflets functioned as instruments capable of generating social effects. Preparing, producing and distributing these discursive artefacts would not have otherwise dominated the time, energy and resources of the Core Campaign Team and local Conservative activists more generally. Once the leaflets had been written and formatted on the computer in the Tory Party office in Dumfries, Party office bearers, staff and other volunteers had to be recruited to help with menial tasks like printing, folding and sorting the leaflets. As the office filled with volunteers who busied themselves with such work, members of the Core Campaign Team were reassured that their efforts to build a political machine behind which political momentum was growing were succeeding as Polling Day approached.

On several occasions, however, senior Conservatives were reminded how contingent and tenuous their efforts were. Some activists and candidates viewed members of the Core Campaign Team with suspicion and treated the *In Touch* leaflet, along with other discursive objects they sought to produce as part of the campaign, with outright hostility. I witnessed one occasion when two incumbent councillors from rural Galloway aggressively demanded that their leaflets should not identify them as Conservatives. In their view, such a label would discourage people from supporting them. 'People won't vote for a Tory!' one of them claimed. An exasperated Conservative MSP tried to respond by explaining that such labelling, appropriately identified with good local candidates and a modern, 'professional-looking' campaign, was vital if the Party was to succeed in 'changing the political culture' of Dumfries and Galloway. However, he was abruptly cut off in mid-sentence by one of the recalcitrant councillors, who told him to 'fuck off'. For the rest of the campaign, these two candidates remained uncooperative with members of the Core Campaign Team, most of whom dismissed their criticism as 'unprofessional'.

As the campaign continued, other challenges arose. For instance, one of the strengths of the *In Touch* leaflet lay in its potential to be crafted for a specific audience, which was usually defined as an individual council ward but could also be an even smaller unit (e.g. a village) within particular Tory 'targets'. However, as the Conservatives nominated increasing numbers of candidates for council, the need to make each individual leaflet 'distinctive' in order to target it effectively to a specific local community became extremely burdensome on a political party with very limited technological resources. Such difficulties manifested themselves in different, and sometimes very dramatic, ways. Ten days before the election, for instance, the worn-out risograph in Castle Street, Dumfries, broke down in the middle of a print run numbering tens of thousands of leaflets. At the same time, local volunteers, many of whom were elderly, were becoming increasingly frustrated about the amount of paper the Core Campaign Team expected them to hand-deliver to local households across the region. Many of them accused senior Tory strategists of 'wasting paper' by producing so many leaflets for distribution. Several refused to distribute any more leaflets on the grounds that it was 'bad for the environment'. By the time Polling Day arrived, many Tory activists remained bitter about this issue and continued to complain about the leaflets for months after the election.

Overcoming the problems precipitated by the broken risograph proved more challenging for key local Conservatives. In search of a new machine, they contacted the Tory office in Ayr but were told that their risograph was in constant use as they worked to produce their own campaign leaflets in South Ayrshire. Local Conservatives then contacted SCCO in Edinburgh where little use was being made of its machine. To clear the backlog of campaign material and print off the remaining leaflets, one senior Tory drove the four-hour round trip to Edinburgh every night for the remainder of the week.[5] As local Conservatives struggled to resolve such logistical problems in the production of so many different leaflets, questions of form emerged partly as a means of mediating such crises before they arose. On these occasions, form involved a 'tunnelling' of vision (cf Scott 1998: 11), in turn producing a number of effects that key Tory strategists generally considered to be positive. For example, by standardising one side of the leaflet with a summary of the Party's local government manifesto, members of the Core Campaign Team sought to reduce the amount of work involved in producing thousands of *In Touch* leaflets. They also recycled copious amounts of textual material between different versions. This exercise became one of satisfying 'the aesthetics of logic and language ... in which language [is] cut, arranged, or inserted to produce appropriate strings of words' (Riles 1998: 386). The repetition of language across these leaflets usually became a question of aesthetic judgement, the patterns for which key Party strategists had to acquire 'an ear and an eye' (Riles 1998: 387). This helped to generate 'a solid linguistic regime' (Riles 1998: 392), bespeaking a rational resolution that served to amplify that sense of getting (being) organised. The visual aesthetic of these leaflets, including the Conservative Party 'swoosh', the bold colours, sub-headings and text boxes, complemented this effect. For members of the Core Campaign Team, the emergence of form as a central concern in the production of *In Touch* came to function as an organising, empowering principle in the making of their campaign, an argument I will develop further in the next chapter. For senior Conservatives, the *In Touch* leaflet came to represent 'a good specimen of a particular genre' (Riles 1998: 381): the modern, 'professional-looking' campaign. In the making and management of paperwork, Tory strategists hoped to make (a) difference.

Notes

1 As Ben Agger (2004: 4; see also 1989) has suggested, reading 'becomes casual because people have neither the time to read carefully nor the critical intellectual skills'.
2 This notion drew on the New Labour ideal of 'joined-up' government, which the sociologist Norman Fairclough (2000) has critiqued.
3 Some anthropologists have recently reflected on the ways in which anthropological theorising itself works on an implicit 'as if' logic (e.g. Levine 2004, Miyazaki 2003, Riles 2001).
4 A risograph is a high-speed, digital printing system. For printing large numbers of copies from the same original, it was often much cheaper to use a risograph than a photocopier or a laser or inkjet printer.
5 It did not occur to Dumfries Conservatives to ask whether the Carlisle Conservatives were making use of their risograph. Carlisle is only 30 miles from Dumfries but across the English Border. There were no elections in England at that time so the risograph was not being used, as the Conservative Party Election Agent for Dumfries discovered after the campaign.

5

The politics of irrelevance

I discussed in the previous chapter how senior Party strategists used the *In Touch* leaflet to invoke a set of connections as they sought to embed (local) Tory candidates in a wider network of (local) social relations. Ironically, however, by seeking to render so explicitly the connections between local Tories and a wider community, this leaflet betrayed an anxiety grounded in a very unsettling assumption for Party activists: that local people considered the Scottish Conservatives irrelevant in the aftermath of devolution and were therefore not interested in what they had to say. This chapter explores this apparent 'crisis' of irrelevance for the Scottish Conservatives. In particular, it describes the ways in which local Tory strategists used press releases and letters to the editors of local newspapers as discursive instruments that they hoped, cumulatively, would generate electoral effects. To this end, members of the Core Campaign Team agreed to highlight a set of 'banal' local issues, including opposition to administrative plans to raise Council Tax, the closure of Brooms Road car park and the removal of a roundabout at a busy intersection in Dumfries. This chapter argues that the local Conservative Party engaged with such issues partly because of a predisposition amongst its activists for wanting to grapple with problems of form rather than the 'substance' of such issues, so to speak.

As I suggested in the previous chapter, local Tories tended to focus more on the logistical and organisational questions constitutive of activist methodology in the production of *In Touch* than the nuances and subtleties of policy. I will now demonstrate how the local issues that made up the content of the Party's press releases and letters to the editor, which were methodically and tirelessly produced and circulated across the region, are themselves best viewed as artefacts of activist labour. However, if the *In Touch* leaflet attempted to make connections and forge new relations, the Party's media strategy sought a different end: to sever other kinds of relations in order to bring a coherent (Tory) whole into discursive view. As I have argued, through form and repetition, the discursive instruments local Conservatives employed in their campaign were treated as if they were capable of persuading local people to back the Tory Party mainly by registering some kind of recognition in the minds of even the most casual and disinterested of voters. Understood in this way, potential supporters were construed as readers.

Although airtime on the local BBC news bulletin, broadcast weekdays at 7.52 am, and ITV Border News were highly prized, local newspapers remained the overwhelming focus of the local Conservative Party's media strategy, for reasons that will become clearer below. Analytically, the ethnographer might approach local newspapers in a number of ways, especially given a longstanding anthropological interest in writing (e.g. Goody 1968, 1986) and literacy (Street 1993) that has, in turn, come to fuel a growing interest in the ethnography of reading (e.g. Boyarin 1992, Reed 2002). Here, however, I will argue that in employing a media strategy, Tory activists articulated a theory of reading *as listening* (cf Fabian 2001) that was also constitutive of making (writing) the local Party campaign. I will begin by discussing how Conservative strategists engaged with local newspapers, in the first instance, to 'read' local politics, which some anthropologists (e.g. Schofield 1968, Tambiah 1968a) have argued *pre-empts* writing.

Reading local politics

In December 2001, I attended the Annual Dinner of the Dumfries Liberal Democrats. Amongst the sixty guests, I was seated at a table with a married couple that owned the Annan-based group Dumfriesshire Newspapers. This was one of the few family-owned newspaper companies left in Scotland at that time and was responsible for publishing four weekly papers: the *Annandale Herald* (known locally as the *Herald*), *Annandale Observer* (the *Observer*), *Dumfries Courier* (the *Courier*) and the *Moffat News*. With the exception of the *Courier*, which was distributed freely on Fridays in Dumfries, these newspapers were sold at local shops in their target communities: Annan, Lockerbie and Moffat respectively. The newspapers often shared the same content and editorial, but their cover stories differed depending on the community in which the newspaper was sold, as did the choice of letters published in the papers' letters pages. As we discussed the challenges of publishing four newspapers in an area that encompassed perhaps seventy to eighty thousand residents, I observed that this seemed like a lot of local newspapers for a relatively small potential market. The couple agreed, asserting that there were more newspapers per capita in Scotland than anywhere else in the world.

Whether or not this claim was true, there certainly seemed to be an overabundance of newsprint in Dumfries and Galloway. Apart from those owned by the Dumfriesshire Newspapers and travelling westwards across the region, local newspapers included the Langholm-based *Eskdale and Liddesdale Advertiser* (or the *E&L*). This was owned by Cumbrian Newspapers, which published the better-known *Cumberland News* across the border in Carlisle, and was read by neighbouring communities in the Scottish Borders. Then there was the bi-weekly *Dumfries and Galloway Standard*, published on Wednesdays and Fridays in Dumfries by Scottish and Universal Newspapers in addition to its sister newspaper the *Galloway News* in Castle Douglas. In the west of the region, the *Galloway Gazette* served the community of Newton Stewart, while its rival *Wigtownshire Free Press*, which also appeared as the *Stranraer Free Press* (or the *Free Press*), was headquartered in Stranraer. Meanwhile, the *Upper Nithsdale News*, known affectionately as the 'Wee Paper', was published every fortnight in Thornhill and enjoyed a small but loyal readership in the communities of Mid and Upper Nithsdale, including Kelloholm, Kirkconnel and Sanquhar. Most of the weekly newspapers appeared on a Thursday or Friday, although the *Free Press* came out on Wednesday afternoons at that time[1] and the *Standard* distributed a thinner, less-read edition on a Wednesday. Moreover, some of these newspaper groups also distributed subsidiary papers, often targeting specific communities. For example, the *Standard* distributed a free monthly paper called the *Georgetown News* in the council wards of Georgetown and Lochvale within Dumfries itself. It also published *Dumfries and Galloway Today* for distribution throughout the region.

Identifying local newspapers becomes even more problematic, though, depending on how they are classified in contrast to, say, a newsletter or pamphlet. The *Glenkens Gazette*, for example, was particularly ambiguous. Printed on an A4 sheet of paper it looked more like a fortnightly newsletter. But I discovered that local Tories regularly faxed press releases to the *Glenkens Gazette*, which might suggest that at least one activist group considered it a legitimate 'newspaper' in its own right. Other local and regional newspapers circulated in the region as well, including the *Cumberland News*. Some were sold in remote areas towards which Party strategists directed little attention. For example, local Conservatives were taken by surprise when the *Cumnock Chronicle* contacted the Castle Street office in Dumfries during the final days of the 2003 Scottish Parliament election looking for comments from Alex Fergusson MSP. Published in East Ayrshire, this newspaper was also sold in Upper Nithsdale, an area many considered a Labour Party stronghold. As a result, local Conservatives had been largely oblivious to the *Cumnock Chronicle*, which claimed a readership in a part of the Galloway and Upper Nithsdale constituency they deemed to lack 'relevance' to an electoral battle primarily waged between the SNP and the Scottish Conservatives.

When I commenced my research in September 2001, I had initially dismissed local newspapers as a distraction from 'real' fieldwork. Reading them did not involve talking to anyone or interacting socially with my research subjects. They were also riddled with factual inaccuracies, mistakes and supposition. They therefore did not initially seem like a useful resource for the ethnographer. When I did consult local newspapers, I focused on advertisements for rental accommodation in Dumfries and Public Notices of political and other meetings that might facilitate contact with potential informants. However, as I regularly read the editorial and letters pages in order to gauge local opinion on a range of issues, I soon found myself methodically reading local newspapers from across the region. Often, despite their banality, I carefully cut out and filed stories about local politics that might prove important later in my fieldwork, sifting them for useful 'nuggets' that might shed light on questions of local politics. Attempting to keep up with this endless stream of words as my office at the Crichton University Campus filled with back copies of old newspapers proved physically exhausting.

I later discovered, however, that engaging with local newspapers constituted for many local readers an important social practice. All of the above newspapers enjoyed loyal readerships amongst the communities in which they were distributed, and this quickly became apparent to me during my fieldwork. I began to notice how a wide variety of people drew on local newspapers as a vital source of local knowledge. For example, the *Standard* was well stocked in local shops, and dog-eared copies could be found lying on tables in local pubs and cafes. One of my informants told me that part of her morning routine on Wednesdays and Fridays was sitting down with a cup of coffee and reading that day's edition of the *Standard*. Another explained that before moving on to other sections of the newspaper she regularly read, she always looked up the Births, Deaths and Marriages. The content of these columns would become the subject of conversations with her mother, neighbours and work colleagues. Meanwhile, several of my male informants started with the sports news on the back pages before moving to the front to read the local news. Stories that appeared in this newspaper as well as its local rival the *Courier* would be discussed over a pint of ale or at the school gate as parents waited to pick up their children at 3pm. Local newspapers could be described as playing a vital role in the making of a (local) public in Dumfries and Galloway.

Like other local residents, Conservative activists devoured local newspapers. Mirroring my own practices as an ethnographer, Party strategists engaged methodically with local newspapers as they sought to monitor the media across the region. Indeed, local Tories maintained an interest in local news across Dumfries and Galloway because they hoped to win 'back' both the parliamentary seats in the region, an aspiration that neither of their principal opponents shared in either of the two constituencies. In Dumfries, for example, most did not consider the SNP to pose much of an electoral threat behind an efficient and well-organised Labour Party. However, the tables were turned in neighbouring Galloway and Upper Nithsdale where the Labour Party was regarded as inconsequential next to an assiduous SNP incumbent. As part of their media monitoring effort, the staff of one Tory MSP had compiled several files of old press clippings dating back to the 1999 Scottish Parliament election. In the absence of an efficient means of indexing such items, the exercise of filing cuttings that were rarely ever read again had become impractical. In neighbouring Galloway and Upper Nithsdale, an elderly volunteer had catalogued articles about local politics in a large and unwieldy scrapbook in the Party's Castle Douglas office over several years. This activity continued throughout my fieldwork even though some Party strategists considered those articles redundant. However, others felt that filing and sorting newspaper stories was an important way to 'give people something to do' and make them feel involved with Party activism.

Moreover, I witnessed many conversations amongst senior Party strategists as they first skimmed and then analysed such coverage of local issues. Tory activists speculated about how local people might read local newspapers, as I will discuss below. However, on several occasions, members of the Core Campaign Team discussed the content of anti-Tory letters to the editor. Often, conversations focused on textual clues – a commonly-used phrase here, a string of words repeated again there – that might indicate whether a letter had, in fact, been ghost-written by Labour strategists and submitted to the local press in the name of a compliant local supporter. As I noted in Chapter 2, this was apparently a common practice in local politics. Senior Tories often submitted material to local newspapers in anticipation of hostile letters, thinking it was better to counter Labour Party domination in the letters pages to reduce their persuasive force as much as possible. As one Party strategist explained to me, placing letters in local newspapers made for important 'mood music' in their wider campaign. But they often complained that their own supporters were less inclined to put their names to ghost-written letters attacking local Labour representatives without wanting to significantly rewrite them.

It could be suggested that key Conservative strategists sought to access in the editorial and letters pages a kind of 'internal reading' of local politics (cf Bourdieu 1991: 152–153). If understood 'correctly', letters ghost-written by the local Labour Party might provide local Tories with 'clues' for anticipating their next 'moves' on a range of local and other issues. Local newspapers also provided a vital, informational resource for senior Party strategists and volunteers as they sought to rebuild their campaign machinery. For example, one crucial section of local newspapers turned out to be Births, Deaths and Marriages, which would regularly contain the names of elderly Tory supporters who had recently deceased. This information needed to be updated regularly on the Party's Blue Chip database of local voters, which I discuss in the next chapter. However, Party strategists also used this information to plan their campaign schedule around the funerals of prominent and well-respected local supporters. With the vast majority of local Conservative volunteers aged over 65, the funeral of a well-known activist would render the majority of their supporters unavailable for campaign activities as they instead sought to pay their last respects.

Finally, Tory strategists drew on local newspapers to explore the motivations of some of their prospective candidates and supporters. In late 2002, for example, a small businessman whom local Conservatives had selected to fight a council ward in Dumfries abruptly ceased all contact with the local Party. Senior Tories speculated for some weeks why their letters and telephone calls to him were going unanswered. Some wondered if, as an office-bearer in the Dumfries Burgh Branch, he had fallen out with a couple of other Party members, most probably two women who reputedly held strong views and were resistant to others encroaching on 'their' decision-making in the branch. Another thought that the small businessman had felt excluded by senior Conservatives when he was refused a key to the Party's office in Castle Street. However, most thought it more likely that he had become distracted by a family emergency. Evidence for this latter possibility appeared to surface a couple of months later. A secretary for one local Tory MSP came across a court notice in the *Standard* concerning a young woman who had been arrested for possession of illegal drugs. The woman, so this secretary knew, was the daughter of the prospective candidate. Upon making this discovery, senior Tories were relieved, satisfied in the (speculative) knowledge that the misfortune of the businessman's daughter, who was now facing a jail sentence, had ended his plans to run for council. In their view, the embarrassment and shame this scandal might cause the candidate plausibly explained why he had cut contact with the local Party. Furthermore, the ability to glean such information from local newspapers was widely considered a particular talent of the staff member mentioned here. Members of the Core Campaign Team had overlooked this story and this, they believed, demonstrated a failure on their part to read local newspapers with thoroughness. 'Reading' meant being able to make connections from details others deemed irrelevant in order to properly grasp (local) social relations.

Silencing the colonel

I have already suggested that local Conservatives faced a crisis of irrelevance at the 2003 elections. Relegated to the political margins locally and nationally, senior Tories hoped that an effective media strategy might help to address this crisis and improve their electoral prospects. In Chapter 2, however, I noted that the Scottish Tories, partly tainted by their (former) opposition to devolution, continued to exercise a (threatening) presence in the imaginations of their opponents. In Dumfries and Galloway, anti-Tory activists often caricatured local Conservatives as an ill-tempered cohort of recalcitrant farmers, upper-class landowners and retired colonels. This served to highlight how 'out of touch' the Conservative Party had become in post-devolution Scotland. Before the Core Campaign Team could frame and implement its media strategy, it had to try and tackle these kinds of stereotypes. However, as they monitored the behaviour of their own activists and candidates in the local press, it became apparent that some Conservatives were indifferent to the desire of key Tory strategists to challenge such caricatures of them. One such prospective candidate was Lt Col. John Charteris.

Lt Col. Charteris had been the unsuccessful Conservative candidate in the Dumfries constituency at the 2001 general election. He had become a committed and sometimes bitter letter-writer to local newspapers in 2002, much to the irritation of key Party strategists. A landowner whose grandfather had briefly been Conservative MP for Dumfriesshire in the 1920s, the retired lieutenant colonel was a veteran of the Gulf War who held strong views about issues relating to defence and the welfare of the Armed Forces. Some senior Party strategists viewed his identification with the wealthy county set of Dumfriesshire and his stubborn determination to argue the case for military intervention in Iraq as an incendiary combination. On 15 November 2002, for instance, the *Courier* published a letter from Lt Col. Charteris in which he criticised the local branch of the Fire Brigade Union (FBU) for joining a national strike and picketing the local Fire Station. Entitled 'Pay Demands Unjustified', his letter provocatively described fire fighters as 'greedy' and 'over paid compared to the pay of our servicemen, the nurses and most civil servants'. Responding with 'disbelief' to the retired lieutenant colonel's 'arrogant rant', local fire fighter Andy Anderson wrote:

> I'm sorry Mister Charteris (retired firefighters don't pretend they are still in the
> job using ranks before their names – when we retire we are just that – proud,

but retired public servants) you as a Lt Col would hardly have been deployed on the street as a stand-in firefighter, that would have [been] beneath a rank like yours ... I doubt your lily whites have ever had a coat of grime on them, never mind handled hose! (*Dumfries Courier*, 22 November 2002)

Mr Anderson then challenged Lt Col. Charteris to join local fire fighters on 'a 42 hour watch' before declaring: 'So he feels the right to feed and clothe our children, keep a roof over our heads and have an acceptable standard of living is greed? I'm sure Mister Charteris has never wanted for anything, and so long as there are EEC and DEFRA agricultural subsidies he never will' (*Dumfries Courier*, 22 November 2002). Putting distance between the local landowner of (rural) Dumfriesshire and the striking fire fighters of (urban) Dumfries, Mr Anderson suggested that the retired lieutenant colonel was removed from, and therefore incapable of understanding, the aspirations and needs of those less wealthy than himself. Continuing with this theme in a letter to the *Standard* a few days later, another fire fighter described Lt Col. Charteris as 'petty' and a 'political glory seeker' before suggesting he 'tunes into the real world' (27 November 2002).

Unrepentant, the local landowner declared 'I'm ready for my fire watch shift' in a letter published the following week:

> Last week I attempted to take up the challenge ... to do a tour with the Dumfries Fire-Fighters. The challenge was made in their letters to The Courier. Unfortunately, nobody was available from their side for the challenge. Why? Because they were all on strike again. (*Dumfries Courier*, 29 November 2002)

Whether or not Lt Col. Charteris had actually turned up at the Fire Station for his 'tour of duty' with the fire fighters, most of the Tory activists to whom I spoke believed he was the sort of person who would have done so. However, what made his letters so 'unhelpful' from the perspective of senior Conservatives was his obvious association with them as the local Party's former candidate at the 2001 general election. After David Mundell MSP, he was probably the most recognisable face of the local Conservative Party at that time. Unlike Mr Mundell, he, by his contribution to the letters pages of local newspapers, was cast in the eyes of many people including some Conservatives as little more than a caricature of a landowning Tory 'toff' who behaved as if he was 'born to rule'. A vocal member of both the Countryside Alliance and the self-styled 'Rural Rebels'[2] that had campaigned against the foxhunting ban, Lt Col. Charteris was also keen to debate other provocative issues. These included the Hunting Bill itself, which had come into force in Scotland in August 2002, and the Land Reform Bill that passed the Scottish Parliament in January 2003 and which only the Conservative Party had opposed.[3]

These were issues with which senior Tories did not want their local campaign to become linked as they risked rendering them 'out of touch' with the concerns of non-Tory voters by clearly identifying local Conservatives with a rural elite. That Lt Col. Charteris continued to write about these divisive issues meant that anti-Tory activists could easily portray him and, by association, his Conservative

colleagues as a 'throwback' to a discredited (rural) past based on ideas of defer-
ence, patriarchy and patronage, further relegating local Tories to the margins
in both space and time. For instance, the SNP candidate for the Dumfries constituency, Andrew Wood, asked in his own letter to the editor whether Lt Col.
Charteris claimed to speak for other Conservatives:

> John Charteris was the Tory candidate at the last general election and what would
> David Mundell have been saying, had Mr Charteris been elected? Fortunately the
> electorate had the good sense in rejecting such a candidate. Truly, this person
> must have been held in high esteem within the Conservative association, to
> have been allowed to stand in the first place, and one begs the question of their
> selection process, or the quality of candidates that they are putting forward into
> Dumfries. (*The Standard*, 18 December 2002)

By making such connections between Party candidates and their maverick
supporters, anti-Tory activists attempted to draw Mr Mundell and his fellow
Conservatives on other issues that were polarising opinion at the time. These
included the FBU strike and the Iraq war, for which the then New Labour government was making preparations. Senior Party strategists strongly resisted
such entanglements, partly because they hoped the difficulties the local Labour
Party was facing on these issues might present them with unexpected electoral
opportunities on Polling Day. Many Conservative activists believed that the local
Labour Party's traditional supporters were probably uncomfortable with the idea
that their government might oppose striking fire fighters or commit troops to a
potentially illegal US-led invasion of Iraq. Relishing the discomfort of their principal opponents in the Dumfries constituency, several Conservatives excitedly
told me that the Labour Party was in 'unknown' political territory. As one MSP
put it, perhaps a little optimistically: 'When the Conservatives were in power, the
Scottish Labour Party got complacent, knowing they always had public opinion
behind them. Now they don't have the public on side and they don't know how to
deal with this new situation.' If drawn by Lt Col. Charteris into debates over the
legitimacy of striking fire fighters or the Iraq war, senior Party strategists feared
that, like the local Labour Party, they might become bogged down on political
issues that refused to settle (cf Jean-Klein 2002: 44).

Another development particularly alarmed senior Conservatives during this
period. In early November 2002, an article had appeared on the front page of the
Glasgow Herald entitled 'Pro-hunt protestors to challenge for MSPs [*sic*] seats'
(4 November 2002).[4] On this occasion, Lt Col. Charteris was named as supporting a political party working 'for the promotion of rural matters'. This party was
allegedly planning to target constituencies in the upcoming Scottish Parliament
elections in which the local MSP had voted for the foxhunting ban. This
potentially included the Dumfries constituency where the Labour incumbent
Dr Elaine Murray MSP had supported the ban. Mr Mundell and other leading
Conservatives in the area worried that if such a candidate contested the seat, local
Tory voters would be divided between rival centre-right, anti-Labour candidates.
In their view, this would have virtually guaranteed victory for the local Labour

Party. Senior Party strategists therefore came to the view that Lt Col. Charteris's erratic behaviour was a problem that required urgent intervention.

Eager to dampen his enthusiasm for writing to local newspapers, senior Tories generally agreed that Lt Col. Charteris should be encouraged to remain within the Party's rank and file. Several activists argued that if he was expelled from the DCCA, a course of action that some favoured, he could inflict even more damage on local Conservatives. Outside the Party, he would have been able to write freely to local newspapers on any issue that attracted his interest, while local voters would continue to associate him with the local Tory Party. Senior Conservatives deployed several informal strategies in an attempt to 'manage' the problems the retired lieutenant colonel was causing. One of the least effective appeared to be a series of stern letters sent to him from the Edinburgh-based chairman of the Scottish Conservative and Unionist Party. However, a better strategy was available to key Party strategists given that Lt Col. Charteris was keen to stand for the local council. Senior Conservatives encouraged his interest for two reasons. First, given their determination to nominate a Tory in every council ward across the region, they did not want to exclude potential candidates in case they later struggled to recruit the required 47 candidates. Second, if the retired lieutenant colonel stood for election, he would have to appoint one of the Party's local Election Agents as his legal representative during the campaign. In such a role, that Election Agent would be empowered to vet all of his campaign material and election comment, including letters to the editor. Lt Col. Charteris was eventually selected as the Conservative candidate for the Lochar ward in northeast Dumfries.

Of course, the difficulties of negotiating with such a strong personality con-sumed time, energy and office resources during the first few months of 2003. Senior Conservatives found this deeply frustrating. Exasperated, one key Party strategist asked an influential member of the county set in Dumfriesshire to 'rein in' the retired lieutenant colonel. 'John Charteris may not be particularly both-ered about [our] chances of getting elected in Dumfries,' he said, 'but he will care very much if he is alienated by his county set mates and they no longer invite him to their parties.' On 21 March 2003, however, a story appeared on the front page of the *Courier* entitled 'War Demo Clash'. According to this story, Lt Col. Charteris had turned up to a small anti-war protest organised by the Dumfries branch of the Scottish Socialist Party and involving the local SNP candidate Andrew Wood. A photograph of the opinionated Tory arguing with an anti-war demonstrator was published with the story. The following day, a large meeting of local Party activists in Castle Douglas voiced anger at what they considered to be Lt Col. Charteris's inability to operate as a team member. One activist declared that he had 'gone too far' while another quipped bitterly: 'All he has succeeded in doing is getting a photograph of the local SNP onto the front page of the *Courier*.' The retired lieutenant colonel himself was not in attendance at this meeting despite having accepted an invitation to turn up. As if chastened, he maintained a low profile amongst his colleagues from then until Polling Day, somewhat to the relief of key Party strategists.

Although senior Tories never fully succeeded in silencing the retired lieu-tenant colonel, the challenge of trying to do so presented them with a paradox. Members of the Core Campaign Team viewed an outspoken supporter like him as both a liability and an obstacle because they would not subject themselves to the discipline that was demanded of a modern, 'professional-looking' cam-paign. What was ironic, though, was that many of the issues about which Lt Col. Charteris wrote so passionately – including foxhunting, land reform, the FBU strike and the Iraq war – were highly 'relevant' to Conservative voters and their opponents. Most Party strategists assumed that many of their 'hardcore' sup-porters shared the retired lieutenant colonel's strong views on these issues. When local Party strategists worked to minimise the voices of the mavericks within their ranks, they potentially rendered themselves less relevant to a local poli-tics in which politically potent Tory caricatures exerted a powerful presence in the imaginations of many local people. However, senior Conservatives believed there was a mismatch between the priorities of their traditional supporters and those of the voters they were seeking to win 'back' in the Dumfries constituency. As they tried to render Lt Col. Charteris and others like him absent from local newspaper coverage, Party strategists sought to create discursive space in which they hoped their media strategy, once implemented, might take effect. As I will now discuss, this strategy attempted to sideline divisive national issues so that emphasis could be placed on local issues that inevitably seem banal in compari-son to, say, the imminent war in Iraq. In their attempts to mobilise such issues, local Conservatives sought to invoke other connections that, once forged, could then be made to do work. As noted in previous chapters, such linkages enable (political) claims to travel. Through their engagement with local issues, banal activists like the Scottish Conservatives hoped to extend the proprietorial reach of their campaign.

Of bus lanes, car parks and roundabouts

Prior to the publication of the Boundary Commission proposals in February 2002, it had been difficult to discern much about the activism of the local Conservative Party from local newspapers. Compared to coverage of the activi-ties of local Labour representatives, the coverage of Tory perspectives seemed to me sparser. I had occasionally read stories featuring the Conservative MP Peter Duncan or either of the two South of Scotland Tory MSPs Alex Fergusson and David Mundell. Less often, Tory councillors might be quoted on a local issue, par-ticularly in Annandale and Eskdale where five of the region's nine Conservative councillors were based.[5] I would later learn that members of the Party's Core Campaign Team also believed that Conservative Party exposure in the local press was not as extensive as it should be. Furthermore, as one Tory parliamentarian explained to me, in no other part of Scotland could the shattered Conservative Party draw on a resource as abundant as the number of local newspapers within Dumfries and Galloway to 'put across' its view. The Core Campaign Team there-fore sought to coordinate a media strategy that would maximise coverage of the

Party in the local press during the run-up to the local government and Scottish Parliament elections scheduled for 1 May 2003.

At one of its first meetings in January 2003, the Core Campaign Team discussed how to put together and implement a 'professional' media strategy. A designated Team member who would be responsible for achieving specific 'targets' in drafting and distributing press releases to local newspapers was asked to volunteer. I agreed to take on this role. This meant working closely with the leader of the council group and Tory parliamentary representatives, who usually made an effort to keep in touch with various local journalists on a weekly basis,[6] to produce at least two press releases each week. The issues about which these press releases would be written were decided under the agenda item 'Media and Campaigns' at Core Campaign Team meetings. These releases would ideally be generic in content and, in the absence of reliable broadband infrastructure across the region, would always be faxed as well as emailed to every local newspaper and other media outlets.

Working from the Castle Street office in Dumfries, I soon discovered that the role of coordinating this media output demanded much frenetic effort at the beginning of each working week. This was because almost all the media deadlines for 'copy' fell on Tuesdays or Wednesdays so that local newspapers could be published and sold on Thursdays and Fridays. Finessing and refining the same press release for different local newspapers and then faxing them to almost a dozen media outlets was very time-consuming. Mr Mundell once complained to me about how exhausting it was to keep up and 'maintain the pace' as far as maintaining his profile in the local press was concerned. Local Tory activists often assumed that the journalists receiving such prodigious amounts of copy found this exhausting as well. Indeed, most local journalists relied heavily on the textual content of press releases in order to fill several pages of newsprint. They would commonly draw information and quotes from press releases, which they would follow up with a telephone conversation with the Tory candidate or representative named in the release. On many occasions, senior Tories were delighted that a press release had been reprinted verbatim as an article in a local newspaper. Local Tories discovered that such occurrences tended to increase in frequency when they emailed their press releases. Responding excitedly to one particular edition of the *Galloway Gazette*, which had reprinted several letters and press releases under what Party strategists considered very favourable headlines, a Conservative MSP emailed me with the simple message: 'The Tories are back!' This led Party strategists to conclude that no press release was ever wasted. The apparent overabundance of local newspapers in Dumfries and Galloway seemed to guarantee that every letter and press release would be published by at least one newspaper and find a wider audience somewhere in the region.

As I will discuss shortly in relation to the issue of Council Tax, the aesthetics of Conservative press releases demanded that their content be crafted with clarity and concision, preferably with a bold and memorable headline. Ideally, stories would be no longer than 300 words, although attachments were sometimes included with a press release. These attachments could be drawn from diverse documentary sources. For example, a press release from a Tory MSP might refer to questions asked in the Scottish Parliament. If so, a copy of the question as it appeared in the Official Record of the Scottish Parliament would be enclosed with the press release. Similarly, the signing of an Early Day Motion at Westminster might have constituted a press release from Peter Duncan MP with the wording of the motion attached separately. Meanwhile, a successful HMI report would provide an opportunity for a press release congratulating a local school and its head teacher. Other sources included the minutes of meetings of the council, NHS board, tourist board and other public bodies, all of which circulated papers to elected parliamentary representatives across the region. Press releases of this kind served to demonstrate that (local) Conservative parliamentarians were fully engaged with a (local) politics of representative-ness.

From January 2003, however, local Party strategists sought to address a set of local issues that would enable them to differentiate a Tory presence on Dumfries and Galloway Council. As I discuss in the next chapter, senior Conservatives worried that local electors failed to distinguish between the Conservative Group on the council and the other political parties that formed the Rainbow Alliance administration. The Core Campaign Team decided that the most effective means of quickly establishing such a contrast through its local media strategy was to highlight Tory opposition to several unpopular council policies. Of the potential issues available to them, few resonated more for local Conservative activists than alleged 'traffic chaos' in Dumfries.

By the end of 2002, the council had introduced a number of initiatives to improve the management of traffic flow through Dumfries' town centre. One of these included the introduction of a bus lane on Glasgow Street, a consequence of which was that other traffic was restricted to one lane as it entered the town along this important access road from the northwest. This led to congestion at busy times of the day. David Mundell MSP decided to 'protest' against the bus lane and had a photograph taken of him standing by Glasgow Street, frowning, with a long line of traffic banked up behind him. This photograph appeared in local media coverage of the issue and was reproduced in a number of campaign leaflets in 2003. Similarly, traffic often became congested at peak times around St Michaels Street roundabout, located at a vital junction for access to Dumfries and Galloway Royal Infirmary and the Crichton University Campus to the south of the town centre. In early 2003, construction work began to replace the roundabout with traffic lights, which were operational by the time of the elections. For many local people, however, these new traffic lights exacerbated problems of congestion on St Michaels Street rather than alleviated them. Mr Mundell and local Conservatives undertook to oppose such 'crazy Council schemes' and campaigned to 'save St Michaels Street roundabout'.

To criticise council officials and representatives of being 'incompetent' and lacking 'common sense' is a familiar theme of local politics in Britain (cf Edwards 2000: 200). However, some might argue that an appeal to 'common sense' in Scotland potentially resonated with broader ideas that Scots see themselves as more practical and community-oriented than the English, who are sometimes

viewed as possessing more conservative and individualistic political values
(Lindsay 1997: 145, cf Hearn 1997, 1998). That local Conservatives sought to
frame their political claims in such terms might therefore be regarded as a coun-
terintuitive move for a political party that many had come to associate with an
anti-Scottish, Anglo-centric Other. However, other scholars (e.g. Herzfeld 1992,
Gupta 1995) have observed that discourses of public accountability in a variety
of liberal democratic settings find forceful expression through a complemen-
tary concern with, and allegations of, corruption or incompetence within state
agencies. I suggest here, then, that a concern with the application of common
sense to local government decision-making constituted an important, perhaps
indispensable, aesthetic for a modern, 'professional-looking' campaign. For
members of the Core Campaign Team, it helped to evoke a powerful sense that
Tory candidates were responsible and responsive to the views of local people.
As the only political group not included in the Rainbow Alliance administration, this enabled them to mark the local Conservative Party as not just different
from its rivals but also *opposed* to unpopular council policies for which they were
'responsible'. An additional attraction of this aesthetic lay in part in how it resonated with the Core Campaign Team's wider efforts to get organised and build
prospective momentum. Arguing for a 'common sense' approach to this local
issue meant engaging in a debate with council 'officialdom' about how to achieve
efficient traffic management in Dumfries. This reinforced the view amongst local
Tories that their prime (policy) concern as (banal) activists lay in addressing the
problems of petty bureaucracy.

Local issues like the Glasgow Street bus lane and the St Michaels Street roundabout also enabled local Conservatives to geographically pinpoint sites of alleged
council incompetence. This enabled them to 'ground' their campaign spatially
and temporally, which in turn generated other kinds of opportunities. During
a campaign tour of the region in April 2003, the deputy leader of the Scottish
Conservatives, Annabel Goldie MSP, was photographed at a number of issue
'hotspots'. These included St Michaels Street roundabout and Canonbie Primary
School in Dumfriesshire, which had been earmarked for closure and which Ms
Goldie visited at 3pm in order to maximise the Party's visibility amongst parents
picking their children up from school. These photo opportunities allowed her to
be pictured with candidates for the local council wards and the Scottish parliamentary constituencies of which they were part. This served to raise the profile of
the Party's candidates by linking them with both a local issue on which they were
pictured and a national Tory politician who might then generate interest from
the press. Thus, it would seem that in the traffic problems of Dumfries senior
Conservative strategists literally found both a metaphor and a means for making
connections between themselves and the people and places they sought to represent. By appropriating (claiming) local issues like opposition to the Glasgow
Street bus lane as their own, local Conservatives were able to extend the reach of
their campaign. The generation of such connections, as I have argued in previous
chapters, is appealing to banal activists.

However, local Tory representatives were careful not to claim all objections to council policy exclusively as their own. During 2002, the council had been considering proposals to build a new leisure complex on the site of a large car park in central Dumfries. Opposition to the closure of Brooms Road car park had been mobilised by Jim Ireland, manager of the Loreburn shopping centre off Dumfries High Street. A petition he organised in late 2002 attracted almost 12,000 signatures. Local Conservatives supported his campaign and facilitated several opportunities for Mr Ireland to raise the issue with national Tory politicians, including the Scottish Conservative leader David McLetchie MSP. This, in turn, facilitated a number of opportunities for Tory representatives to be photographed with Mr Ireland and his petition in the local press. As a result, local Conservatives were able to associate themselves with opponents of the closure of Brooms Road car park without encroaching on the proprietorial claim that Mr Ireland, one of the local business elite, had already made to this issue. 'We have to be careful not to tread on his toes and take this issue over', one Tory MSP explained to me. 'We don't want to risk alienating him.'

Such caution appeared to be justified when a front-page story entitled 'Shopping Centre in Poll Row' appeared in the *Courier* on 11 April 2003. In that story, Ashley Banks, a young journalist with a reputation for exaggeration, proclaimed:

> A political storm broke out today over a campaign board displayed in Dumfries' main shopping centre. There were claims the impartiality of the Loreburn Centre had been breached. Labour leaders today attacked Centre manager Jim Ireland for his opinions over the council's controversial traffic management system in the town, proposed leisure site row at Brooms Road and school closures. (Dumfries Courier, 11 April 2003)

The campaign board to which Ms Banks referred contained several dozen clippings and commentary from local newspapers concerning alleged council incompetence and was located by the escalators at one entrance to the Loreburn Centre. In the article, Mr Ireland was reported as saying:

> I am not one to tell people who or what to vote for but if the same councillors are voted in the next election they will see the decisions made so far as a vote of confidence and this is clearly not the case ... Wasted money has been spent on the useless bus lane at Glasgow Street, traffic lights at St Michaels Street and Nith Place and to top it all off their [sic] is still the possibility of losing our busy Brooms Road car park for a leisure centre. Taxi drivers and business people are complaining, people are sick of being late for their work and waiting in the long queues. (Dumfries Courier, 11 April 2003)

According to senior Tories who knew him well, Mr Ireland had allegedly received an aggressive telephone call from the local Labour Party Election Agent shortly after the campaign board was erected. What apparently appalled local Labour activists was the board's argument that local people should use their votes to 'send a message' to incumbent Rainbow Alliance councillors – just like they had to an unpopular Tory government at the 1997 general election. This suggestion was especially poignant for local Conservative activists. Several were in the

Castle Street office stuffing envelopes on the Friday evening when this edition of the *Courier* arrived at their doorstep. Over beer and slices of pizza, activists took turns reading the article aloud. They humorously invoked the tones of Winston Churchill as they mocked Ms Banks' melodramatic claims that the 'impartiality' of a Dumfries shopping centre 'had been breached', as if this precipitated a major crisis. On a more serious note, one Tory MSP observed that Mr Ireland's activism on this issue might be a portent of electoral success to come. He explained to me that the manager of the Loreburn Centre was just the kind of local elite the Tories had lost to Labour in 1997. He now wondered if Mr Ireland might have 'come back' to the fold. Had the tide turned in favour of the Conservative Party?

The emergence of form

In the previous section, I described some of the local issues the Core Campaign Team sought to mobilise as part of their media strategy. Implementing this strategy took place at the same time as they tried to silence maverick supporters like Lt. Col John Charteris. This parallel effort to create discursive space in which their media strategy could take effect reminded me of the political philosopher Michael Oakeshott's famous 1962 essay 'Rationalism in Politics', where he described 'the conduct of affairs, for the Rationalist' as 'a matter of solving problems':

> Thus, political life is resolved into a succession of crises, each to be surmounted by the application of 'reason'. Each generation, indeed each administration, should see unrolled before it the blank sheet of infinite possibility. And if by chance this tabula rasa has been defaced by the irrational scribblings of tradition-ridden ancestors, then the first task of the Rationalist is to scrub it clean. (1991[1962]: 9)

Drawing on Oakeshott's observations, the efforts of senior Tories to gag their more stubborn supporters amounted to a kind of 'scrubbing clean' of the Party's discursive identity in the local media. Only then could they seek to instil what they viewed as an amateurish local Party organisation with professional standards of organisation more generally. This was reflected in part by the choice of local issues Party strategists made in their campaign and media strategies. It also manifested itself aesthetically, in terms of the forms of the discursive instruments senior Tories crafted to promote their media strategy. I now discuss these aesthetics and how they emerged in the months leading up to Polling Day.

I have already described how senior Party strategists worried that local people did not differentiate between members of the Rainbow Alliance administration and their Conservative opponents on Dumfries and Galloway Council. In addition to identifying local issues on which to oppose the administration, one of the Core Campaign Team's earliest decisions was to re-format and standardise press releases from the Tory group of councillors. The new media release was headed by the title 'Conservative Opposition – Dumfries and Galloway Council' followed by contact details of the Tory council group leader, thus naming the local Conservative Party as 'the Opposition' to a council administration that senior

Party strategists hoped had become unpopular with local voters. To the left of the title was the logo of the Scottish Conservatives, a lion sketched in red, white and blue.[7] At the bottom, the telephone number for the Conservative contact or 'spokesman' for the story in the press release would be highlighted above the slogan 'Time for a Change'. The names of all the incumbent Tory councillors were listed at the foot of the release.

Members of the Core Campaign Team hoped that these features would rein-force to local journalists the distinction between the Tory group and other local councillors as they wrote up stories in the local press. In the weeks that followed, Party strategists concluded that their media strategy had succeeded in generating positive effects because several local newspapers started to regularly describe the Tory council group as the official opposition to the Rainbow Alliance admin-istration. This was partly a consequence, in their view, of a common practice amongst journalists whereby they regularly plagiarised – literally, by 'cutting' and 'pasting' text – into newspaper articles. To take full political advantage of this practice, senior Tories placed emphasis on well-written press releases with bold, clear headings. In turn, this encouraged local Party strategists to place emphasis on matching the aesthetic clarity and visual simplicity of the press release with precision in its message. As I have previously noted, banal activists like the Scottish Conservatives preferred to concentrate on questions of form, method and organisation rather than on policy issues that might be viewed as complex and controversial. This focus was particularly obvious in relation to the issue of opposing 'hikes' in Council Tax, which the council administration planned to raise in early February 2003. Senior Tories believed that this issue demanded a disciplined response from the local Conservative council group, one that could be articulated and reinforced clearly and simply in a series of press releases.

Local Tory councillors were initially reluctant to oppose the Rainbow Alliance administration on Council Tax. Several leading Conservative councillors wanted to reach agreement with their opponents on how much Council Tax should be increased for the financial year 2003–4. In doing so, they hoped their non-Tory colleagues would interpret their actions as 'prudent' and sensible. According to the Conservative councillors who shared this view, this would have enabled the administration to address various financial pressures and invest in new facilities, such as the proposed leisure centre at Brooms Road car park. However, senior Party strategists like Peter Duncan MP and the two Tory MSPs believed that with an election just months away it would be more politically compelling for the council group to oppose an increase in Council Tax higher than inflation. Throughout January 2003, the Core Campaign Team debated how to proceed on this issue. Councillor Allan Wright eventually committed himself and his colleagues to supporting a 'freeze' on Council Tax 'at the rate of inflation' and opposing administration proposals for what the local Conservative Party called 'inflation-busting Council Tax hikes'. This policy commitment was presented as a major 'point of difference' with the Rainbow Alliance administration. Some Tory councillors continued to worry about whether their position on Council Tax put the council's finances at risk. Nevertheless, they realised that with just nine votes out of 47 in a full council meeting, they could exert very little influence on the debate over Council Tax anyway. A series of press releases were therefore issued on their behalf, under headings that declared local Tories would 'freeze Council Tax' in an oversimplification of the Party's stance. Downplaying references to pegging Council Tax at the rate of inflation, the Party's media campaign also misleadingly implied that local Conservatives were empowered to be able to decide the Council Tax rate for 2003–4.

Ironically, it was perhaps precisely because they could not influence the outcome of this vote that they were able to 'claim victory on Council Tax' in a press release issued after the full council meeting of 13 February 2003. The text of this press release placed emphasis on the 'consistency' of the Conservative Party's position, highlighting in bold the Tory commitment to 'freeze Council Tax at current levels'. This served to further differentiate local Tories from the Rainbow Alliance administration, which senior Party strategists sought to present as 'chaotic', 'cynical' and 'incoherent'. Such apparent clarity of purpose enabled local Conservatives to claim that they had been victorious in the debate over setting new rates of Council Tax:

> There can be no doubt that our early commitment to freeze Council Tax at the rate of inflation forced the Administration to think again … [The] only reason why some semblance of common sense has prevailed on this occasion is because the Administration has caved into the arguments that the Conservatives have been making now for weeks. Only the Conservatives have been consistent on this issue.

Riles (1998: 394) has argued that complexity can most clearly be brought 'into a single encompassing view' through the imposition of form on a text. Government bureaucracies, political parties and other institutions produce texts in which language adheres 'to a predetermined format … borrowed from other documents while producing its own variations on the standard form' (Riles 1998: 381). I suggest that in a discursive instrument like the press release, the emergence of form can be seen to function as an empowering principle for senior Tories as they sought to bring their campaign discursively and organisationally into view. Much like the *In Touch* leaflet discussed in the previous chapter, the press release described here constituted for the Core Campaign Team a good specimen of a specific genre: the modern, 'professional-looking' campaign. Indeed, once particular phrases and patterns of language had been perfected during the drafting of the press release, they could be reproduced in other documents, including *In Touch* leaflets and letters to the editor. However, this cut two ways as the forms of the discursive instruments senior Conservatives employed in their campaign made their own demands of language and party policy, ruthlessly distilling and simplifying the Tory position on Council Tax, for example, so that it could be communicated more clearly, easily and frequently with a potentially disinterested electorate. Many senior Conservatives welcomed this outcome partly because it enabled them to impose a level of discipline on an otherwise reluctant and sometimes sullen Tory council group.

The politics of irrelevance

Local journalists and newspaper editors became increasingly sensitive about accusations of political bias during the final weeks of the campaign. Newspaper coverage of the political issues that were animating local politics declined during April 2003. In contrast, the number of party political leaflets distributed in Dumfries rose significantly as Polling Day approached. Tory volunteers noticed a dramatic increase in the amount of Labour Party and other campaign literature delivered through their letterboxes, which several then forwarded to the Castle Street office. Members of the Core Campaign Team and other senior Tories were reassured that their efforts to reassert the Party's electoral credibility in local politics had succeeded when they examined such material. This was particularly the case when they read leaflets attacking the Conservative Party. I had initially thought that such literature might be discomforting for them. Rather, senior Tories often concluded that rival parties had employed this tactic because they believed that the Conservatives had come to reconstitute an electoral threat. For instance, a story entitled 'Labour Investment versus Tory Cuts' appeared in the *Dumfries Constituency Rose*, the Labour Party's glossy Election Address delivered to local households just days ahead of Polling Day. Posing questions that Conservative Party strategists had been keen to avoid, it asked:

> Have you ever wondered why Tory MSPs locally never talk about the Conservative Party's policies? What is it they are trying to hide? ... While local Tory MSPs pretend to want more spending on local services, in the Scottish Parliament they always oppose Labours' [sic] measures to invest and improve public services and now they plan to cut that investment. The Tories must be the only people who think we need fewer doctors and fewer nurses, fewer teachers and fewer police in Dumfries Constituency. Don't let the Tories take us back with cuts to schools and hospitals.

Some elderly Conservatives reacted with disgust at what they said were 'Labour lies' and interpreted such attacks as evidence of the underhand tactics of increasingly desperate and ruthless political opponents. However, several members of the Core Campaign Team seemed more sanguine at this late stage of the campaign about the Labour Party's attempts to re-introduce what they saw as national issues into the local contest. Indeed, the suggestion that a victory for Mr Mundell in the Dumfries constituency would herald massive cuts in public services locally seemed ridiculous to them. After all, even if the Scottish Conservatives succeeded in Dumfries and Galloway it was extremely unlikely that they would win enough votes nationally to form a government in Scotland. Furthermore, some Party strategists hoped that by making reference to national politics, the local Labour Party risked inflicting political damage to itself by failing to maximise its distance from the Blair government and, by implication, its more divisive policies on Iraq and other issues. From the perspective of local Conservatives, the implausible claims and reckless attacks of the Labour Party demonstrated that they were contenders in the Dumfries constituency. 'If ever we needed proof that we are relevant, this is it,' one Party strategist told me excitedly.

'They are afraid of us. They know we can win.'

Building on this theme from the *Dumfries Constituency Rose*, another leaflet contained on its back a 'personal message' from the local Labour candidate. Its second paragraph warned:

> On May 1st you will have a choice between voting for continued investment in schools and hospitals with Labour or putting at risk the foundations Labour have laid. A vote for any other party in Dumfries Constituency – or worse still, no vote at all – will simply let the Tories back in. I hope therefore that you will use your votes.

Leaflets of this kind nonetheless spurred many Tory activists to do more in the final weeks of the campaign. Most activists seemed upbeat and talked of victory, believing that the tone of such appeals betrayed desperation and panic amongst Labour activists. The electoral 'threat' the local Labour Party believed the Scottish Conservatives posed was articulated even more starkly in a target letter from Dr Murray delivered just days before the election:

> Only Scottish Labour is committed to improving our public services and transforming our communities. A vote for any other party – or worse still, no vote at all – will put at risk the foundations Labour have laid by simply letting the Tories back in here in Dumfries Constituency. It is easy to forgot [sic] how bad things were under the Tories, who starved our schools and hospitals of investment, and who presided over record high unemployment, high mortgage rates and high inflation. There is no doubt that the Tories would try to take us back to … those years of massive spending cuts and that would mean fewer teachers, fewer nurses and fewer police.

From these leaflets, senior Conservatives speculated that the SNP, which was opposed to the Iraq war and supported the FBU strike, now presented the local Labour Party with an additional threat and may have been siphoning some of their disillusioned voters (see Chapter 6). Confirmation that the Labour Party felt the need to pull rank with its own supporters appeared to come in the form of an article in Labour's Election Address entitled 'Only Labour can keep the Tories out – Just look at the result the last time!' 'In 1999, we said only Labour could beat the Tories,' so the narrative went, 'and we were right. The election in Dumfries Constituency is a clear two horse race between Labour and the Tories.' Others, though, saw in this story an appeal to anti-Tory supporters of other political parties to use their votes tactically against the local Conservative Party:

> The other parties are much too far behind – and their support is falling. The only way to be certain of keeping the Tories out of Dumfries Constituency is by voting to keep Elaine Murray as your MSP. The result will be very close, so make sure you use your vote. And make sure you use your vote for Scottish Labour.

That the Scottish Conservatives had become the explicit focus of Labour attacks was unsettling for some Tory activists. Many felt that local Labour activists possessed an impressive political machine that should never be underestimated. Following the Labour Party's outburst against Mr Ireland and the Loreburn Centre, they concluded that Labour activists were now fully engaged and committed in their fight to defeat the local Tories. In addition, those activists who were sceptical of the optimism of their colleagues pointed to another article contained in the Labour Party's Election Address. Entitled 'Divorce is an Expensive Business: The UK is stronger together, weaker apart', the story attacked the SNP and described the Scottish Tories as 'completely powerless to stop the SNP in Scotland'. An appeal for anti-SNP Conservative voters, this article seemed to contradict the Labour Party's arguments against voting Tory in Scotland by underscoring their electoral irrelevance. Furthermore, such anxieties were amplified when they read a letter distributed on 8 April 2003 by the Election Agent for the local Labour Party Colin Smyth, who was standing for election in the Lochvale ward. In the letter, he declared that he opposed the incumbent Independent councillor for voting to close Brooms Road car park. He also described the spending of £300,000 to dig up the old St Michaels Street roundabout and install new traffic lights as an unnecessary expense that could have been avoided through 'consultation with local people'. When one elderly Conservative read this letter in the Castle Street office, she reacted with horror to what she considered an audacious and dishonest claim by a local Labour activist. 'They're stealing our issues!' she exclaimed, noting that the Labour Party formed part of the Rainbow Alliance administration in the council. In her view, they could therefore not plausibly claim ownership of such an issue. For other activists, though, Mr Smyth's appropriation of these local issues provided evidence that the local Conservative campaign was progressing in the right direction. 'It shows you the Labour Party knows we have identified the issues that local people really care about,' crowed one senior Tory.

Of course, such seemingly banal issues were attractive to local Conservatives partly because they were readily accessible to them as they sought to mobilise from the margins of local and national politics. That these issues could be discerned and framed relatively quickly rendered them even more appealing as Tory activists struggled within various financial, logistical and technological constraints in their efforts to organise a modern, 'professional-looking' campaign. In addition, their positions on local issues could be articulated clearly and efficiently in short press releases with punchy headlines about 'freezing' Council Tax or 'saving' Brooms Road car park. These were the simple building blocks with which local Tory activists built their media strategy. Moreover, campaigning against the closure of a car park or the removal of a roundabout enabled local Conservatives to make connections with a wider public that could easily understand these issues. In effect, these issues became conduits through which local Tories could make (political) claims. However, local Conservatives could not render exclusive their claim to local issues. Deploying such issues was a tactic equally available to rival activists. To their dismay, local Tories discovered this when, in their view, the local Labour candidate Mr Smyth 'stole' the issue of St Michaels Street roundabout from them. With the Labour Party seeking to mobilise on local issues too, could the Tory Party maintain momentum and snatch victory from them on 1 May 2003? With this question in mind, many Party activists approached Polling Day with a mixture of excitement and trepidation.

Notes

1 This newspaper is now published on Thursdays.
2 This protest group appears to have confined its activities to southwest Scotland. Recognisable in orange boiler suits, the short-lived 'Rural Rebels' employed direct action tactics, at one point dumping dead livestock on the M74 in Dumfriesshire.
3 For more on the history of land reform in Scotland, see Callander and Wightman 1997, Hunter 1976, 1991 and 1995, McCrone 1998, and Wightman 1997 and 1999.
4 Along with the *Scotsman*, the *Glasgow Herald* is one of Scotland's two main daily broadsheet newspapers. Their sister papers are the *Scotland on Sunday* and *Sunday Herald* respectively.
5 The visibility of the Party's candidates was therefore higher in the pages of Dumfriesshire Newspapers, which were more widely read in the communities served by these councillors.
6 Through their personal dealings with local Conservative representatives, some journalists had been identified as either supportive of or, more commonly, opposed to the Party. Conservative representatives often invested considerable time in making sure that those local journalists and newspaper editors considered sympathetic to the Party were well informed about their activities.
7 In fact, this emblem was slightly out of date. The Party had issued a new version of it, a clearly drawn lion. However, local activists could not find an electronic copy of this new image so they improvised with the older, readily available version.

6

Disaggregating the secret ballot: electioneering and the politics of self-knowledge

In this chapter, I explore a set of documents as technologies available to Conservative activists attempting to forecast the political allegiances of voters in an election by secret ballot. During their campaign for the 2003 local government and Scottish Parliament elections, local Tories faced the challenge of building up a detailed database of potential supporters who could then be 'targeted' for mobilisation on Polling Day. I will examine how they sought to address this challenge through their interactions with a range of discursive materials, which senior Conservatives hoped would produce positive electoral effects for Party candidates running in the elections scheduled for Thursday, 1 May 2003. Almost inevitably, activists became preoccupied with the banal concerns of designing, producing and distributing these documents at the expense of deliberating on the arguments and issues that might successfully persuade possible supporters to vote for Tory candidates in the forthcoming elections. Their engagement with these discursive materials in the aftermath of catastrophic failure provides an opportunity to analyse how the instrumental possibilities of such documents are enacted in practice and contributed to the making of a local Tory politics of self-knowledge.

Grounded in the day-to-day micro-practices constitutive of electioneering, this chapter describes a *dossier* of documents (cf Hetherington 2008) – the survey, the canvass return and the target letter – that the Core Campaign Team deployed in its attempts to locate and target its supporters. This group's efforts to canvass and survey local voters resonate with an argument Bertrand *et al.* (2007) have articulated in which they resist equating the secret ballot with the free expression of individual political choice. However, while they urge scholars to disaggregate the technology of the secret ballot to understand how 'separable and even contradictory traits … can be reassembled in variable socio-historical circumstances' (Bertrand *et al.* 2007: 2–3), the Core Campaign Team sought to disaggregate the electoral roll to identify the political allegiances of thousands of local voters.[1]

Senior Conservatives hoped to render the electoral register transparent, breaking up one whole – the parliamentary constituency – to apprehend and then mobilise at least one of its (emergent) component parts – the Conservative electoral base. As I will demonstrate, however, the knowledge that senior Tories generated about their base was unstable; the new Conservative whole threatened to disintegrate into smaller, less useful parts if Party strategists failed to take preventative action.

Many Party activists considered the documents described in this chapter as 'new' and 'vital' additions to their discursive armoury. They were deployed within various legal constraints as set down primarily in the Representation of the People Act 1945 [1983] and the Political Parties, Elections and Referendums Act 2000. This legislation restricts campaign finance and the use of parliamentary resources in elections. However, the legislation also seeks to protect the integrity of the secret ballot as both a universal and an individual political act. I suggest that the documents considered here might therefore be prosthetic in function, extending the Conservative campaign within (and potentially around) this legal framework while feeding a Conservative politics of self-knowledge. In the process, they provided a means for senior Tories to attempt to rebuild politically towards electoral recovery. In particular, they were used to generate information for Blue Chip, a database of local voters drawn from the electoral register. As I have already argued in Chapter 4, the engagement of Party activists with such discursive tools served to invest Conservative efforts with a sense of getting organised and building prospective momentum in their knowledge-making. This was an experience that was particularly empowering and reassuring for supporters of a political party working from the margins of local and Scottish politics. Firstly, I will discuss the Local Opinion Survey, which was central to local Tory efforts to determine quickly and efficiently the voting intentions of local people across the region.

Disaggregating the electoral roll

The Core Campaign Team's use of this survey in generating knowledge about the Conservative electoral base foregrounds its use as a prosthetic means by which senior Tories attempted to reach 'out' to their supporters. This understanding of a body of Conservative (self) knowledge also rendered their electoral base external to the Party. Through the Local Opinion Survey, however, Party strategists anticipated such a fledgling Conservative whole. I will later describe how senior Tories imagined this whole as somehow unstable, the threat of its disintegration ever present. Before they could apprehend the Tory electoral base as a whole, however, Party activists had to first extend the reach of their claim to representative-ness, as I now discuss.

As they began preparations for the 2003 elections to local government and the Scottish Parliament, key Conservative strategists sought to improve the reliability of canvass data the Party had collected from the mid-1990s onwards. Old files of such information from the 1992 general election, which the Conservative Party had won, could not be located and were, thus, not available to activists. In any event, one Party strategist told me that he doubted the hypothetical value of the data anyway, given that it would have been a decade out of date. To build up a new database of canvassed voters, several surveys had already been distributed throughout the region by January 2003, while several more were planned for the months leading up to Polling Day. The Local Opinion Survey I describe here was organised by David Mundell MSP, the Scottish Conservative candidate for the Dumfries constituency, which he was contesting for the second time. The survey was scheduled for delivery via Royal Mail in February 2003. It sought the views of local householders on a series of generic issues including crime, proposals to close rural schools and priorities on road maintenance. A Freepost envelope was enclosed with the survey. Readers were encouraged to send it back to the Party's Castle Street office in Dumfries using this envelope, which would ensure that the survey recipient would not incur any costs for its return postage to the local Tories. Senior Conservatives anticipated that these surveys would be returned during March–April 2003, giving them an opportunity to input data to Blue Chip. In practice, this proved a time-consuming and labour-intensive exercise for those activists involved.

I now consider the physical form of the Local Opinion Survey, which bore similarities to other discursive exercises, such as a government census, polling or quantitative research in the social sciences.[2] Like some of these other artefacts, the survey enabled explicit instrumental possibilities when considered together with the covering letter on the back of which it was printed. The letter was authored by Mr Mundell and was addressed personally to a member of a local household. The identities of those who chose to respond to the survey could therefore easily be discerned by turning it over to check the name of the addressee in the top left-hand corner of the letter. Given that two of the survey questions concerned the former and current voting intentions of the respondent, this was actually the point of the survey: it was explicitly designed to identify Tory voters and other potential supporters. Understood as a discursive instrument, the Local Opinion Survey could, in fact, be reduced to these two questions alone. Senior Conservative strategists thus often viewed the function of this survey purely in these instrumental terms; all other information it generated was considered surplus to requirements.

The covering letter from Mr Mundell was primed to solicit a response from sympathetic readers. Subtitled '2003 Scottish Parliament and Council Elections', his letter outlined a series of issues on which he claimed his Conservative colleagues in the Scottish Parliament had been campaigning for local people. The letter noted:

> From our previous surveys we know many people are concerned about the priorities of the new Scottish Parliament. Local people are particularly concerned about the Central Belt bias of the Parliament and the lack of attention it pays to rural areas like Dumfries and Galloway. Conservatives in the Scottish Parliament have consistently spoken out on important local issues such as jobs, the future of Chapelcross [nuclear power station near Annan], the state of local roads, the

difficulty in recruiting medical staff and dentists to the area, farming after Foot and Mouth Disease, and [the] future of services in rural areas more generally. However, we would appreciate hearing your views on the issues that you believe are the most important to you and your family.

Mr Mundell's listing of the 'issues' highlighted during previous contact with 'local people' enabled him to give voice to a set of interests thought to make up a (coveted) whole: the Dumfries constituency in the Scottish Parliament. This constitutes a claim to representative-ness; the act of listening[3] to 'local opinion' empowers Mr Mundell's claim to knowledge about the local area and its people, which also serves to make a proprietory claim to the constituency, as I discussed in Chapter 3. However, foregrounding a Conservative paper trail generated through previous surveys is a further reminder of the 'responsiveness' of the aspiring representative. Mr Mundell thus inverts his claim to representative-ness, reminding local people of their past contact with local Tories before asking them (again) for their views. In turn, such a claim serves to invite local people to extend a proprietary claim to Mr Mundell as 'our' representative. Senior Conservatives who assumed that Tory voters would already identify with Mr Mundell hoped that this letter would be a further incentive for their support. The letter sought to connect the Conservative candidate with his potential supporters 'out there'.

The Local Opinion Survey and its covering letter therefore extended the reach of the local Party's campaign. However, the claim local Conservatives made to representative-ness could only be asserted partially, as becomes apparent in the next paragraph:

> Our feedback is that local people are also very disappointed by the performance of the current Council Administration. The Conservative Group is the Opposition on this Council and is well placed to lead the Council after this year's elections. The Conservative Group's aim is to deliver quality services, while keeping Council tax under control. Instead the Rainbow Alliance of Labour, SNP, Liberal Democrats and Independents that control the current Council Administration are getting involved in the disastrous projects such as the nonsensical school closure programme. Again your thoughts on the Council issues most important to you would be greatly appreciated.

This paragraph reveals several anxieties that senior Conservatives shared. In particular, members of the Core Campaign Team considered it vital to distance Conservative representatives from the council administration. As I have previously noted, the anti-Tory Rainbow Alliance administration comprised Independent, Labour, Liberal Democrat and SNP councillors. One Party strategist expressed his frustration to me that members of the Tory Group on the council remained reluctant to criticise their opponents. This was because, he said, they remained sensitive to the grouping of every single other councillor that had been forged to exclude them from the administration following the 1999 local government elections. This strategist explained that failing to define themselves as the Conservative Opposition on Dumfries and Galloway Council meant that local people might perceive them as similar to candidates from other political parties. This, he feared, could potentially weaken later efforts to mobilise their supporters to back Conservative candidates. In addition, senior Tories worried that the 'loyalties' of some supporters might be 'divided' between local Conservatives and other high-profile candidates with whom they might be connected through the myriad associations to which activists and others belong in small, rural communities, as has already been discussed in previous chapters. In other words, some local Tory voters might make a proprietary claim to a non-Conservative candidate in the upcoming elections. I discuss later how in council wards where Tory candidates challenged Independent incumbents, some Conservative strategists considered this question particularly problematic and sought to address these concerns directly through the target letter. Before they could embark on such an exercise, however, Party activists needed to process the information they were receiving from the Local Opinion Survey. I now examine this survey further to explore some of the logistical difficulties that local activists encountered as they attempted to consolidate the voting data they were gathering.

Inputting the data

As noted, the survey was designed to solicit information about voting intentions that could later be put to instrumental ends. In the weeks following the delivery of the Local Opinion Survey to households in the Dumfries constituency, thousands were returned in the enclosed Freepost envelope. The overwhelming majority of respondents pledged to vote for the Conservative Party, which suggested that the primary purpose of the survey in identifying Tory voters in particular had been realised. This rendered the Local Opinion Survey one of the most effective instruments in the local Party's discursive armoury. During March and April 2003, Conservative activists added to the Blue Chip database of local electors the names of hundreds of previously unknown supporters. Further, they were also able to confirm the voting intentions of many of those already listed as 'pledged' Tory voters.

However, the idea that the Local Opinion Survey might be explicitly crafted as a political tool was not generally obvious to everyone who read it. Some recipients condemned it for not achieving other ends. A literary scholar residing at that time in Dumfries complained to me that the survey she received was not 'objective' as the identities of potential respondents could easily be ascertained, therefore removing anonymity from the survey results. She did not realise that this was the point of the survey and, thus, considered it a failure for its incapability of generating a 'robust', statistical view of local opinion. Some Party activists shared her view. I witnessed a heated discussion between one member of the Core Campaign Team and an elderly volunteer who had spent several hours adding data to Blue Chip. Asserting the survey to be a waste of time, the latter noted that she was being asked to process voting intentions to the exclusion of all other data. She then expressed frustration about the significant amount of information Party strategists were discarding in the process. The volunteer argued that the views of local householders about the importance of a range of local and Scottish Parliament issues, which they were asked to rank in the survey's first two questions, should also be noted on Blue Chip. However, the senior Tory strategist with whom she argued thought this irrelevant and potentially wasteful of limited time and resources. After all, as I have already noted, the Conservative Party office in Castle Street, Dumfries, suffered from a lack of modern equipment and resources. Although there were several desktop computers, Blue Chip could only be accessed through one machine with limited memory on its hard drive. Unable to run several applications at the same time, this computer often crashed while volunteers were inputting Blue Chip data, a problem that was further exacerbated whenever local Conservatives tried to process a lot of information electronically. The view of the senior Conservative mentioned here was that the Party simply lacked sufficient technical and volunteer support to process such additional information, which he felt had to be viewed as superfluous to the primary exercise of inputting voting intentions.

Not everyone who responded to the Local Opinion Survey expressed support for the Scottish Conservatives. Those who refused to declare their voting intentions and asked to be removed from the Party's mailing list were widely considered to have other political allegiances. The surveyors would classify these households on Blue Chip with an 'A' for being 'against' the Scottish Conservatives. However, senior Tories generally considered any indication of voting intentions useful as, in theory, a declared Labour voter could be removed from future mailings, which would help the Party conserve money and time for more targeted campaigning activity. Furthermore, Conservative strategists had incorporated into Mr Mundell's letter another means for identifying anti-Tory voters that proved very effective. Several dozen surveys were returned to Castle Street in the Freepost envelope with their names and addresses torn off from the top left-hand corner of the covering letter. For senior strategists, it was self-evident that anti-Conservative activists trying to waste the local Tory Party's resources had returned these surveys, which were sometimes covered in graffiti. To discern the identities of such antagonists, Conservative activists relied on an inconspicuous eight-digit number printed to the right of Mr Mundell's signature at the bottom of the letter. This constituted the electoral registration number of the voter to whom the letter had been individually addressed. Once matched to the electoral roll, the name and address of the survey respondent could easily be determined. A Party volunteer would then mark that individual's voting intentions on Blue Chip with an 'A', therefore removing them from future mailings.

Firming up the whole

Senior Conservatives, through their careful cultivation of information obtained through the Local Opinion Survey, imagined much of this set of data as lacking stability and, therefore, requiring corroboration. One means of double-checking and verifying the data they were gathering was through canvassing, which was conducted either in person, 'door-to-door', or over the telephone. However, Tory efforts to canvass in this way proved problematic. For reasons that I now consider, Party volunteers were often reluctant to help as canvassers. This had a disabling effect, curtailing the Conservative Party campaign from reaching new, prospective supporters as local volunteers imposed their own limits on what kinds of activities they were willing to undertake.

Elderly Tories were particularly reluctant to canvass in council estates and urban areas that they considered 'rough' or 'unsafe', arguing that such political territory usually remained immune to the 'attractions' of Scottish Conservatism. A powerful argument for many Party activists lay in the form of their still-fresh memories of the 1997 general election, which had of course been very discouraging for many of them. As noted in Chapter 2, one individual who had been amongst the few to have gone 'door-stepping' in that campaign told me how she had found the experience very stressful. She claimed that she had been spat on and verbally abused one evening whilst canvassing a council estate; she refused to help with such efforts in 2003. Members of the Core Campaign Team also failed to convince many activists to assist with telephone canvassing, even after offering financial reimbursements to volunteers willing to telephone people from their own home. In fact, by the end of the campaign, only one Conservative supporter – a woman from the small town of Annan, 15 miles southeast of Dumfries – had regularly volunteered for this task. Many local Tories simply considered distasteful the idea of 'cold calling' strangers to ask them how they intended to vote. Conservative campaign strategists had little choice but to deploy office staff to this task.

To counter such attitudes of class-based exclusivity amongst their supporters and encourage them to help with the Party's canvassing effort, local Tory strategists called upon one of their colleagues from nearby South Ayrshire to address an activist training day held in February 2003 at the Aberdour Hotel in Dumfries. They drafted in Murray Tosh MSP, an approachable Conservative with years of campaigning experience in local government elections. In a presentation to an audience of around 40 activists, he outlined tactics that canvassers could use on the doorstep to discern the voting intentions of even the most hostile of householders. For example, when confronted with someone who had expressed anti-Tory views on the doorstep, he explained that a canvasser might ask: 'So I take it you will be voting Labour again?' Such probing proved a surprisingly effective tactic in 'flushing out' Labour supporters, who would almost always identify themselves in response, and Nationalist voters, who would react to the idea of voting Labour with disgust. Mr Tosh then went on to explain how it was both 'easy' and 'important' to use a standard alphabetical code for listing such intentions, as volunteers could then process this information into Blue Chip more efficiently. To further streamline this process, he emphasised the need for the prompt return of canvass forms to Castle Street to facilitate the use of the most accurate figures to 'get out the vote' (GOTV) on Polling Day (see Chapter 7). But he also cautioned his audience against making too many assumptions about who constituted a Tory voter and where they might live. 'I know some Conservatives who decide that a resident is a supporter if they live in a posh house or have a Mercedes sitting in the driveway,' he observed. 'But some of the rudest people I have ever met live in *big hooses* and vote Conservative while some of the nicest are the folks you'll meet going door-to-door in the Council schemes.'

I was struck by Mr Tosh's comments, which were delivered as if no members of his audience lived in a big house or drove an expensive vehicle. But what they revealed was a set of assumptions, perhaps borne of his canvassing experiences, about the prejudices of Conservative voters. Many senior Tories I met shared these assumptions. The idea that their supporters might shut themselves off in large estates and respond with hostility to strangers knocking on their door seemed especially evocative to them. Indeed, such an image served to underscore the need for the Local Opinion Survey discussed earlier, which was designed to reach out to Conservative voters, overcoming obstacles to communication that were sometimes erected by local Tories themselves. Nevertheless, relying on members of staff, a handful of committed office-bearers and activists as well as individual council candidates, Party strategists were able to deploy a reasonably expansive network of canvassers across Dumfries and Galloway. Armed with a clipboard listing the names and addresses of local residents, with printed notes on their voting history attached if known, small groups of up to six canvassers would move methodically through a handful of streets, knocking on doors and quizzing householders about their voting intentions in the forthcoming elections. Double-checking the data already gleaned from the Local Opinion Survey in the process, senior Conservatives reassured themselves of the effectiveness of their information-gathering efforts as they saw the Tory vote 'firm up' along the way.

However, no amount of checking and crosschecking addressed a couple of basic flaws that had been overlooked when Party strategists developed their canvass and survey methodology to render their supporters visible through the electoral roll. Canvassers rarely distinguished between the voting intentions of the local householders they quizzed, often assuming that a Tory voter would support Conservative candidates in both the local government and the Scottish Parliament elections. Senior strategists later realised that they could not be sure Conservative supporters would refrain from splitting their votes between different parties, particularly if they had a personal connection with a rival candidate. Tory voters in council wards represented by Independent incumbents were thought to pose a particular challenge, given that many of them, believing that Independents were 'closet' Conservatives, were therefore tempted to vote for them. This problem was complicated even more when the Castle Street office received Local Opinion Surveys from households in which more than one adult lived but to which only one survey had been sent. Party strategists also came to realise that they could not rely on other kinds of assumptions; for example, it was not given that a husband and wife would vote identically in the coming elections. More perplexingly for senior Conservatives, the identity of the individual who had filled out the survey on behalf of such households could not always be ascertained either.[4]

Mobilisation

Having amassed the names and addresses of thousands of 'pledged' and sometimes 'probable' supporters, senior Conservatives focused on another problematic: how to mobilise Tory voters to 'turn out' on Polling Day and support Conservative candidates. As the election approached, members of the Core Campaign Team sought to achieve this outcome through a series of GOTV or target letters. There were many different examples and versions of these letters, most of them distributed in the final week of April. At least 10,000 target letters had been distributed in the Dumfries constituency alone by the end of the campaign, each pledged supporter receiving several different versions to constantly remind them of the importance of voting. In this way, a concern with continuously checking and re-gathering voting data came to be replaced with the need to cultivate, prime and reinforce the (Conservative) whole in order to mobilise it on Polling Day. To this end, some letters had been posted much earlier. In February 2003, for instance, a target letter had been sent to those who had already pledged support to the Scottish Conservatives as part of a campaign to maximise the number of committed Tory voters registered for postal ballots. The idea behind this 'postal vote campaign' was to mobilise as many pledged Conservatives before the election as possible. This could then allow for the Party's limited personnel and other resources to be concentrated on targeting the remainder of the Conservative electoral base on Polling Day and increasing turnout from Tory voters.

The local Tory campaign was very successful in persuading Conservative voters to apply for postal ballots, which helped contribute to the Dumfries constituency registering the highest number of postal votes in the 2003 elections (cf Burnside *et al.* 2003). Members of the Core Campaign Team attributed this success in part to a target letter signed by Lord Monro, the popular Tory 'grandee' and former MP for Dumfries. In that letter, he argued that Conservatives needed to vote in the Scottish Parliament elections:

> I voted No-No in 1997 [for the devolution referendum] and have seen nothing to change my mind. However the Parliament is not going to go away and the only way to change it is to have more Conservatives in it. The only way to do that is to vote Conservative in next year's elections. Not voting will simply allow more Labour, Liberal and SNP members to be elected with their left-wing anti-rural agenda. We will just get much more of what we have seen over the past three and a half years. I urge all local Conservatives to ensure they vote.

Throughout the first few months of 2003, senior Conservatives reinforced this message repeatedly through leaflets, letters and speeches to Conservative Party audiences including the Dumfries Ladies Lunch Club and the Dumfries Burgh Branch, which organised a series of 'political suppers' at which guest speakers included Peter Duncan MP, Alex Fergusson MSP, Lord Monro, David Mundell MSP and Murray Tosh MSP. But in highlighting this message, senior Conservatives revealed lingering doubts about the willingness of their supporters to participate in an election for an institution most of them had opposed in the 1997 devolution referendum. However, by April 2003, most of the senior Conservatives to whom I spoke felt that, despite the views of a recalcitrant minority as expressed through the Local Opinion Survey, their supporters had come to accept the importance of voting in the coming elections. One Conservative MSP told me about one sign that he considered encouraging, which demonstrated that many local Conservatives had reconciled themselves to the Scottish Parliament. This was the large number of volunteers from the Dumfries Ladies Lunch Club who had enthusiastically come into Castle Street to help with the stuffing and sorting of thousands of documents and leaflets, including the Local Opinion Survey, during the campaign. Knowing that many of these predominantly elderly women had opposed devolution a few years previously, this Tory MSP said that he had been 'genuinely touched' by their support. Members of the Dumfries Ladies Lunch Club, it seemed, had extended a proprietary claim to their Party's campaign in the local government and Scottish Parliament elections even if they did not support the latter institution and saw it as unrepresentative of their interests and views.

Pulling rank

A greater cause for anxiety amongst senior Conservatives, however, was how to encourage Tory voters to support the Party's candidates in the local council elections. As I have already noted, this was a particularly pressing tactical problem when Conservative candidates stood against Independent incumbents that many local people thought possessed conservative views. Some of my informants observed that the endurance of Independent councillors harked back to a tradition of electing 'non-aligned' representatives – the so-called 'Colonels' juntas' – that dominated county politics in Dumfries and Galloway throughout the twentieth century (McCulloch 2000: 517). Many Conservative voters had helped to perpetuate this tradition through their continued backing of Independent councillors. As a result, Tory Party strategists assumed that many of their supporters had voted for Independent candidates in the 1999 local council election. They therefore believed that the view amongst some Conservatives – that backing an Independent candidate for local council was acceptable – needed to be challenged. Party strategists therefore drafted target letters from well-known and respected figures from the local and national Conservative Party organisation to endorse candidates engaged in such contests. In doing so, they hoped to mobilise a network of Tory names and, by association, local knowledge and political capital to reinforce support for the Party's candidate amongst the Conservative electoral base.

For example, Conservative voters in the Moffat ward received several target letters from David Mundell MSP, Lord Monro and the (then) Scottish Conservative leader in the Scottish Parliament, David McLetchie MSP. These letters were sometimes designed to appeal to Tory voters on a more personal level, dispensing with the formal professionalism many might have associated with earlier Party correspondence like the Local Opinion Survey. Indeed, the letter from David Mundell that encouraged local supporters to vote for the Conservative candidate

Safa Ash-Kuri was typewritten on yellow paper. This rendered it distinctive from the many items distributed previously in the campaign and conveyed a sense that Mr Mundell had penned it at his own home in Moffat before hand-delivering it to local households. To emphasise this local (personal) connection, he used his residential address in the top right-hand corner of the letter. This further marked it out from official Party correspondence, displacing Mr Mundell's earlier identity as Conservative representative for a more 'personal' voice.

Mr Mundell began his letter by mentioning Safa Ash-Kuri's 'solid experience in business' and described the local Tory Party as being 'very fortunate' to have found a candidate with 'the expertise and the common sense' that the council 'clearly lacks'. But the letter was written with a specific 'threat' in mind, that which the Independent councillor poses:

> [It] is particularly important that Conservative supporters vote Conservative in the Council elections. Our local 'Independent' Councillor voted against Conservative proposals that would have kept Beattock Primary open and guaranteed Moffat Academy's future as an all-through school. Independent Councillors claim to be non political yet they have formed themselves into a party group on the Council and vote together as a party in coalition with Labour and the SNP. Accordingly, I can assure you that voting Independent is not the equivalent of voting Conservative. If you want both an excellent local Councillor, well qualified to fight for the needs of our communities and to change the Council, vote Conservative, vote for Safa Ash-Kuri in the Council elections on 1st May.

The Independent councillor constituted a threat to Conservative candidates largely because many of the Party's supporters believed that they were closet Tories. In Moffat, a council ward that was widely considered a 'natural' Conservative seat, local supporters often reported that the Independent incumbent Billy Lockhart had privately told them that he too held conservative views. Embedded in the community and bound through kin-based and other networks with the Conservative voter base, Councillor Lockhart also enjoyed the support of several local Party members who actively campaigned for him against the Conservative challenger. This further blurred the boundary between Tory and non-aligned councillor. Senior Conservatives therefore tried to discursively 'pull rank' against a web of local associations and interconnections between their supporters and rival (Independent) candidates, urging them to back the Party's endorsed candidate. In part, this was attempted by highlighting Councillor Lockhart's association with anti-Tory political groups in the administration, which served to symbolically sever his own networks amongst some Conservative supporters. Accusing Independents of voting 'with Labour and the SNP', the letter drew a strong link between Councillor Lockhart and the other groups that made up the Rainbow Alliance administration. By associating with the Independent councillor, some Conservative activists in Moffat also risked becoming complicit in the local administration's policy legacy, which Party strategists condemned as a 'record of failure'.

Mr Mundell's letter also sought to both consolidate and mobilise Conservative electoral support for Mr Ash-Kuri by implicating him in a wider social network of his own. Mr Ash-Kuri, a retired oil company executive from the Middle East, had recently moved to Moffat, joining the Conservative Party campaign only four weeks before Polling Day. Senior Tories reasonably assumed that he might not be as well known as his Independent opponent. By endorsing him, Mr Mundell and the highly respected Lord Monro brought their own names, political capital and, by association, local knowledge and networks together to reinforce Mr Ash-Kuri's candidacy amongst the local Tory electoral base. In this way, they asserted he was a worthy representative deserving of their support. Mr Mundell and other senior Conservatives sought to extend their own proprietary claim to Mr Ash-Kuri that they hoped the Conservative electoral base in Moffat would in turn mimic. In effect, this constituted a claim of ownership over 'our' candidate, similar to the kinds of proprietary claims that I detailed in Chapter 3, as well as a solicitation to Tory voters to extend their own claim over a candidate like Mr Ash-Kuri. Indeed, senior Conservatives were very explicit about their reasons for generating such associations. In the last couple of weeks before Polling Day, one Conservative MSP explained to me that he felt he could 'deliver' a number of council wards to Tory candidates through such personal backing. This individual treated the target letter as an extension of his own, albeit partial, claim to representative-ness, reaching out to encompass Conservative candidates running in the local government elections. A discursive tool charged with the power to 'pull rank' locally and realign political relations, the target letter was therefore thought to be able to cumulatively generate electoral and social effects. Senior Conservatives hoped that such effects might last beyond Polling Day.

SNP-free in 2003!

I have already described how Conservative canvassers were encouraged to use an alphabetical code in order to identify the political allegiances of local house-holders for Blue Chip. That code included the following identifications: C for Conservative, S for Labour,[5] L for Liberal (Democrat), A for Against, T for Labour waverer, P for Probable Conservative, I for Independent/Other, N for (Scottish) Nationalist, Z for Nationalist waverer, W for Won't Vote, and M for Liberal (Democrat) waverer. Some senior Conservatives in Dumfries and Galloway speculated that there might be potential in targeting supporters of a rival party, particularly those that had been classified as waverers, in a campaign to attract tactical votes to the Scottish Conservatives. Several Party activists argued that a campaign of anti-Tory tactical voting had had a devastating impact in the 1997 general election. In the final two weeks before Polling Day, the Core Campaign Team made a fledgling, improvisational effort to mobilise such potential support.

Prior to Christmas 2002, the MP for Galloway and Upper Nithsdale, Peter Duncan, had been toying with the idea of encouraging anti-SNP Labour and Liberal Democrat voters in his constituency to support the local Conservative candidate Alex Fergusson MSP in order to 'wipe Nationalism off the map of southwest Scotland' in the upcoming Scottish Parliament election. Although there was some scepticism as to whether Labour supporters would actually vote

Conservative to achieve this aim, local Tory activists generally approved of the idea. Around the same time, Mr Fergusson had been thinking about the SNP slogan from the 1992 general election. Campaigning under the banner 'Scotland free in 1993!', they had mounted a vocal but ultimately unsuccessful campaign to defeat the (then) incumbent Conservative MP in Galloway and Upper Nithsdale, Rt Hon. Ian Lang. While he was driving home one night, a new slogan suddenly occurred to him: to make Galloway and Upper Nithsdale 'SNP-free in 2003!'

At least one key Party strategist disliked the pun while a handful of other activists thought it was unnecessarily provocative. But Mr Fergusson was adamant that he wanted to use the phrase in his leaflets at a time when many activists believed the SNP might be underestimating the Conservative Party's chances of winning the constituency. Senior Tories thought that the SNP was taking the election for granted. Although the incumbent SNP candidate was credited with an excellent 'press operation' in the local newspapers, his failure to acknowledge his opposition was interpreted by many Conservative activists as a sign of complacency.[6] Furthermore, these observations potentially resonated with my own notes of the Scottish Nationalists' campaign in Galloway and Upper Nithsdale. For example, 24 hours before Polling Day, I spoke to the parliamentary researcher for Alasdair Morgan, the SNP MSP for Galloway and Upper Nithsdale, at the opening of postal ballots in Loreburn Hall. 'It is one thing for the Tories to beat an unknown SNP candidate at the [2001] general election,' he declared, 'but they would have to get really lucky to beat Alasdair Morgan.' Hoping that they might catch an overconfident local SNP off guard, the Scottish Conservatives decided to introduce their invitation to marginal voters to make Galloway and Upper Nithsdale 'SNP-free in 2003' in the last month of the campaign. This would leave the Scottish Nationalists with little time in which to respond. Highlighting the ability for local Conservatives to work as a 'team' at both Holyrood and Westminster should they win the constituency, Mr Fergusson wrote:

> Peter Duncan has provided a strong voice to the people of Galloway and Upper Nithsdale in Westminster and it is now time to match that with equally strong representation in Holyrood. Give me your support on 1st May and together we can make Galloway and Upper Nithsdale SNP free in 2003!

These two closing sentences were repeated on much of the Conservative Party's literature – in campaign press releases, *In Touch* and other leaflets as well as target letters to supporters and potential voters – during the final days and hours of the campaign. Local Party strategists remained uncertain as to whether many people would be persuaded by this appeal. However, they felt that making the connection between Mr Duncan, who had narrowly won his constituency in a surprise victory over the SNP in the 2001 general election, and Mr Fergusson would help galvanise Tory supporters to vote on Polling Day. In the last week of April 2003, though, members of the Core Campaign Team were encouraged by anecdotal reports that some Labour Party activists were planning to vote Tory in order to 'wipe Nationalism off the map of southwest Scotland'. With just days to go, the brother of a Labour Party councillor from Stranraer wandered into the Wigtownshire office of Peter Duncan MP. Chatting to a member of his staff there, he explained that for the first time in their lives he and others were telling their friends to vote Conservative to make the constituency 'SNP-free in 2003', a slogan that they apparently particularly relished.

Getting Labour out

Meanwhile, Mr Mundell and members of the Core Campaign Team viewed the tactical challenge in Dumfries quite differently. In the first week of April 2003, Dumfriesshire Newspapers described the constituency as a potential four-way marginal seat. This view was based on the results of the 1999 Scottish Parliament elections, where the SNP and the Liberal Democrats polled 19.81% and 16.39% respectively behind Labour (36.64%) and the Conservatives (27.15%). Indeed, senior Tories believed that their chances of winning the Dumfries constituency partly depended on the ability of the local SNP and Liberal Democrats to mount strong challenges to siphon centre-left voters away from the Labour Party incumbent. However, at that late stage in the campaign, the Liberal Democrats had only just selected a candidate. This did not inspire much confidence amongst local Conservatives about the kind of campaign they would be able to mobilise. Moreover, the apparently erratic behaviour of the local SNP candidate, Andrew Wood, had been a cause of some concern to Tory activists for several months.

For instance, a story had appeared in the *Standard* on 31 January 2003 entitled 'Safety struggle' in which Mr Wood argued for the removal of a 'dangerous' roundabout in the small village of Dunscore. Ambiguously described as 'the Prospective Scottish Parliamentary Candidate', Mr Wood was instantly rebutted in the article by the local Tory councillor Allan Wright. To local Conservative activists, the reasoning behind Mr Wood's interest in this roundabout was unclear. They initially greeted his intervention with humour. After all, Dunscore is located roughly ten miles northwest of Dumfries in the neighbouring Galloway and Upper Nithsdale constituency. It was therefore not within the parliamentary seat that Mr Wood was contesting in the upcoming elections. Indeed, the incumbent SNP MSP Alasdair Morgan was defending the constituency to which the small village belonged. Following a discussion at one of their Monday morning meetings, the Core Campaign Team decided not to write a letter to the editor in response to the story because they assumed that the Labour Party would probably use the opportunity to attack the SNP themselves. A common view amongst senior Tory strategists was that the Labour Party considered their biggest electoral weakness to lie in the potential for the SNP to poach votes from them. The local Labour Party was therefore thought to have a strong interest in discrediting the local SNP candidate whenever the opportunity arose. Furthermore, senior Conservatives were deeply reluctant to become embroiled in a dispute with the SNP and were regularly baffled when the Scottish Nationalists sought to initiate one, such as when Mr Wood had attacked Lt Col. Charteris about the fire fighters' strike, as discussed in the previous chapter. With the local branch of the FBU on strike and with growing opposition to a potential war with Iraq, there appeared to be some potential for the Scottish Nationalists to draw support away from the Labour Party and weaken its electoral base. Put simply, local Tory strategists believed that to succeed in 'getting Labour out' of Dumfries, the Scottish Conservatives and the SNP both had to make the local Labour Party their target and not each other.

Throughout my fieldwork, I was conscious that some Conservatives were engaged in discussion with activists from other political parties. Sometimes, these discussions took place through local kin-based networks, but senior Tories often enjoyed good relations with influential activists from rival groups. In Galloway and Upper Nithsdale, for example, routine informal contact took place between a couple of Stranraer-based Labour Party councillors, including the one whose brother was mentioned earlier, and the local Conservative MP Peter Duncan. Discreet communications also occurred between Mr Duncan and a SNP councillor from Wigtownshire. Even in Dumfries, local Tories were able to quietly exchange information with key activists from other political parties. Mr Mundell spoke regularly with a Liberal Democrat councillor from Langholm who would later defect to the Conservative Party at the 2007 elections for Dumfries and Galloway Council. Having himself been a Social Democrat councillor in Lockerbie during the 1980s, Mr Mundell had joined the Scottish Tories some time after his former party merged with the Liberals to form the Liberal Democrats in 1988. He continued to stay in touch with a number of his former colleagues. Furthermore, one member of staff in the Conservative Party's office in Castle Street was dating at that time Ian Anderson, the general secretary and main spokesman for the local branch of the FBU. Mr Anderson was also a member of the Scottish Socialist Party, led by the Glasgow MSP Tommy Sheridan, which had recently opened two branches – in Annan and Dumfries respectively – and selected an energetic local candidate who would often spend Saturday mornings selling the *Socialist Worker* in Dumfries High Street. This personal connection provided another useful channel for exchanging gossip and other information about local politics and, especially, the local Labour Party.

In contrast, however, local Conservatives did not have much contact with the SNP in Dumfries. My own Scottish Nationalist contacts were much better than those of my Tory Party informants. When I spoke to two SNP activists a couple of weeks after the above story about the Dunscore roundabout appeared in the *Standard*, I asked why they were not targeting the Labour Party more in their material and whether they intended to do so in the future. Despite the SNP leadership adopting a strident anti-war stance, they told me that the situation in Iraq was an issue about which they had to be 'very careful' and that they did not want to get 'too personal' in their attacks on local Labour Members of Parliament. On another occasion, I had spoken to the parliamentary researcher quoted earlier, a young man who was an important activist in Alasdair Morgan's campaign. I had suggested to him that a view I had encountered amongst local Conservatives was that it was in their mutual interests to try to get the Labour Party out of the Dumfries constituency. If achieved through a Conservative Party victory, the

SNP would then be provided with an opportunity to target centre-left voters in a Tory-held constituency. As a result, local debate could be polarised between Scotland's most ardent Unionist party and its obvious ideological nemesis, at least on the issue of independence: the Scottish Nationalists. According to such a view, the Dumfries constituency could then be approached as a winnable prospect for the SNP in the medium to long term. As I put this argument to him, I was a little surprised when the SNP activist politely changed the subject. It was as if such a strategy had never occurred to him or could not be entertained for reasons that remained unspoken.

Local Tories who were familiar with this reluctance to engage in what they saw as a 'professional' political strategy despaired at the Nationalists' alleged lack of 'sophistication'. One Tory candidate explained to me that if SNP voters were more 'sophisticated', he could directly appeal to them for their votes by explaining that it was 'in their interests to get Labour out of first-past-the-post constituencies'. He did concur with an observation I made that after eighteen years of unpopular Tory rule SNP voters were perhaps not ready to cast their votes tactically against the Labour Party. However, he nevertheless hoped that there might come a day when such a direct appeal for the support of Scottish Nationalists might be possible. Indeed, while canvassing local households just days before the election, he 'found' one SNP voter in Dumfries who said that she was voting for him to 'get Labour out'. This discovery prompted some excitement and he promptly telephoned to tell me about this 'development' just to prove that there might be some potential in a long-term strategy of targeting Nationalist votes in the constituency.

The politics of self-knowledge

The daily production of thousands of canvass returns, letters and leaflets began to take its toll on the Party's limited office and volunteer resources as the day of the election approached. Staff members were unable to keep up with escalating demands from activists and candidates for reliable, up-to-date information. In response, they concentrated on processing as many of the voting intentions gleaned from the Local Opinion Survey as possible. At the same time, the focus of Conservative activists began to narrow on GOTV materials as they sought to mobilise their electoral base. Telephoning Conservative 'pledges' in order to 'get out the vote' on Polling Day, volunteers checked the accuracy of their Blue Chip canvass data yet again as they chatted with their supporters. During such conversations, Party activists placed emphasis on the importance of voting Tory 'three times': twice for the Scottish Parliament, to which representatives might be elected via two different voting systems, and once for the local council. Through these and other strategies, Conservative activists made efforts to discipline and maximise the turnout of their electoral base. As they engaged in these practices of disciplining, mobilising and targeting local voters, Tory activists encountered the limits of their self-knowledge.

Post-election, Party strategists would again check the veracity of their Blue

Chip data following the publication of the so-called 'marked' electoral register. This was a list of all eligible voters in the constituency that identified the names of those who had voted in the election against those who had 'stayed at home'. The marked register provided Party professionals with an opportunity to compare the actual turnout of their pledged vote to the projections that had informed their earlier GOTV campaign, which I will discuss in the next chapter. Accordingly, they would find that a handful of supporters who had said that they would vote in the election had not done so. Generally, however, senior Conservatives were encouraged that the overwhelming majority of the people they had sought to mobilise had, in fact, voted on Polling Day. 'There might have been another 500 votes we could have squeezed out of the Dumfries constituency,' one Conservative strategist would later explain to me, 'but I am convinced we did everything that we could.'

Such efforts served to generate a sense amongst members of the Core Campaign Team and Tory activists more generally that the local Conservative Party was getting better organised. For the first time since the 1997 general election, they felt able to extract a list of pledged Conservative voters from Blue Chip and with some confidence apprehend and gaze upon a reassuring whole: the Conservative electoral base. On its own, the base was not a large enough part of a greater whole – the Dumfries constituency – to ensure that a Conservative candidate would be elected first-past-the-post for the Scottish Parliament. In the final days of their campaign, they therefore also made a fledgling, improvisational effort to court support from those of their opponents who might have preferred to see the Conservative Party win over their principal opposition. In the Dumfries constituency, this meant trying to appeal to anti-Labour SNP and Liberal Democrat voters. Meanwhile, in Galloway and Upper Nithsdale, local Tory strategists hoped that Labour Party hostility to the Scottish Nationalists might deliver additional support to the Scottish Conservatives on Polling Day.

Importantly, senior Conservatives could now quantify and 'see' their electoral base, convinced of the reliability of the voting data they had accumulated through the Local Opinion Survey and their wider canvassing effort. Such a Tory 'whole' was nevertheless unstable; the need to constantly 'target' it underscored the potential for the whole to disintegrate into Conservative and non-Conservative (Independent) parts in the council elections. Key Party strategists had to act to safeguard against this disintegration, which meant that the task of re-gathering voter information was never complete. Their attention to detail was required in maintaining Blue Chip *vis-à-vis* the threat of further disaggregation. Addressing this threat thus imbued the Conservative campaign with a sense of prospective momentum borne of vigilance. Local Party strategists had generated this sense through their breakdown of the electoral roll and subsequent cultivation of a solid, new (Conservative) whole. When they later reflected on their efforts after Polling Day, they would find in such methods and organisation a retrospective sense of having made progress from their disastrous result at the 1997 general election. They were able to imagine a future in which they could embellish their knowledge of themselves and the Conservative electoral base 'out there' through additional canvassing and surveys. In the continuous cultivation and updating of such data, Conservative activists anticipated a time when they would be able to successfully mobilise their pledged vote, persuade 'probable' supporters to back them and reclaim at least one parliamentary constituency lost in 1997: Dumfries. Whether that day would arrive on 1 May 2003 remained to be seen.

Notes

1 The local Authority updates the electoral roll each year and publishes a version in electronic form, a copy of which political parties and other interests can purchase. The activities of Conservative strategists described here could be said to mirror the work of council officials, whose maintenance of the electoral roll requires constant attention.
2 In the colonial past, for example, the census was used as an instrument of governmental control (cf Cohn 1987, 1996).
3 For more on the art of listening, see Back (2007).
4 Rightly or wrongly, Conservative volunteers would normally assume that a husband would complete a Local Opinion Survey on behalf of a married couple.
5 Most Tory activists took 'S' to stand for 'Socialist,' a label many of them used to describe Labour Party members and activists. Supporters of the Scottish Socialist Party, lacking much of an electoral presence in Dumfriesshire, would be listed under 'Other' along with supporters of the Scottish Greens.
6 Some local Tories held a contrary view: that the SNP never mentioned the Conservatives because they had become utterly irrelevant in post-devolution Scotland.

7

Counting on failure:
Polling Day and its aftermath

On Friday 29 April 2003, I attended a breakfast meeting at the local McDonald's, just off the A75 ring road around Dumfries. Those in attendance included the Tory MP Peter Duncan and the young Conservative Party Election Agent for Dumfries, Alan MacLeod. David Mundell MSP, who was also planning to join us, was running late. After ordering bacon and sausage McMuffins with coffee, we discussed the performance of a handful of council candidates who had become 'difficult' during the final weeks of the campaign. Mr Duncan drolly attributed their awkward and erratic behaviour to an attack of 'candidatitis', a mock psychological condition that accounts for the anxiety and stress candidates feel in the last days before the election. Our conversation then progressed to the importance of trying to gain an objective, 'outside' view of the performance of the local Conservative Party's campaign in the elections for both Dumfries and Galloway Council and the Scottish Parliament. To help develop such a perspective, Mr Duncan had reformatted the Core Campaign Team's spreadsheet entitled 'Council Candidates', which I discussed in Chapter 4, to contain additional canvass data drawn from Blue Chip. This data set was broken down to ward level, for each of which the number of Conservative Party 'pledges' and 'possible' voters were listed as 'raw' numerical information as well as a percentage of the overall potential vote. Nominal 'counts' were also included for opposition parties, although these figures tended to be viewed with considerable caution. In contrast to the totals for the canvassed Tory vote, most Party strategists regarded these figures as widely inaccurate. In council wards held by non-Conservatives, the shortfall between the 'known' Tory vote and the respective incumbent's total support from the previous election was also highlighted along with the percentage 'swing' the Conservative challenger would require to defeat the sitting councillor. This spreadsheet, in effect, provided a summary of the projected Conservative vote, broken down by council ward, which could then be compared with the actual vote the party managed to achieve on Polling Day.

The provision of such 'benchmarks', Mr Duncan explained, would assist the Core Campaign Team in its post-election analysis. Indeed, by comparing their 'result' on Polling Day with what senior Conservatives anticipated to be their projected vote, the performance of individual council candidates could be evaluated. Put simply, a candidate who exceeded their 'target' based on the projected Tory vote on Polling Day might be considered 'strong' or 'successful' even if they failed to win their council ward overall. Those who fell short of the expected total Conservative vote in their respective wards could be described as having 'failed'. Underachieving candidates could then be identified and, Mr Duncan hoped, weaknesses in the party's overall campaign could be pinpointed – indeed, personified. Following the election, this would then give the Core Campaign Team an opportunity to discern where the fault lines lay within their campaign apparatus. They could then identify what had and had not worked in their campaign by enabling them to interview individual candidates about their performance, identifying 'best practice' amongst those who had succeeded, while also 'flagging' issues on which local Conservatives might seek to improve in future elections. In addition to identifying how many votes Tory candidates needed to win their respective council wards, Mr Duncan had been mulling over another 'numbers game' during our discussion: how many ballots did Mr Fergusson and Mr Mundell require to win their respective first-past-the-post constituencies in the Scottish Parliament? Turning to Mr Mundell after he arrived, he asked him how many votes he thought the Conservative MSP could secure. With Mr Mundell declaring that he thought he could get '14,000 votes', Mr Duncan glanced over his spreadsheet thoughtfully and responded: 'That should be enough.' Mr Mundell's target certainly seemed achievable when the projections for each council ward in his constituency were combined to give an overall total for the Conservative Party's nominal vote in Dumfriesshire.

In crafting such a document, Mr Duncan, a senior Conservative, drew on his professional experience of business and management in order to develop a means for auditing the Party's campaign for the 2003 elections to Dumfries and Galloway Council and the Scottish Parliament. As Jean-Klein (2002: 50) has observed, audits have become 'the dominant means by which, in contemporary and self-avowed liberal democracies, the performance of corporate organisations and public institutions are measured, and the allocation of critical resources – material as well as symbolic and/or ideological – is structured'. Mr Duncan's efforts to mount an audit of the party's local campaign employed a notion of transparency, which promised fellow Conservatives a 'full view of the organisation of one's productivity' (Jean-Klein 2002: 50). At the same time, such efforts mimicked the practices of new organisational elites such as the bureaucrats and civil servants tasked with running elections.[1] Through close observation of what did and did not happen on Polling Day, Tory Party strategists hoped to gain an overview of what did or did not work. Such an overview would then allow the Core Campaign Team to hold individual Party activists and candidates accountable.

If someone did not achieve what was projected for them in Mr Duncan's spreadsheet, key strategists would at least know where to look – or who to interrogate – in order to determine what had gone wrong. Following the anthropologist Bill Maurer, the critical enterprise inspired by the spreadsheet is perhaps analogous to an accountant's balance sheet: 'as a process of abstracting from a field of practice, it will always overlook some phenomena to make visible others. For accounting, the result is an open-endedness belied by the apparent stability of the balance sheet' (Maurer 2002: 646). Notwithstanding the anxieties of Tory activists over the accuracy and quality of their canvass data, which I discussed in the previous chapter, Mr Duncan's spreadsheet offered an illusion of certainty. Matching the names of individual candidates to specific council wards and local communities before listing reassuring quantities and percentages of Tory support across the region, the spreadsheet brought both the local Conservative activist network and campaign into view. However, even if the numbers contained within the spreadsheet could 'speak for themselves', local Conservatives were soon to be reminded that they conveyed anything but stability.

Of course, the idea that Mr Duncan's spreadsheet might be used to benchmark success assumed that some candidates would fail to achieve the targets projected within it. The spreadsheet therefore anticipated a degree of failure in the Party's campaign across the region. However, the predicament that faced local Conservatives at the 2003 elections differed from that which confronted, for example, the Japanese financial analysts who, Miyazaki (2003) argues, anticipated that in failure they might learn something useful about the inadequacies of their own financial instruments and models. It would be disingenuous to suggest that local Conservatives aspired to learn, through their own failure, something new about electoral theory and practice. Even if the various instruments they devised anticipated that some aspects of the Party's campaign machinery would be found wanting, most Conservative activists hoped that their campaign would be successful. Indeed, the hope to which several Tory activists clung was for their own expectations to be exceeded through an overwhelming, and unexpected, Conservative victory. Ironically, such success would have eclipsed the benchmarks contained within Mr Duncan's spreadsheet and rendered it ineffective and redundant. From this perspective, some Tory activists might have privately hoped that their spreadsheet would 'fail' in the sense that it would no longer have anything relevant to say about their campaign. Put simply, their desire for accuracy in their canvass data was generally viewed as a prerequisite to defeating a slick Labour Party machine in Dumfries. However, they nevertheless hoped to surprise both themselves and their local Labour opponents – 'pulling the rug' from under the feet of their antagonists, as one of my informants put it – and having their collective anxieties about belonging to the new political landscape of post-devolution Scotland dashed. For Tory activists confident of an electoral breakthrough, however, Polling Day contained several surprises. But unlike the Japanese financial analysts Miyazaki describes, local Tories had many incentives, financial and otherwise, to hope for success.

This chapter describes how key Party strategists sought to assess the Tory campaign in terms of its internal mechanics as well as its external effects. Despite the promise of apprehension contained within the spreadsheet described above, the methods they devised for judging their 'progress' on Polling Day itself and the Election Count that followed remained largely impromptu and informal.

This was because the challenge of obtaining an 'outside' view from a location within the local party's machinery proved doubly problematic for members of the Core Campaign Team, not least because the election results did not conform to Mr Duncan's or the local Conservative Party's generally optimistic projections. Indeed, the various strategies local Conservatives used to 'read' what was happening around them produced some surprising and potentially unsettling results. This was partly because of their inability to predict the outcome of the elections in the light of all sorts of diverse factors, such as the weather. Furthermore, Polling Day was marked by a sense that rival parties had by now maximised momentum in their respective campaigns. This heightened for some local activists the unnerving possibilities borne of other potential outcomes, such as electoral defeat. Some Tory strategists suspected that the local Labour Party, which many Conservatives now felt was probably 'coming from behind' and struggling to 'catch up' with a modern, 'professional-looking' Conservative Party campaign, enjoyed more support than they had previously been willing to acknowledge. I suggest that the methodological failure of senior Tory Party strategists to anticipate and effectively account for their electoral failure would, in turn, reinforce their marginal status in Scottish politics, mainly by rendering redundant their attempts to generate knowledge about themselves and a local political culture they deemed hostile to Conservatism. On Polling Day itself, more methodical attempts at auditing the party's campaign across Dumfries and Galloway were quickly abandoned as old anxieties returned to the ranks of local Conservative activists.

Shadow boxing

Tory activists and candidates began to contemplate what the result of the election might mean for them as they counted down the final days, hours and – for those unable to sleep on the eve of the poll – minutes before the election. Most members of the Core Campaign Team assumed that local Conservatives would enjoy some degree of electoral success on Polling Day. Generally, most party activists seemed upbeat about the campaign, believing that 'the tide had turned' and that the Scottish Conservatives were now 'setting the pace'. Few seemed to entertain the possibility that Mr Mundell would fail in his campaign to wrest the Dumfries constituency from the local Labour Party. In early April 2003, one senior Tory told me that while he thought Mr Fergusson was 'not going to make it' on Polling Day, Mr Mundell would win 'by about 1000 votes'. A Tory candidate for a council ward within the Royal Burgh of Dumfries was in the habit of declaring that the Labour incumbent Elaine Murray was 'finished' and that Mr Mundell would win 'with a 2,000–3,000 vote majority'.[2] The optimism of local activists was highly infectious, and even those with little direct involvement in the campaign seemed to anticipate some kind of victory.

As Polling Day approached, however, some Conservatives became uneasy. In the final couple of days of the campaign, activists in Dumfries began to see signs of Labour Party activity. As they deposited eve-of-poll and GOTV leaflets on the doormats of town centre households, some campaigners noticed Labour Party and other campaign materials stuffed through the same letterboxes. As if shadow boxing with their local Labour opponents, there was a sense amongst some activists that others were now mimicking their efforts and that their political rivals were sometimes lurking around street corners, just a few steps ahead (or behind) them. In addition, party activists widely suspected that their efforts were under constant observation from their political opponents. This led some to speculate as to whether or not the local Labour Party in particular had discerned the strengths or weaknesses of their campaign before they had themselves. This made several activists uneasy, reminding them of how they had borne the brunt of a slick Labour Party operation in the past. Some activists counselled their colleagues 'never to underestimate the local Labour Party machine', a view that was regularly reinforced to me by my non-Tory informants. Furthermore, Mr Mundell was becoming agitated. During a car journey in Dumfriesshire towards the end of April, I asked him how he was feeling about the upcoming elections. His reaction was tense:

> I have no idea. It's just too close to call. I just have to accept that there is not a single person in the entire world who could give me an objective opinion on how the election will go on Thursday.

Mr Mundell then pointed out that the local Labour Party possessed 'a formidable machine', which had already beaten him once before in the previous Scottish Parliament election. He also restated from earlier conversations with me his 'clear' belief that there was more potential support for the Labour Party in the Dumfries constituency than there was for the Scottish Conservatives. Just because the local Labour Party did not appear to be doing very much, he explained, did not mean it was therefore doing nothing. As the campaign neared its endpoint, senior Tories like Mr Mundell increasingly felt the need to remind themselves that, regardless of what had happened in the days and weeks beforehand, only the events of Polling Day itself would decide the outcome of the elections.

For Mr Mundell, Polling Day and the count that evening in Easterbrook Hall would provide a rare opportunity to glimpse the electoral impact of the Tory campaign at the micro-local level. I have already noted that Mr Duncan's spreadsheet provided a projected summary of the Conservative vote across the region. Broken down to ward level, these projections were based on canvass data drawn from Blue Chip. However, these data could be broken down to smaller units, such as the village or street. According to Mr Mundell, there was only one opportunity to test the veracity of the data, and this required a Conservative observer at the count to be present for the opening of the box of ballot papers from a particular polling station. Although the count would officially begin when polling closed at 10pm, it would proceed in a seemingly ad-hoc fashion as boxes were transported to Easterbook Hall during the evening.[3] The police would escort the first boxes from nearby Carlaevrock, Cresswell and Georgetown to the count shortly after 10pm. The last box, from Drummore – over 80 miles away near the southernmost tip of Scotland in rural Galloway – would probably appear around midnight.

These boxes would then be opened as they arrived and the ballot papers sifted for any obvious 'spoiled' papers, which would be removed at this early stage. Ballots would then be added to a large pile through which other polling officials would be working, sorting them into smaller bundles of support for different candidates and parties. As I discuss below, the opening of the boxes presented local Conservatives with a fleeting opportunity to view the papers before the identity of the polling station from which they originated was lost in the wider count. A rough count of what papers a Tory activist could see would give senior strategists an idea of how a small community served by a lone polling station had voted. This could then be compared with the canvass data on Blue Chip to determine the data's accuracy.

Mr Mundell was particularly interested in a handful of rural communities where he had personally 'invested' a lot of campaigning effort. The village of Beattock, just across the M74 from Moffat on the A701 to Dumfries, was one such community. With a primary school that had been earmarked for closure and a significant number of local residents living in former council housing, this community was not 'natural Tory turf', according to some senior Conservatives. However, the Conservative Party had campaigned strongly against the closure of small rural schools. Members of the Core Campaign Team thought that this strategy had probably improved the electoral fortunes of the party, particularly in the local government elections. They therefore proposed Beattock as a 'litmus test' for whether this strategy had been successful. Furthermore, in Mr Mundell's view, the opening of the ballot box from Beattock polling station could indicate whether local people generally not considered 'natural' Tory voters might be persuaded to support the Conservative Party if they campaigned on local issues important to specific communities. Strong support for the Conservatives in Beattock might suggest that 'sticking our necks out to save their local school', as one senior Tory put it, had been a good strategic decision during the campaign.

In the rest of this chapter, I describe the events of Polling Day, much of which I spent in the company of one member of the Core Campaign Team, the Conservative Party's Election Agent for Dumfries Alan MacLeod. During the day, we engaged in GOTV activities around the constituency before assisting with efforts to scrutinise the counting of ballot papers in Easterbrook Hall that evening. We also remained in contact by mobile telephone with other Tory activists and a number of interested observers.[4] The forces at work on Polling Day were very rarely within view. Mr MacLeod and I only ever caught glimpses of the campaigning activity being waged across the region that day. Nonetheless, such glimpses formed the basis of speculation about the morale and organisation of the Conservative Party's opponents. What we saw most often were the artefacts of the Labour Party's activist effort, discursive artefacts that sometimes evoked a mirror image to the activism of Tory volunteers and pointed to the efforts of their opponents. Such activism had remained largely out of sight of local Conservatives. For the local Labour Party and others, the stuffing of envelopes, the leafleting of streets, the telephoning of households and the canvassing of doorsteps would have been as labour-intensive an exercise as it had been for the local Tories. On

Polling Day, glimpsing the work of rival activists through the products of their labour was highly suggestive and very unsettling for local Conservatives. As they focused their attention on their principal opponents in Dumfries – the Labour Party – that sense of prospective momentum, which local Tories had succeeded in generating during the previous weeks and months, began to falter.

Polling Day begins

Polling stations opened at 7am on Thursday 1 May 2003 and closed at 10pm. There was an air of expectation that morning as I left my town centre flat and walked into the Conservative Party office in Castle Street around 8.30am. When I arrived, I was surprised at how quiet it was after weeks of so much frenetic activity. The telephones were silent and there was none of the background noise of the volunteers from previous weeks. Even the background murmur of BBC Radio Two seemed eerie. With a media blackout enforced on Polling Day itself, the banal sounds of DJ banter and popular music felt out of place.

Mr MacLeod was alone in the office, pottering about amongst the many piles of leaflets, literature and empty boxes that had accumulated during the course of the campaign. When he saw me, he explained that other staff members were out in the constituency leafleting and that they would be returning to the office later that morning to commence the telephone 'knock-up'. Sitting down with a cup of coffee, I felt somehow like I had missed the action by an hour or so, the electoral 'battle' now raging on the streets of Dumfries and in the villages of Dumfries and Galloway. I imagined dozens of activists out letterboxing local households with GOTV materials as local Tories sought to mobilise their electoral base. Meanwhile, David Mundell was travelling to key polling stations in Dumfriesshire to chat with local supporters before returning to his home in Moffat to conduct his own telephone 'knock-up' that afternoon. A handful of volunteers had come forward to telephone other parts of the constituency, including the activist from Annan mentioned in Chapter 6 who was passionate about telephone canvassing, while a couple of staff members at SCCO in Edinburgh had also been assigned to the telephone 'knock-up'. This would commence later that morning. The Tory Party agent decided that our time would be best spent going door-to-door in Dumfries to help 'get out the vote'.

After locking the office, Mr MacLeod drove me to Georgetown, a large private housing estate to the southeast of the town centre. Local Conservatives generally considered Georgetown to be a 'swing' area in which there was a significant Tory voter base that was marginally outnumbered by Labour supporters. Key Party strategists generally believed that if the Conservatives lost Georgetown on a ratio of 2:3 votes to the Labour Party, their prospects of winning across the Dumfries constituency were strong. They therefore hoped that the opening of ballot boxes from polling stations in Georgetown would thus provide an early clue as to how the election count would proceed that evening.

As we drove, we passed a large four-wheel-drive Land Rover sporting bright red posters stuck to its back windscreen. We then started to notice other vehicles with the same poster, an A4 sheet of coloured paper declaring support for the local Labour Party incumbent Dr Elaine Murray. Mr MacLeod fell silent as we drove. It seemed as if every third or fourth vehicle we passed was involved in this public display of support for the Labour Party. Furthermore, I did not see a single car displaying a poster for Mr Mundell. This helped to create the strong impression that residents of Dumfries were firmly backing the Labour candidate, prompting the Tory Party agent to state that there were more posters on display than he would have liked to see. Only when we drove past Georgetown Library, which was being used as a polling station, did his mood begin to improve, encouraged by the sight of the Tory council candidate for the Lochvale ward standing by the door with her blue Conservative Party rosette pinned to her blouse. Standing next to her was the incumbent Independent councillor, whereas the local Labour candidate was absent. This seemed like a positive sign to Mr MacLeod.

In Georgetown, we turned down a side street and parked the car. The Conservative Party agent gave me a list of house numbers in which people lived who had pledged their support to the Conservative Party. These were homes whose telephone numbers were not publicly available and which would therefore not be called during the telephone 'knock-up' scheduled to start later that morning. Grabbing some Polling Day leaflets, I headed for the three or four houses that had been highlighted on my list in a small cul-de-sac. Mr MacLeod went to the next street as I knocked on the first door. Nobody answered and it quickly became obvious that no one in the street was at home. I stuffed Polling Day leaflets into the letterboxes of each of the empty houses on my list. This did not take me long. Walking back down the street, Mr MacLeod approached me in his car. When I climbed into the passenger seat, he said: 'I've just seen Colin Smyth!' At that moment, Mr Smyth – the local Labour Party's Election Agent for the Dumfries constituency and council candidate for the Lochvale ward – walked around the corner into the street. He was wearing a red Labour Party rosette and carrying his own bunch of Polling Day leaflets along with a clipboard. 'I think we should go to another part of Georgetown,' Mr MacLeod said.

As we drove past him, Mr Smyth glanced at us before quickly averting his gaze, as if pretending not to have seen us. Mr MacLeod drove to another part of Georgetown where, according to Blue Chip, there was a concentration of Tory voters. Parking at the entrance to another cul-de-sac that led uphill to a number of large houses, I got out of the car and started walking up the street. Like the other street, this one seemed very quiet. Most of the driveways were empty and I glanced around me, alert to the possibility of spotting another Labour Party activist. The day was bright despite being overcast and it might have been warm had it not been for a slight breeze; the clouds on the horizon threatened rain. As I walked, however, I noticed a leaflet hanging from the front doorknob of the house nearest to me. It looked like a big red question mark, shaped similarly to a 'Do Not Disturb' sign one might find on the doorknob of a hotel room. I then saw another of these red question marks, dangling from the door of another house. Stopping in the middle of the street, I scanned the front doors of all the houses around me. Almost every single one of them had one of these signs hanging from their front doors. Given that there were only about ten houses in this street, I was able to see from my list that the two or three houses I had been asked to 'knock up' were amongst the very few that did not have such a sign. My curiosity aroused, I jogged up the driveway of the nearest house and looked more closely at the red question mark. As I suspected, it was the Labour Party's Polling Day leaflet, which simply stated 'Remember to use your votes for Labour today'. 'Knocking up' the remaining houses on my list, I reflected on the significance of these leaflets, displayed on the front doors of those houses omitted from my list. Two points were obvious. First, while local Conservatives had been busy identifying their own supporters in the electorate, the Labour Party had been doing the same. It now seemed like there were more Labour voters 'out there' than local Conservatives had often assumed in daily conversation. Second, local Labour Party activists had leafleted these streets shortly before our arrival and might still be in the area. Together with the Elaine Murray posters we had seen earlier, the presence of the red Polling Day leaflets on the doorknobs of nearby houses contributed to the impression that the local Labour Party was marking out its territory, making its own political (proprietorial) claim to Dumfries: this was Labour turf.

I caught up with Mr MacLeod, who had also noticed the red Polling Day leaflets. We drove down the hill and pulled up outside a house with an overgrown garden, which he asked me to letterbox with the Tory Party GOTV leaflet. When I returned, he said: 'We've been spotted.' 'Where?' I asked. Glancing up the street behind us, I saw two young women standing near the crest of a hill, both wearing Labour Party rosettes and carrying clipboards. According to Mr MacLeod, they had been talking to each other before one of them spotted us further down the street. Now both watching us, one of them was speaking into her mobile phone. 'They will be reporting into Labour Party HQ, telling them they've spotted Conservative activity,' Mr MacLeod explained. 'I think we'd better go somewhere else.' So we drove to the other side of Georgetown.

The weather turns

After 'knocking up' a few more households, the sky darkened and it started to rain. Rather than drive straight back to the office, Mr MacLeod suggested that we tour the streets of Dumfries to see if we could spot any more Labour activists. We drove for some time around the Carlaevrock ward without seeing anything of interest before heading back into Dumfries Town Centre. During our drive, the Tory Party agent outlined a theory that many of his colleagues used to 'read' the activity of their opponents. Such readings depended on where rival activists were seen: 'your' council wards or 'theirs'. Mr MacLeod explained:

> If you see the Labour Party in your areas, then you know you're in trouble. That would be a sign that they are really confident and don't have to worry about getting their vote out. If you saw them out in places like Marchmount and Maxwelltown [where Blue Chip identified concentrations of Tory voters] at this time of day, it would be a really bad sign. Of course, if they were in trouble, you would expect

to see them out in their areas. If they know they're going to have a bad election, they will be working hard in places like Lochside, making sure that they got their hard-core supporters out.

Put simply, if they were struggling to motivate their electoral base, the Labour Party would have to focus their campaign resources on persuading their supporters not to stay at home on Polling Day. Such a scenario would be positive for local Tories if they could get their own vote out in significant numbers because they would then stand a strong chance of winning the election. According to Mr MacLeod, mobilising a party's electoral base in this way was a particularly effective strategy if there was low voter turnout in the election. Noting that we had seen Labour activists 'knocking up' Georgetown, which senior Conservatives considered a 'swing' area, I asked Mr MacLeod how his theory might explain their efforts. 'I have no idea,' he replied.

We then decided to drive across town to Lochside, an impoverished council housing estate in which there were high levels of unemployment, drug misuse and crime. Driving down the Whitesands, we passed the Friars Vennel, an historic shopping district that runs up to the Burns Statue at the top of the High Street.[5] The local Labour Party office was located a few doors along the Vennel. All the blinds were drawn. Mr MacLeod speculated that this probably meant Labour Party activists were out, mobilised somewhere in the constituency. Alternatively, they might have been busy 'knocking up' their supporters over the telephone, their blinds drawn to discourage interest from passing members of the public. The rain was intensifying so it did not seem like promising weather in which to be mustering support door-to-door.

As we entered Lochside, we passed a church on our left that was being used as a polling station. Mr MacLeod pulled over and decided to check on voter turnout. As the Tory Party's Election Agent, he could enter any polling station in the Dumfries constituency. I waited for him in the car. A few minutes later, he returned with the news that turnout had been very low so far that day. This fact was encouraging, he said, as it indicated that the local Labour Party might be struggling to get its vote out. It also suggested that the election might be fought on a low turnout, in which case Mr Mundell might win the seat if Tory voters were successfully mobilising elsewhere in the constituency. Buoyed by this development, Mr MacLeod drove further into Lochside looking for signs of the local Labour Party. I noticed one or two cars displaying Elaine Murray posters as well as some others plastered on the front windows of nearby flats. Then, with some surprise, we suddenly came upon a large number of Labour activists, soaked in the downpour, huddled under umbrellas and pointing at dampened maps and canvass sheets by the side of the road. We counted five or six of them before spotting a couple more down a footpath. The group included Dr Elaine Murray and several other well-known Labour activists from Dumfries. We drove down the road before turning at a junction to drive past them a second time and get a better look at what they were doing. The Tory Party agent was jubilant at spotting the local Labour Party marooned in such large numbers in the middle of heavy rain. Furthermore, they had been sighted in one of 'their' wards, which fuelled his excitement even more. If his theory on how to read the activity of rival activists on Polling Day was correct, then the Conservative Party might be poised to win the Dumfries constituency by a landslide. The low turnout detected at the local polling station combined with the sighting of local Labour Party activists caught and seemingly lost in the rain might have confirmed that for which key Party strategists had been most hoping: that 'the wheels had fallen off' the local Labour Party machine and they were now heading for defeat.

Following a 'celebratory' lunch at McDonald's on the way back into town, Mr MacLeod and I returned to the party office in Castle Street. It was now unrecognisable from the empty place we had left that morning. Various members of staff had returned from their earlier tasks, as had a handful of volunteers. They were now working through lists of telephone numbers and making hundreds – indeed, thousands – of telephone calls to 'get out the vote' across Dumfries and Galloway. There were five telephone lines from the office, but not all of them were in use at the same time. For example, one was a parliamentary line, which could not be used for political campaigning; this was kept free so that activists and members of the general public could call the office if there was a need for them to do so. Another was the fax line, which was later utilised by one enthusiastic volunteer who decided to help with the telephone 'knock up' in the evening. Secretarial staff and volunteers were using the three remaining lines as they methodically worked through their lists. Operating from a script that had been composed in the final days of the campaign, Tory activists rang people who had previously indicated their willingness to support the Conservative Party during the canvass and survey efforts described in Chapter 6. The script therefore assumed that the vast majority of the individuals telephoned during the 'knock up' would be supportive. Short and succinct, the primary piece of information sought in the script was whether or not the individual had voted and, if they had not, whether or not they intended to vote. When it had been established that someone had voted, their name would be crossed off the list with a pencil and ruler. Activists would then use this opportunity to confirm that the individual to whom they were talking had voted Tory to check again the accuracy of the canvass data on Blue Chip. This information would usually be confirmed in the right-hand column of the sheet.

I asked one volunteer how the telephoning had been progressing. She responded that the people to whom they had spoken seemed very supportive. Most of them had already voted or would be voting. In fact, they had now almost completed their lists and were about to commence some telephoning for Alex Fergusson in the Galloway and Upper Nithsdale constituency, for whom lists of Conservative 'pledges' around Stranraer had been faxed through to Castle Street. These results seemed to suggest that much of the locally pledged support for the Conservative Party had already voted. This appeared to contrast with the seemingly low turnout in Lochside, an electoral 'stronghold' for the local Labour Party. If Conservative voters were motivated and the party was succeeding in mobilising them, Tory activists in the office thought it likely that they were now forging 'ahead' of the Labour Party at that time of Polling Day. That it was now raining heavily was considered a further boost for the party's electoral prospects as this could only compound the difficulties of Labour activists trying to mobilise supporters reluctant to make their way to the polling station in the rain. Despite the apparent success of the telephone 'knock up', however, the volunteer to whom I spoke stated that some people had been 'annoying'. Indeed, some Conservatives were adamant that they would not be voting in either election because in their view 'it made no difference'. When he heard about this, Mr MacLeod seemed unnerved and asked the volunteer what respondents had meant when they made this statement. She said that she did not know.

With all the telephone lines in use, there was little for us to do in the office. We decided to return to the streets of Dumfries. Just before we left, another volunteer received a telephone call from SCCO in Edinburgh, which a local supporter had contacted in search of a lift to her nearest polling station. The Tory Party agent offered to give this elderly woman a lift so she could vote. It was still raining as we drove to her house. On the way, we discussed the reasons why some Conservatives were refusing to come out and vote. During previous weeks, we had both encountered a handful of local Tories who possessed mixed feelings about their local candidate for the Scottish Parliament. For some, Mr Mundell was not a 'traditional Tory' and did not possess views that, for them, were 'right-wing enough'. Others still considered him a 'turn-coat' from the days he represented Lockerbie as a councillor for the Social Democrats in the 1980s. However, we both thought that a more likely explanation for reluctance amongst some Tories to vote that day lay in their disinclination to reconcile themselves to Scottish devolution. Before the campaign, Mr MacLeod had received a couple of letters from disgruntled supporters who refused to cast a vote in the Scottish Parliament elections because they felt that to do so would give an institution to which they remained opposed some legitimacy.[6] While he did not believe many local Tories shared this view, he expressed the worry that in a close contest, 'every vote could matter'. Mr MacLeod seemed to believe that if the Scottish Conservatives were to win the Dumfries constituency that day, it would be with a very small margin.

However, there was another, troubling, possibility: could it be that some local voters, whether Conservative supporters or not, had declined to participate in the election because they believed their vote would not make a difference in changing the government of Scotland? Despite the best efforts of the SNP, Labour's principal opponents in the Scottish Parliament, few really thought that after Polling Day a government would form that did not include the Scottish Labour Party or the Liberal Democrats. In such a political landscape, what real incentive was there for local people to turn out and vote? Indeed, just how *could* a Conservative MSP make a difference in Dumfries, even if he or she was elected? After all, a Tory representative would still be marginal in the wider political landscape of post-devolution Scotland. It was possible that, by declaring their intention not to vote at all, some local Conservatives had come to this conclusion. Considering all of these possibilities, however, Mr MacLeod stated that he simply had no idea why some Tories refused to vote on Polling Day. For him, this problem was particularly vexing given that most activists seemed to agree Dumfries was one of the few Scottish parliamentary constituencies the Conservatives could actually win from the Labour Party. Nor could he know whether the result would be close that night and, therefore, whether the refusal of some local Tories to cast their votes would deny the Party victory. Our discussion amounted to little more than speculation.

We arrived at our destination and picked up the elderly supporter. Mr MacLeod stayed in his car while I accompanied her to the polling station. Carefully avoiding a young Labour Party activist standing by the door with a clipboard in her hands, we made our way to the desk at which a couple of polling officials sat. They then assisted her while I waited. After returning the supporter to her home, we decided to drive out of town to see if we could identify any opposition activity in rural Dumfriesshire. According to Mr MacLeod, this might help us develop a better idea of how the Labour Party's campaign was progressing that day. We drove through the Heathhall and Lochar council wards in northeast Dumfries. Beyond the burgh boundary, we turned off the A75 and headed towards Ae, a tiny community famous for possessing the shortest name of any town or village in the United Kingdom. As we expected, the Ae polling station seemed deserted. We then drove back towards Lochmaben and then Lockerbie, again without seeing much political activity from Labour, Tory or other supporters.

Mr MacLeod then decided to drive to Annan through the rural council ward of Hoddom and Kinmount. This ward contained a high number of Conservative supporters and was represented by the popular Tory councillor Andrew Bell-Irving. An affable local landowner whose family had a long association with the area, Councillor Bell-Irving was once described to me by one of my non-Tory informants as 'a likeable bloke' who played the role of 'the fat country squire' very well. 'You could just imagine him', she had said, 'in bygone days, sitting on horseback and chatting to the peasants.' In addition, the Tory Party agent had explained to me that Councillor Bell-Irving was self-consciousness and perhaps slightly embarrassed about apparently fitting a certain Tory stereotype so perfectly. He had commented to him on a previous occasion that he would not have been able to get elected to council in any ward other than Hoddom and Kinmount, where there was a strong concentration of wealthy, landowning families living in *big hooses*. As we drove by a number of gates and gatehouses to secluded, wooded estates, glistening in the emerging sunlight, the rain stopped completely and the sun punctured the sky. When we passed a small church covered in Scottish Conservative banners, Mr MacLeod's mood improved dramatically. 'This is the Tory heartland of rural Dumfriesshire!' he proclaimed excitedly. Driving on to the small town of Annan, there were no further visual clues to suggest it was Polling Day. However, as we joined the A75 to return to Dumfries fifteen miles away, we passed a field on the outskirts of town with a huge 'Vote Conservative' poster mounted within it. The Tory Party agent cheered. A few miles further along the A75, we passed another massive poster, this time attached to the back of a piece of farm machinery by the side of the road. Mr MacLeod noted that the owners of the farm to which the machinery and poster belonged were friends of the retired lieutenant colonel John Charteris, whose awkward and uncooperative behaviour had previously caused so many difficulties for Party strategists, as I discussed in Chapter 5. But now, his reputation momentarily improved in the eyes of the party agent: 'I always knew he would come good in the end!'

'Labour voters come out at night'

It was early evening by the time we reached Dumfries. Driving up the Whitesands on our way back to the Castle Street office, we took a short detour down the Friars Vennel past the local Labour Party office. Dozens of people were walking down the middle of the cobbled street and there were a couple of cars parked near the office itself, which narrowed our passage considerably. Just as we passed the front entrance to the office, it suddenly opened and over half a dozen prominent Labour activists came running out, surrounding Mr MacLeod's car as if they had been waiting in ambush. But they apparently did not notice us and climbed instead into the two cars parked by the office. We stopped at the bottom of the Vennel to turn right onto the Whitesands, the two vehicles pulling up behind us. Amongst the activists we could see in the first car, we identified several Labour candidates for the council elections as well as the local Labour MP Russell Brown. Watching them in his side mirror, Mr MacLeod wondered aloud where they might be going. Once we had turned right, we saw them turn left in our rearview mirrors. This route could take them to Georgetown or perhaps out of town altogether as they headed southeast of Dumfries. 'Do you think they're going to Annan?' I asked. 'I don't know,' the Tory Party agent responded. After a pause, I said: 'Where do you think they are going?' 'I don't know,' Mr MacLeod repeated, looking tense.

Several people were still making telephone calls from the Conservative Party office when we arrived there a few minutes later. The telephone 'knock up' would continue until 8pm, two hours before the close of the poll. Because many Tory supporters were elderly, it was generally thought that ringing them any later than this time would be rude and disrespectful. Senior Conservatives also assumed that if their supporters intended to cast their votes on Polling Day, they would have done so by then. If the Conservative Party campaign had been fully mobilised that day, it seemed as if it was now winding down. In contrast, based on what Mr MacLeod and I had observed at the Labour Party office, it appeared that local Labour activists were gearing up for a final push to get out their vote that evening. An anxious-looking Mr Mundell had also turned up at the office around the same time we arrived. Mr MacLeod withdrew to his office while I spoke to the Scottish parliamentary candidate in the reception area. I told him about the Labour activists we had seen earlier that day as well as what we had just witnessed outside the local Labour Party office. This was not a positive development in Mr Mundell's view. 'Well, it's too bad the rain has stopped,' he said. 'This is the time when the Labour Party can get its vote out. Labour voters come out at night.'

Shortly afterwards, one of my non-Tory informants rang my mobile. I moved to the small boardroom that the Core Campaign Team had used for its weekly meetings over the previous months. My caller then explained that she had voted earlier in the day and was now at her parents' house in Lochvale. In the background, I could hear some excited activity. She said that a young Labour Party activist had just knocked on the front door of the house and had asked her parents, who were both Labour Party supporters, if they had voted yet that day. Responding that they had not, the young woman then asked if they would mind coming down to the polling station at Georgetown Library and casting their votes. The local Labour Party expected the result, she said, 'to be extremely close' in the Dumfries constituency. Her parents agreed and were in the process of putting on their coats before heading out with the young woman. Looking out of the front window, my informant then told me that she could see several other Labour activists knocking on doors further down her parents' street.[7] My thoughts returned to the local Labour activists we had seen hastily leaving the Friars Vennel less than an hour earlier.

I received two more calls on my mobile that evening. One was from a young Tory candidate who lived in Stranraer and was running against an Independent incumbent for a council ward in his local area. He told me that he was feeling positive and was in the process of driving across the region to attend the count at Easterbrook Hall. He also planned to stay in Dumfries that evening so he could attend the counting of ballot papers for the local council elections, which would take place in Loreburn Hall the following day.[8] I then spoke to Alex Fergusson, the Scottish Conservative candidate in Galloway and Upper Nithsdale. He was also feeling upbeat as he, too, drove to the count. While travelling around his prospective constituency on Polling Day, he had passed many 'Scottish Conservative' posters in farmers' fields along the A75. Many of the farmers who had erected such posters were personal friends and acquaintances of his, a point he found especially 'gratifying'. Later, Mr MacLeod and I headed over to Easterbrook Hall as well. On the way, we dropped into the Cresswell Community Centre, which was being used as a polling station. The Tory Party agent returned to the car once he had checked the voter turnout, which seemed to him low. He cautiously welcomed this fact since Cresswell was a part of Dumfries in which the Labour Party was thought to enjoy a lot of support. Not known for his optimistic outlook on the Tory Party's chances of winning these elections, it seemed that even Mr MacLeod anticipated some kind of success that evening.

Counting on failure

In the week before Polling Day, local Conservative candidates in the 2003 elections had appointed polling and counting agents. While a polling agent was entitled to enter polling stations to, for example, take notes on voter turnout, a counting agent was allowed to observe the counting of ballot papers to ensure that there were no 'irregularities'. I had been appointed a counting agent for Mr Mundell. The Returning Officer – a senior council official – had posted the relevant paperwork to each counting agent a couple of days before Polling Day. My pack included, amongst other items, a pass with which to enter the count, guidelines on conduct during the evening and instructions on what constituted a valid ballot paper. It also included a floor plan of Easterbrook Hall. The count took place in the main Hall. Most of the Hall remained 'off limits' to counting agents, who were left with a small area near the stage in which to mingle. Some local journalists circulated amongst the counting agents, although most were in an upstairs seating area that had been kept free for local and national media, including representatives of ITV Border and BBC radio. In the main body of the Hall, several dozen council employees sat along portable trellis tables, ready and waiting to commence the sorting and counting of ballot papers. Other senior council officials were engaged in discussions at the back of the hall, as were a handful of police officers.

A number of counting agents for the local Conservatives had arrived before us. Some other activists were already there, too. I saw the SNP candidate for the Dumfries constituency Andrew Wood and his Election Agent, who was loading up a laptop in one corner of the main hall where they had found an unused power point. There were no Labour activists at the count yet except for the Dumfries incumbent Dr Elaine Murray and her husband. Those Tories who had already arrived were unsure whether this meant that her supporters were confident of victory. Local Conservatives had told me on previous occasions that the local Labour Party always turned up to the count late if they thought they were going to win. Dr Murray's presence suggested that at least some of them were uncertain of how events would unfold that evening.

Key Party strategists considered the role of counting agents crucial. Not only were they necessary for ensuring that the count itself remained 'transparent'; as I have already discussed, counting agents could also help to identify sources of Tory electoral strength at the micro-local level if present during the opening of the ballot boxes as they arrived from polling stations. Armed with pencils and clipboards, counting agents mimicked the polling officials sorting and counting the ballot papers to produce their own mock 'count'.[9] At the end of the night, individual counting 'sheets' would then be collected to try to get an overview of where the Conservative Party vote was concentrated. If this was done well within the initial stages of the count, senior Tories also hoped that they might gain an early indication as to how the election would eventually turn out. Of course, this process could only provide a crude sketch of the contours of electoral support across the constituency. The accuracy of this count varied amongst individuals depending on the age, ability and eyesight of Tory activists. Most of the Conservatives present were very elderly and were easily distracted from the task, particularly if they were struggling to read the ballot papers over the shoulders of polling officials. Members of the Core Campaign Team found this frustrating. At one point, one senior Tory asked me to interrupt a conversation that was taking place between three or four elderly activists while a crucial ballot box was being opened in front of them – to which they had been completely oblivious.

The first boxes arrived shortly after 10pm. As police and security escorted them into the building, the Returning Officer announced that these boxes had come from polling stations near or within Dumfries and that others would continue to arrive during the night. He also took this opportunity to introduce a small group of middle-aged men in leather jackets, who were standing at the edge of the Hall. These six or seven individuals were polling officials from Albania who had come to observe the count. One Tory activist turned to me and observed that the men resembled Soviet-era secret policemen. 'I wouldn't like to meet one of those men in a dark alley,' he whispered mischievously.

The boxes were checked and verified out of view of the counting agents before being distributed and emptied at various tables. I stood talking to a local BBC radio journalist, who had asked me what kind of result I anticipated that evening. Conscious of nearby Conservative activists eavesdropping on what I was saying, I stated that the result was too close to call but that the political story of the night might be one of a Tory revival in southwest Scotland. Meanwhile, a Tory council candidate standing next to me declared (not for the first time, as I have already noted) that 'Elaine Murray was finished' as David Mundell would win 'by 3,000 votes'. Other activists, including several Liberal Democrats and Scottish Nationalists to whom I spoke that evening, seemed to think he would probably lose. Such views were consistent with earlier observations conveyed to me by non-Tory activists, who had described the local Labour MSP as 'assiduous' and unlikely to lose her Scottish parliamentary seat. On a previous occasion, for instance, one local Labour activist had explained to me that an elected representative 'would really have to do something wrong to lose their seat', which meant that in his view Dr Murray would probably get re-elected.

Around this time, a cohort of local Labour activists arrived *en masse* and, as a result, the mood of some Tory activists darkened. Counting agents from all the political parties present moved towards the tables where polling officials had started opening boxes. The first of these were from Georgetown, which senior Party strategists were keen to see. As counting agents scratched down notes while they observed the ballot papers from these boxes getting sorted, the figures looked promising: the Labour Party appeared to be ahead of the Tories on the ratio of 3:2 votes. There were some other encouraging signs contained within other boxes as well. For example, when the box for Beattock polling station was opened about thirty minutes later, the result appeared to overwhelmingly favour Mr Mundell. For senior Tory strategists, this appeared to vindicate the local party's policy commitment to 'saving' Beattock Primary from closure.

Just after midnight, however, there was some anticipation that a result was imminent for the Dumfries constituency. By this point, the mood of many Tories in the Hall appeared to have become tense. It certainly seemed to me that most Conservative activists had lost the enthusiasm they had felt earlier that day. Mr Mundell looked distracted as he talked to the Returning Officer on the other side of the Hall. Supporters speculated that the local Conservatives had, once again, 'fallen behind' the Labour Party. One activist told me that 'there's only 500 votes in it', but no one knew who was ahead. The faces of local Labour activists were equally attentive and solemn. Dr Elaine Murray, who was also talking to the Returning Officer, seemed to be wiping away tears. About ten minutes later, the candidates for the Dumfries constituency approached the stage at the front of the Hall. Standing behind the Returning Officer, Mr Mundell clutched his wife's hand as she fought back her own tears. The fears of local Conservatives were confirmed when the Returning Officer read out the number of votes cast for each candidate: Dr Murray had won the Dumfries constituency by roughly 1,000 votes. Local Labour activists roared with celebration as the result was declared while some began heckling Mr Mundell as he took the microphone to concede defeat. Nonplussed, he congratulated Dr Murray on her victory and thanked his supporters. Then, he asserted that the result in the Dumfries constituency was a 'huge success' for local Conservatives, who had secured a 10% swing against the incumbent Labour Party.[10]

Many of Mr Mundell's supporters were clearly disappointed. However, attention quickly turned to the count in Galloway and Upper Nithsdale, which was taking place on the other side of the Hall. Within minutes of the declaration of the vote in the Dumfries constituency, there were mutterings amongst Conservative and Labour counting agents that the result in the neighbouring constituency was 'too close to call'. Indeed, SNP and Tory activists from the west of the region looked pensive. I walked over to Mr Fergusson, who was standing with a small group of his supporters. 'I'm about 100 votes ahead,' he said to me, clearly agitated and excited at the same time. 'There's going to be a re-count.' Mr Mundell now joined the Conservative MP for Galloway and Upper Nithsdale Peter Duncan as they rallied the party's counting agents around the tables. 'We're going to have to watch every ballot paper because they [the SNP] will be watching ours,' one activist told me. At that moment, the Returning Officer issued instructions to those polling officials tasked with re-sorting the papers ahead of a re-count. He explained that they needed to check every ballot in every bundle to be sure that they had not accidentally included any 'spoiled' papers. They would then need to re-count each bundle to make sure they each consisted of exactly 100 ballots. Baskets of bundled papers were then distributed along the tables. As they were sorted again, one polling official 'found' a stray basket containing a lone bundle of ballot papers at the back of the Hall. After conferring with the Returning Officer, this stray bundle was then added to the large pile of votes for the incumbent SNP candidate. The margin now appeared to be just nine votes. The possibility that Mr Fergusson might suffer a narrow defeat to the SNP increased as the political stakes for local Conservatives just grew higher.

Conservative and SNP counting agents watched intently over their shoulders as polling officials carefully re-sorted and re-counted the ballot papers in each bundle. The Hall had become much quieter. Even Labour activists from the Dumfries constituency were transfixed by the re-count in Galloway and Upper Nithsdale. Every now and then, a 'spoiled' ballot paper that had been included in the initial count would be discovered and removed. Almost as frequently, an SNP ballot that had been accidentally filed amongst the hundreds of votes for the Scottish Socialist Party would be added to the Scottish Nationalist pile. For roughly twenty tense minutes, the margin between Mr Fergusson and Mr Morgan seemed to grow and diminish by a handful of votes as the re-count continued. Then, another polling official suddenly discovered another stray tray with another stray bundle of ballot papers in it. The candidates conferred again with the Returning Officer, this time for several minutes. Activists watched from a distance. The SNP incumbent looked worried while Mr Fergusson appeared stony-faced. The Returning Officer then added the stray bundle to Alex Fergusson's pile of ballot papers. From their shell-shocked expressions, it was apparent that local SNP activists were giving up hope. The final tally saw the Tory candidate win the constituency by 99 votes.[11] In a victorious speech following the declaration of the result, Mr Fergusson observed that the Galloway and Upper Nithsdale constituency had rejected Scottish Nationalist representation after only one term in the Scottish Parliament. This, he said, confirmed a pattern of SNP electoral failure in southwest Scotland, where they were unable to hold the local Westminster seat longer than one term in 1974 and 2001. The defeated SNP incumbent Alasdair Morgan retorted that as a newly elected Regional List MSP for the South of Scotland, he would spend the next four years 'shadowing' Mr Fergusson in his old parliamentary constituency.[12] In effect, he promised to stalk Mr Fergusson in the same way that the Tory candidate had when he had been elected through the Regional List after losing to Mr Morgan at the previous election.

There were even more surprising results for local Conservatives the following day, when the ballots for the local council elections were counted at Loreburn Hall. On a high turnout, local Tories had won a greater share of the vote (31%) than any other political party. They were re-elected in the nine council wards they had held before Polling Day, with increased majorities in eight of them.[13] However, in spite of all their campaigning efforts during the months leading up to the elections, local Conservatives won just two additional council wards as only a tiny handful changed hands across the entire region. One such ward was Moffat, which included the village of Beattock and for which the Conservative candidate Safa Ash-Kuri had been selected less than a month before Polling Day. The other was Criffel ward, where the Tory challenger Bruce Hodgson had succeeded in his four-year campaign to unseat the Independent incumbent that had beaten him in the 1999 election for Dumfries and Galloway Council. This seemingly 'mixed' result disappointed local Conservatives who were bemused by the fact that only their longest-running and most recently recruited candidates had been elected. Once the results were known, it appeared to one senior Party strategist that contrary to the assumptions that had informed much of their campaign, the electoral momentum had, in fact, been behind the anti-Tory council administration all along. 'We would have run our campaign very differently had we known that,' he later told me. Then, another result was announced towards the end of the count in Loreburn Hall: an obviously relieved David Mundell had just been re-elected to the Scottish Parliament through the South of Scotland Regional List.

At the beginning of this chapter, I described how local Tories had anticipated electoral success on 1 May 2003 and had also looked to Polling Day as an opportunity to carry out a mock audit of their campaign. However, the methods and strategies they devised for assessing their party's 'progress', in terms of both their campaign's internal mechanics as well as its external effects, were all rendered redundant on Polling Day. Afterwards, I never once heard Mr Duncan mention again the spreadsheet he had prepared for the McDonald's meeting with which I commenced this chapter. Nor did senior Conservatives spend much time discussing the performance of individual council candidates against the benchmarks and 'targets' that Mr Duncan's spreadsheet had contained. Instead, such documents were discarded as old anxieties returned on Polling Day and the elections produced unexpected results that many local Tory activists found unsettling. In their explanations 'for what went wrong', one contributing factor in particular eventually came to stand as a symbol for the uncertainties inherent to the entire process: the weather. Indeed, one key Party strategist simply concluded that if the rain had continued to fall in the evening, Mr Mundell would have won the Dumfries constituency. According to this view, 'Labour voters come out at night' and would have been discouraged from voting by the poor weather. Many Conservative activists found this explanation convincing. After all, by early afternoon on 1 May, those involved in the telephone 'knock up' felt that most of the pledged Tory support had already voted. If the local Conservative Party could be said to have forged 'ahead' at that point in the day, they speculated that the local Labour Party had been struggling to 'catch up' – until, that is, the rain stopped and the skies cleared. For Tory activists, Polling Day had been marked by a sense of losing the very prospective momentum that they had succeeded in generating during the previous weeks and months. And as I discuss in the next chapter, it was unclear from the observations they had made on Polling Day and the count that followed what, in particular, had contributed to the local Conservative Party's electoral success or failure.

Notes

1 For an analysis of similar practices observed from a location amongst polling officials in Bosnia-Herzegovina, see Coles (2004, 2007).

2 On one occasion, Mr Mundell overheard this candidate predicting such an overwhelming result in a conversation with local activists. 'Well, I would be happy with [a victory of] two votes!' he quipped.

3 Easterbrook Hall is located on the Crichton Estate (part of which is the Crichton University Campus) on the southern edge of Dumfries. The site was home to the Crichton Royal Hospital until 1989, which began its institutional life as a lunatic asylum opened in 1839.

4 Activists were discouraged from calling each other on their mobile telephones during Polling Day. Senior Tories felt that this could potentially distract activists from engaging with local electors on a day when, they said, mobilising 'every vote mattered'. Instead, communication by text message was the norm. Activists would exchange information about voter turnout at key polling stations throughout the day or sightings of Labour Party (and other) activists.

5 The Friars Vennel is one of the oldest streets in Dumfries and, according to local historians, the oldest shopping 'precinct' in Scotland (Fortune and McMillan 2005).

6 These individuals often took a similar view towards voting in elections for the European Parliament, the existence of which many also opposed.

7 Several houses had displayed red 'Elaine Murray' posters on this street, which one local Tory candidate had described as 'a hotbed of socialism'.

8 The count had to be moved from Easterbook Hall on Friday 2 May, because the venue

had been previously booked for a wedding reception. As the last stragglers left the count in the early hours of Friday morning, staff had already begun clearing the room and setting up tables for the next event scheduled for the popular venue later that day.

9   This reminds me of Amy Levine's argument (2004: 92) that South Korean government officials mimic the practices of human rights activists and other representatives of civil society (and vice versa) in the pursuit of 'transparency'.

10 The official results were: Elaine Murray (Labour) – 12,834 votes (40%); David Mundell (Conservative) – 11,738 votes (36.6%); Andrew Wood (SNP) – 3,931 votes (12.2%); Clare Hamblen (Liberal Democrat) – 2,394 votes (7.5%); and John Dennis (Scottish Socialist Party) – 1,213 votes (3.8%). For more on the results of the Scottish Parliament elections, see Burnside *et al.* (2003).

11 The result in Galloway and Upper Nithsdale was as follows: Alex Fergusson (Conservative) – 11,332 votes (38.2%); Alasdair Morgan (SNP) – 11,233 votes (37.9%); Norma Hart (Labour) – 4,299 votes (14.5%); Neil Wallace (Liberal Democrat) – 1,847 votes (6.2%); Joy Cherkaoui (Scottish Socialist Party) – 709 votes (2.4%); Graham Brockhouse (Scottish People's Alliance) – 215 votes (0.7%). For more, see Burnside *et al.* (2003).

12 Both Mr Fergusson and Mr Morgan had headed their respective Party tickets for the South of Scotland Regional List. This virtually guaranteed their re-election to the Scottish Parliament since both Parties anticipated strong support across southern Scotland that would translate into Regional List seats.

13 In the Thornhill ward, no one had stood against the incumbent Tory councillor, who was re-elected automatically.

8

Return of the lesser-spotted Tory

'Politics has changed and politics is changing.' (South of Scotland Conservative MSP Alex Fergusson, addressing local Tory Party activists in February 2003)

In this chapter I will briefly sketch some of the incidents that took place in the aftermath of the 2003 elections to ask whether local Conservatives had successfully addressed their crisis of irrelevance. One question with which senior Tories sought to grapple was what, if anything, had changed as a result of their campaign? With much resting on the reading of a letter published in a local newspaper or a few words exchanged in a car on the way to a Party function, the grounds on which Conservative activists assessed their own knowledge of local politics as well as that of what did or did not 'work' in their campaign were sketchy and uncertain. I suggest that local Party strategists had to struggle to make 'change' appear. In an election where every Scottish parliamentary representative in Dumfries and Galloway had been re-elected to fight another day, rival activists might reasonably have argued that the political status quo had been preserved. Using the same discursive instruments and media skills they forged during their campaign, senior Conservatives acted quickly to persuade their supporters that local Tories had, in fact, 'won' the election. These efforts appeared to be effective. Then, bringing the chapter up to date with more recent political events, I will conclude by observing that the Scottish Conservatives continue to confront many challenges in their quest for political relevance in Scotland. Ironically, since the victory of the Scottish Nationalists at the 2007 Scottish Parliament elections, it could be argued that the presence of the Tory Party is more keenly felt in Scottish politics than it has been since the 1990s. After all, only with the tacit support of the Scottish Tories can the minority SNP administration govern in the face of uncooperative Labour and Liberal Democrat MSPs. However, the electoral fortunes of the Conservative Party north of the English border at best remain mixed. The future of the lesser-spotted Tory continues to look uncertain.

Tories bounce back

After the counting of the council ballot papers at Loreburn Hall on Friday 2 May, a handful of Tory activists returned to the Party's office in Castle Street,

Dumfries. Amongst those present were a couple of unsuccessful candidates for council as well as Tory councillor Ivor Hyslop, who had been re-elected with an increased majority in his ward. Several members of staff and other volunteers were also present, as were the Conservative MSP David Mundell, the Election Agent for Dumfries Alan MacLeod and one of Mr Mundell's sons. Several other key Party strategists, including Peter Duncan MP and Alex Fergusson MSP, had decided to go home instead, no doubt to recuperate and relax after a couple of stressful days with very little sleep.

Ostensibly a quiet 'celebration' following the election, the mood of the gathering was reflective. One candidate was clearly disappointed that he had not won his council ward, although he remained in typically good *fettle* (spirit). Mr MacLeod kept disappearing into his office to answer the telephone but was similarly subdued. Meanwhile, Mr Mundell looked relieved to have retained his seat in the Scottish Parliament. Given the emotion-charged weeks that had preceded and culminated with Polling Day, everyone seemed a little deflated. Furthermore, they all seemed unsure whether the local Conservative Party could be said to have won an important victory or endured a defeat, particularly given their disappointment at the outcome of the council election. Wine and champagne were opened and a number of activists became more talkative after an alcoholic beverage or two. Events and observations from the previous two days were discussed while humorous stories from the campaign itself were remembered. Mr Mundell's son recounted the *Courier* news story in which it was claimed that the political 'impartiality' of a local shopping centre 'had been breached' in the run-up to the election. Most fellow activists had found this story hilarious while others thought it a little bemusing.

As activists broke into smaller conversations and groups, Mr Mundell and I discussed the results from the local council election as well as his own in the Dumfries constituency. Surprised that local Conservatives had not won more than eleven council wards, he felt able to make a few initial observations. In his view, Independent candidates had 'cost' local Conservatives victory in several key 'target' wards. The fight to 'wipe the Independents off the political map' and change the political culture of local politics would have to recommence in earnest, he said. Furthermore, the election of two additional Tory councillors, including Mr Ash-Kuri in Moffat, would serve as a lesson to all future candidates that only through hard work and establishing their 'local' credentials early in the campaign could they become confident of their chances of success.

However, Mr Mundell felt that local Conservatives had probably miscalculated on some key questions of strategy. In hindsight, he felt that there had not been much appetite amongst local people to vote out the Rainbow Alliance administration of Independents, Labour, Liberal Democrat and SNP councillors in Dumfries and Galloway. 'The mood was not with us,' he said. But his mind was already turning over new possibilities. Having just held on to his Scottish parliamentary seat through the Regional List for the South of Scotland, he was contemplating how the contest in the Dumfries constituency might have turned out differently if the rain had continued to fall into the evening. Senior

Conservatives were confident, he said, that 'Tory supporters had come out and voted by the end of the morning.' Nevertheless, 'when the sun came out around 4 o'clock in the afternoon, I knew I had lost. The Labour Party get their vote out in the evening, so the election was there for them to win.' Despite this outcome, though, Mr Mundell was pleased that he had secured an electoral swing to the Scottish Conservatives of almost 10%. This was by far the biggest shift of votes to the Tory Party anywhere in Scotland and was greater than that which was achieved in the three first-past-the-post seats the Party won: Ayr, Edinburgh Pentlands, and Galloway and Upper Nithsdale. For Mr Mundell personally and the local Conservative Party generally, there was considerable mileage that could be extracted from this apparently promising result. For the Tory MSP, the seeds of a new challenge were forming in his head as we spoke. 'I think it might be time for me and Russell Brown to go head to head,' he said in an early indication that the idea of running for election to Westminster had crossed his mind. 'The more I think about this result, the more I think it might have a real upside.'

About 30 minutes later, an activist entered the room having picked up a copy of that evening's *Courier*, which had just been delivered on the Castle Street doorstep. It was the first local newspaper to publish any coverage of the election results, which were summed up with a simple headline on the front page: 'Tories Bounce Back'. Upon reading this, the mood of the activists present brightened considerably. 'It's a good headline and a great result for Alex,' observed Mr Mundell. 'And if Alex had not been elected in Galloway and Upper Nithsdale, I may not have been either.' Indeed, Mr Fergusson had topped the Tory Party's 'ticket' for the Regional List in the South of Scotland. Even if he had been unsuccessful in Galloway and Upper Nithsdale, his re-election to the Scottish Parliament had been virtually assured. But in such a circumstance, he may have knocked Mr Mundell out of the Scottish Parliament altogether, given that his name had appeared further down the list of nominated Conservative candidates in the South of Scotland. Mr Mundell's hopes of re-election had been deeply invested in a victory for Mr Fergusson in Galloway and Upper Nithsdale.

Then, turning to me, Mr Mundell proclaimed: 'Congratulations! You made a difference!' At first, I was a little taken aback by the idea that someone might attribute me with some credit for the success of the local Conservative Party campaign in Galloway and Upper Nithsdale. On reflection, though, I realised that in a tight contest in which the SNP incumbent was defeated by just 99 votes, it was possible to argue that everyone – indeed, everything – had 'made a difference'. Even the possibility that some key Labour activists had tactically voted for the Tory challenger in a bid to 'wipe the SNP off the map of southwest Scotland' had to be taken seriously as a contributing factor to Mr Fergusson's success. In their post-election analysis, which would take several weeks of private conversations and group discussions amongst activists across (and even beyond) the region, key Party strategists could not reach agreement on which factors and issues most contributed to their success. In my own mind, I eventually came to acknowledge the difficulties of identifying what discursive instruments and issues had been 'decisive' in the election of Mr Fergusson in Galloway and Upper Nithsdale. All factors, no matter how small, appeared to have been decisive, and each factor appeared to have been as decisive as every other. Here, analysis and knowledge failed. It was impossible to generate a sense of what had or had not been more important; there were no hierarchies, no levels, no discernible 'cause and effect'.

Conversely, reflecting on what contributing factors and issues made a difference in Galloway and Upper Nithsdale invited activists to consider further what did not work in the Dumfries constituency. This would prove even more problematic for local Conservatives because so much activity had been reproduced across the region as part of the local council campaign, which had been constitutive of the region's two Scottish Parliament campaigns. Some blamed the weather on Polling Day. Others pointed out that the SNP and Liberal Democrat campaigns had completely collapsed. This meant that the Scottish Nationalists had not played the vital role local Tories had hoped they would in siphoning electoral support from the Labour Party on issues like the Iraq war and the fire fighters' strike. Furthermore, some blamed the Core Campaign Team itself for failing to coordinate the Party's campaign effectively in the last days before the election. For activists who subscribed to this view, the breaking down of the risograph machine the week before Polling Day was clear evidence that senior Conservatives had been overly ambitious and had overreached in their campaign: they produced too many leaflets and expected their exhausted (elderly) volunteers to do too much work. It was also impossible for Party strategists to make any kind of judgment as to whether their otherwise strong performance in Dumfries might have been the result of many SNP voters switching to the Tory Party in order to vote tactically against the local Labour Party. Losing by a little over 1,000 votes in Dumfries, it was very difficult for local Conservative activists to discern what, if anything, could have made (up) the difference. As in the Party's success in neighbouring Galloway and Upper Nithsdale, the ground on which any kind of political analysis could be based ultimately eluded them.

Return of the lesser-spotted Tory

On Thursday 8 May 2003, the *Galloway News* printed a letter from a Scottish Nationalist supporter in Kirkcudbright in which she asked:

> Why, oh why do the people of Galloway and Upper Nithsdale feel so akin to the policies of the Conservative party? Do they not realise what letting the Tories in wholescale [sic] would mean? They would privatise your health services, leaving the less well off to get their hospital care in a second rate service. And they would make the rest of you pay through the nose.

Furthermore, for her, the election of a Conservative MSP in Galloway and Upper Nithsdale amounted to a return to the way things had *ae been* (always been). From the perspective of this letter-writer, this constituted a perpetuation of Tory hegemony in southwest Scotland:

> It's time people woke up and realised what they are voting for. Take an interest and not just vote for what their fathers and grandfathers believed in. People have

no right to moan if they are willing to elect a man who stands for a party that represents old money and old beliefs. It's time to think about what is REALLY needed in Galloway. And it certainly isn't a Tory MSP.

Had this letter been published before Polling Day, it might have constituted a passionate attempt to persuade local people to avoid 'going back' to a discredited, Tory past. Appearing in newsprint seven days after the election, however, it read more like a lament to me. Inverting the idea that the lesser-spotted Tory might have 'returned' to rural Galloway, it mourned the fact that southwest Scotland had apparently 'gone back' to the Conservative fold. But others relished what they saw as the re-establishment of political 'normalcy'. I was in the pub a week later with a Labour activist and one of his Tory acquaintances, a retired fire fighter. 'That was a good [election] result,' the latter whispered to me conspiratorially while the Labour activist was buying his round of ale. 'Things seem to be moving back in the right direction.' Even some anti-Tory activists were pleased with the outcome. In the days that followed, a young academic at the Crichton University Campus who supported the Scottish Socialist Party congratulated me on the success of the local Conservative Party. 'I'm sure you had a hand in it,' he said, mischievously:

> And anyway, now we can return to the natural order of things. Everyone needs a nemesis, like Sherlock Holmes and Professor Moriarty. It's better to have the Tories back in Scotland. It's like welcoming back an *auld enemy* [old enemy]. Now we know whom to hate.

Around the same time, negotiations commenced between Tory councillors and other political parties eager to form a new council administration. These negotiations continued against the advice of senior Party strategists, who reminded local councillors of an earlier undertaking, to which their leader Allan Wright had agreed, not to seek to form an administration unless at least fifteen local Conservatives were elected. On this occasion, however, a new 'Rainbow Alliance' administration was created. This time, it would be led by Independents with the support of the Tory council group while the local Labour Party was excluded. On brokering these new arrangements, one Tory councillor declared excitedly: 'We did it! We changed the Council!'

Meanwhile, a few weeks later on 26 June 2003, the Boundary Commission for Scotland published a notice detailing revised boundaries for parliamentary constituencies in southern Scotland. It also released the Assistant Commissioner's report and the transcript from the public inquiry in Dumfries. As I noted at the end of Chapter 3, the Boundary Commission decided to persist with its plans to abolish the Dumfries constituency. However, it decided to rename the proposed, new PCA constituency Dumfriesshire, Clydesdale and Tweeddale (DCT) and agreed to combine the two council wards in Northeast Dumfries with the rest of the town in the new parliamentary seat of Dumfries and Galloway. These wards were traded for another two, Caerlaverock and Nithsdale East, which now became part of the DCT constituency. This time, though, Provost Cameron and his supporters in Northeast Dumfries offered no major objections despite opposition from some 700 local people, including many Labour activists, who argued that these new proposals would also 'tear the heart out of *oor toon*'. Nor did the local Conservative Party see a need to make any more of its own submissions to the Boundary Commission. As one senior Party strategist explained to me, local Tories had 'nothing more to say' about the new boundaries.

Banal activism and ethnography

When I commenced my fieldwork in September 2001, I tried to maintain links with all political groups in order to try to get a better sense of the political 'big picture' in Dumfries and Galloway. I quickly became aware that, as another individual trying to make sense of what was happening politically in post-devolution Scotland, the practices I employed as an ethnographer were not dissimilar to those of the local Conservative activists that became the focus of my study. As a result, my own perspective on local politics eventually transformed from being that of 'the outsider' to belonging to someone on 'the inside', especially after I became involved in the local Tory Party campaign. During meetings of the Core Campaign Team, senior Conservatives would sometimes ask me for 'an objective view' about their chances. After a few weeks, my advice became 'semi-objective' in their eyes until they stopped asking for my opinion altogether. Perhaps even to them, it had become obvious that my efforts to gather information about local politics in Dumfries and Galloway were rarely different from their own. The knowledge on which I based my judgments about local politics across the region was gleaned using many of the same skills and techniques that were also at their disposal. Like me, members of the Core Campaign Team busily studied local media and discussed political gossip picked up 'out there' in order to second-guess what was happening around us.

Indeed, it was very reassuring to learn that by closely reading local newspapers, for example, I was mimicking a set of knowledge-making practices in which my ethnographic subjects were similarly engaged. However, the excitement I felt at such moments of discovery was always mitigated by an uncertainty generated from these same practices. After all, what perspective could an ethnographer contribute to an understanding of political change at the local level in rural Scotland that could not be gleaned from one of my more articulate and self-aware informants? Some have argued that communities in Britain are 'less like each other than we may popularly suppose' (Cohen 1982: 9). However, I am inclined to agree with Jeanette Edwards (2000: 248) that 'the ways in which we conceptualize our social worlds and locate ourselves within them are much more alike than our constant strategies of differentiation would suggest'. This point seems especially relevant when the knowledge-making practices of the ethnographer are contrasted with those of the local Tory activists I encountered in Dumfries and Galloway, many of whom saw themselves as political outsiders in post-devolution Scotland. Furthermore, in their efforts to know, local Conservatives sought to reproduce those same practices in which they perceived rival, more-successful activists to be engaged. One consequence of this was that Tory activists had to strain in order to appear novel and different from their opponents.

In Chapter 1, I suggested that a political campaign fought for a parliamentary election could be analysed as a 'new' ethnographic object. My argument concerning Tory activists in Dumfries and Galloway has focused on the practices they employed that led them to embrace what I have called 'banal activism'. For local Conservatives, this involved an engagement with the making of a range of discursive artefacts: the *In Touch* leaflet, the press release, the survey and the target letter. Local Conservatives credited these with instrumental possibilities, believing that they would produce positive electoral and other effects in the aftermath of the Party's catastrophic failure in the late 1990s. As I have observed, one of these effects was to bring the Conservative Party campaign into view as an analytical object towards which the ethnographer and the would-be activist could both direct attention. This campaign could be said to have possessed a social life, which came to a quick and quiet end during the dying hours of Polling Day. However, some anthropologists might find a focus on these artefacts and the string of minor crises and other micro-events that were constitutive of the Tory campaign in Dumfries and Galloway somewhat frustrating. What I have described in this book has been a set of practices and concerns that some might regard as everyday, mundane and potentially inconsequential. As a result, not all anthropologists might recognise these materials as sufficiently 'ethnographic', as they appear to lack a kind of socio-cultural 'thickness', to paraphrase Clifford Geertz (1973). But as Bruno Latour (1993: 48) has observed, 'the modern world ... permits scarcely anything more than small extensions of practices, slight acceleration in the circulation of knowledge, a tiny extension of societies, minuscule increases in the number of actors, small modifications of old beliefs'. Moreover, successful ethnographers take their cues from the people they choose to study. In Dumfries and Galloway, that meant concentrating on the issues, practices and questions that most occupied the minds of local Conservative activists. As I have described, these were fundamentally ones of form and activist methodology.

Notably, as they sought to address these questions, my research subjects were subjected to a kind of tunnelling of vision. For example, a discursive artefact like the *In Touch* leaflet came to be seen as a substitute for social relations, invoking and mediating in a very literal sense connections between person, place and political party. Of course, whether or not this leaflet was capable of producing the effects that activists claimed it would is another question entirely. Indeed, some activists argued that *In Touch* was a waste of time, incapable of making (a) difference. As I came to apprehend these discursive materials in the same way as my Tory informants, I too was subjected to a tunnelling of vision. In turn, this left little analytical space in which to conceive of other possibilities for reworking the discursive objects on which my ethnographic subjects and I were focused. The limits of my own analysis reproduced those that my research subjects had imposed on themselves. However, this is not to diminish the significance of the discursive artefacts described in this book for the local activists I encountered in Dumfries and Galloway. After all, in early 2003 these artefacts came to grip the imaginations of Tory activists. This was despite there being little evidence that they were capable of producing the electoral effects senior Party strategists and supporters desired. The production of these materials eventually monopolised the work of Conservative activists, who became enchanted by the possibilities of using documents and paperwork as technologies. As a consequence, a whole series of small, quasi-bureaucratic events and practices became imbued with significance greater than the sum of them as individual events (parts) to bring a new whole into view: the Conservative Party campaign. For my argument, this was the most compelling effect of such discursive work. In this book, I have tried to explore these artefacts and practices to demonstrate how they contributed to the making of that whole, which in its own right constituted a 'new' ethnographic object.

Looking to the future

Strathern has argued that social science has a 'regenerative capacity' to constantly 'build up the conditions from which the world can be apprehended anew' (Strathern 1988: 19–20). I suggest that this capacity is equally available to the activist and the ethnographer. Furthermore, this is one of the great attractions of banal activism for politically disenfranchised and poorly organised groups like the Scottish Tories. As one senior Conservative put it to me, 'we had to do something' in the absence of better ideas. The enabling possibilities of leafleting, local issues and mobilising local media were within easy reach. The Core Campaign Team understood that most of their (elderly) activists were intellectually capable of grasping (national) controversies that should be avoided and identifying (local) issues on which to build a political campaign. Most of them were also physically able to stuff envelopes, take notes and work the risograph. These practices were integral in the making of the discursive artefacts that gave the Party's campaign material form. They were also accessible to a political organisation that had collapsed following their annihilation at the 1997 general election. From the perspective of senior Tories, even the most disinterested of Conservative voters could be cajoled into contributing some kind of effort to the campaign. Those activists who did invest labour and time into the local Party's 2003 campaign found these experiences empowering. While the Core Campaign Team found in the aftermath of the elections that the local Tory Party's knowledge and organisational base was weaker than they had imagined before Polling Day, the busy work of the banal activist had propelled and sustained them during the campaign.

In Dumfries and Galloway, the Scottish Conservatives continue to face uncertainties and anxieties about the future. However, the sense of organisation that members of the Core Campaign Team achieved in 2003 gave many local Tories a new 'spring in their step', so to speak. It was with a feeling of optimism that they were able to approach a future in which they could now imagine one day winning the Dumfries constituency 'back' from the Labour Party. Their first electoral test came the following year, when two by-elections were called in council wards the Tory Party had won in 2003. The first of these was in Moffat, where Councillor Safa Ash-Kuri resigned to take up new employment in the Persian Gulf only a year after winning his council ward from the Independents, as I discussed in earlier chapters. In neighbouring Hoddom and Kinmount, the untimely death of the affable, incumbent Conservative councillor Andrew Bell-Irving, a middle-aged man with a young family, shocked activists of all political persuasions. Councillor Bell-Irving had harboured ambitions to eventually stand for Parliament himself and many local Tories considered his passing a massive loss to the Scottish Conservatives. However, running with the slogan 'looking to the future', the Conservative Party held both council wards despite a strong challenge from the former Independent councillor in Moffat.

The following year, a general election was held on the new parliamentary boundaries. While the fortunes of the Scottish Tories did not improve across the country, David Mundell MSP won DCT against lacklustre campaigns from the Labour Party and the Liberal Democrats, although both parties claimed to be contenders in the new constituency. Mr Mundell subsequently resigned from the Scottish Parliament, his seat being filled by the young accountant Derek Brownlee, who was the next candidate endorsed on the Tory ticket for the South of Scotland List. However, the contest Mr Mundell imagined between himself and the Dumfries Labour MP Russell Brown had never eventuated. The latter had opted to run against the Tory MP Peter Duncan for the new, Westminster seat of Dumfries and Galloway. Although he improved his electoral base by over 6,000 votes, Mr Duncan lost that election by 3,000 votes. Mr Mundell therefore took his place at Westminster as Scotland's only Conservative Member of Parliament.

In 2007, the system for electing local councils across Scotland was changed. New, multimember council wards were adopted for which election would proceed via proportional representation (PR). Although the Scottish Conservatives had opposed PR, this new system benefited them greatly in Dumfries and Galloway. They made significant gains, particularly against the Independents, to become the largest political group on council, with at least one Tory elected in every council ward across the region. They then formed a coalition with the Liberal Democrats and currently administer Dumfries and Galloway with the support of SNP councillors, who also significantly increased their representation under PR. In addition, Alex Fergusson MSP was re-elected with an increased majority in Galloway and Upper Nithsdale whereupon he became Presiding Officer of the Scottish Parliament. However, the Labour Party held the Dumfries constituency again despite losing seats to the Scottish Nationalists elsewhere in Scotland. In fact, the Labour–Liberal Democrat Scottish Executive lost their majority. A minority SNP administration formed in the weeks following the election, which now governs Scotland with the support of the Greens and the Scottish Conservatives. For many Scots, this is an unlikely alliance.

Afterword

A couple of months after this manuscript was completed, a UK general election was called on Thursday 6 May 2010. The outcome of that election was remarkable. A hard-fought campaign by all parties produced a hung parliament in which the Conservative Party narrowly fell short of the 326 seats required to achieve an outright majority in the House of Commons, although they nevertheless emerged the 'winner' in terms of obtaining the most parliamentary seats (306) and the largest share of the popular vote (36.1%). In the aftermath of the election, some leading members of the outgoing Labour government, which had returned 258 MPs on 29% of the popular vote, had hoped that a (minority) Progressive Alliance could be forged with the Liberal Democrats. However, the Labour Party had simply not won enough parliamentary seats to form a workable majority with the Liberal Democrats, who had won 57 seats with 23% of the vote. These hopes were dashed when the latter entered into a seemingly unimaginable coalition arrangement with the Conservative Party. The new Cabinet includes members of both parties, with the Liberal Democrat leader Nick Clegg now serving as deputy prime minister. The new Liberal Conservative government, as the new prime minister David Cameron likes to call it, is the first coalition government in the United Kingdom since the Second World War.

However, the electoral gains of the Conservative Party in England and Wales were not reproduced in Scotland. Indeed, for the third general election in a row, the Scottish Tories failed to win more than one seat at Westminster. In 2010, the incumbent Conservative MP David Mundell managed to retain the DCT constituency he had won in 2005, marginally increasing his majority over the local Labour Party after a dogged fight with both that party and an insurgent Liberal Democrat campaign in Peeblesshire. In the neighbouring constituency of Dumfries and Galloway, Mr Duncan failed in his bid to defeat the Labour MP Russell Brown, who managed to more than double his majority to almost 7,500 votes in an election that more-usually saw large swings registered against the Labour Party in England and Wales. As a result, it would seem that Dumfries is no longer a 'wee Tory *toon*', while the rest of Scotland continues to remain hostile to Conservatism – the Scottish Conservative and Unionist Party suffered convincing defeats, often to Labour incumbents, in all their other target seats. In a pattern that must now deeply worry senior Tory strategists north of the border, no parliamentary seats changed hands at all, with the Labour Party returning the most MPs (41 out of 59) from Scotland.

Following the election, the difficulties facing the Scottish Conservatives were compounded further. The *Daily Telegraph* newspaper reported on 11 May 2010 that SCCO was being forced to move from the Abbey Business Centre in Princes Street, Edinburgh, to the second floor of a New Town house owned by the Party's Edinburgh North and Leith Association. The office accommodation in Princes Street was thought to be worth about £100,000 per year in rental income and is owned by Lord Laidlaw of Rothiemay. Lord Laidlaw had both been a major donor to the UK Conservatives and provided space in the Abbey Business Centre as a donation in kind to the Scottish Tories so that they could house their headquarters there. However, in February 2010, he announced that he would no longer provide financial support to the Conservative Party because his offshore tax status had become a source of embarrassment to them. And then, as if to rub salt into the electoral wounds of the Scottish Tories, the *Daily Telegraph* went on to report that former government minister and loyal acolyte of Margaret Thatcher Lord Tebbit declared that the time had come for the Conservative Party 'to pack up north of the border'.

The Scottish Tories having failed to make any significant electoral break-throughs in Scotland, it would be easy to dismiss as ineffective and irrelevant their campaigning efforts, which I have described in this book. However, it is possible that the banal activism of local Party strategists and volunteers in Dumfries and Galloway and some other areas of Scotland has played a crucial role in sustaining a core Tory vote. The 16,501 votes Peter Duncan mustered for the Conservatives against Russell Brown were not, after all, an insubstantial sum, especially when considered against the many other parts of Scotland where there is virtually no Tory presence in local or Scottish politics at all. In other pre-1997 strongholds like Edinburgh Southwest, Renfrewshire East and Stirling, Conservative candi-dates each exceeded 10,000 votes, reconfirming the Tory Party's position in those constituencies as the primary challenger to the incumbent party. Meanwhile, the local Conservative MSP in Roxburgh and Berwickshire appeared to follow Mr Mundell's example from the 2005 general election and succeeded in building an impressive tally of just over 16,500 votes, although he, too, was ultimately unsuccessful in his bid to secure the Westminster seat. Senior Tory strategists might therefore point to those practices I have called banal activism and argue that, like the introduction of PR to the Scottish Parliament elections in 1999 or Lord Laidlaw's considerable financial support for the Party throughout the early 2000s, it has served to ensure that the Scottish Conservatives did not disappear entirely from the political landscape of Scotland.

It seems reasonable to suggest that, in the face of continuing uncertainty about their future electoral prospects, the Scottish Tories have exhausted the pos-sibilities with which banal activism presented them. Buffeting against the limits of what they can achieve through their focus on local-level activism and issues, they have successfully postponed the kind of vexing philosophical and policy debates that would have no doubt exacerbated internal divisions but remain essential to any attempts by the Party to argue that it has undergone change and renewal. The contrast between the failures of the Scottish Conservatives and the stronger electoral performance in 2010 of their Tory counterparts south of the border is now stark. In the Scottish media, the Conservative Party claimed to be targeting eleven parliamentary seats in Scotland. Had the Scottish Tories won all their target seats rather than just the one they were defending in 2010, they would have boosted the number of Conservative MPs to 316 in total. This would have still been short of the 326 required for a single political party to form a government with an overall majority, but it would have strengthened the argument that a minority Tory administration could have governed with (some) stability.

For the new prime minister David Cameron, however, the coalition Liberal Conservative government provides the benefit of some legitimacy in terms of Scottish representation. With the same number of Scottish MPs (eleven) as the last UK Tory government had when it lost power in 1997, the Liberal Democrats are the second largest party in terms of Westminster representation in Scotland and the third most successful in terms of the popular vote, behind Labour and the SNP but ahead of the Conservative Party. The new UK government therefore includes twelve Scottish MPs with Michael Moore, the Liberal Democrat MP for Berwickshire, Roxburgh and Selkirk, becoming Secretary of State for Scotland and Mr Mundell his junior minister. A coalition with the Conservatives at a time when the Labour Party north of the border has demonstrated its electoral resilience presents the Liberal Democrats in Scotland with their own share of challenges and threats. But in their new allies the Scottish Conservatives may have found a new political opportunity to 'detoxify' the Tory brand in Scotland. Whether he wants to or not, the Liberal Democrat Secretary of State for Scotland could end up providing political cover for the Scottish Tories when the UK government begins implementing cuts in Scottish public spending in line with its plans to tackle a public deficit of £700 billion. While the Liberal Democrats take the heat for these spending cuts, the Scottish Tories might finally be able to engage in that long-postponed internal debate about the direction, identity, philosophy, and policy agenda of their party. In doing so, they may finally find a way to transcend the banal activism that has characterised their political campaigns in recent years and reassert their political relevance as a force for centre-right politics in Scotland.

Bibliography

Abeles, Marc (1988). 'Modern political ritual: Ethnography of an inauguration and a pilgrimage by President Mitterrand' *Current Anthropology* 29: 391–404.

Agger, Ben (1989). *Fast Capitalism: A Critical Theory of Significance* (Champaign, IL: University of Illinois Press).

—— (2004). *Speeding Up Fast Capitalism: Cultures, Jobs, Families, Schools, Bodies* (Boulder, CO: Paradigm Publishers).

Alter, Peter (1994). *Nationalism* (2nd edn) (London: Edward Arnold).

Arendt, Hannah (2007 [1963]). *Eichmann in Jerusalem: A Report on the Banality of Evil* (Harmondsworth: Penguin).

Aronoff, Myron J. (1977). *Power and Ritual in the Israel Labor Party* (Amsterdam/ Assen: Van Gorcum).

Askew, Kelly, and Richard R. Wilk (2002). *The Anthropology of Media: A Reader* (Oxford: Blackwell Publishers).

Austin, J. L. (1962). *How To Do Things With Words* (Oxford: Oxford University Press).

Back, Les (2007) *The Art of Listening* (Oxford: Berg).

Bechhofer, Frank, David McCrone, Robert Kiely and Richard Stewart (1999). 'Constructing national identity: Arts and landed elites in Scotland' *Sociology* 33(3): 515–534.

Bell, Florence, John Luffrum, Frank Peck and Sarah Manuel (2002). *Review of Post Foot and Mouth Disease Recovery Plans on the Anglo-Scottish Border* (University of Northumbria, Carlisle Campus: Centre for Border Studies).

Benthall, Jonathan (2000). 'Civil society's need for de-deconstruction' *Anthropology Today* 16(2): 1–3.

Bertrand, Romain, Jean-Louis Briquet and Peter Pels (2007) 'Introduction: Towards an historical ethnography of voting', in Romain Bertrand, Jean-Louis Briquet and Peter Pels (eds) *Cultures of Voting: The Hidden History of the Secret Ballot* (London: Hurst and Company), pp. 1–15.

Billig, Michael (1995). *Banal Nationalism* (London: Sage).

Bloch, Ernst (1986). *The Principle of Hope* (Cambridge, MA: MIT Press).

Bloch, Maurice (ed.) (1975). *Political Oratory in Traditional Society* (London: Academic Press).

Bogdanor, Vernon (1999). *Devolution in the United Kingdom* (Oxford: Oxford University Press).

Borneman, John (1992). *Belonging in the Two Berlins: Kin, State, Nation* (Cambridge: Cambridge University Press).

— (1997). 'State, territory, and national identity formation in the two Berlins, 1945–1995' in Akhil Gupta and James Ferguson (eds) *Culture, Power, Place: Explorations in Critical Anthropology* (Durham, NC: Duke University Press).

Boundary Commission for Scotland (2002a). *Fifth Periodical Review of Parliamentary Constituencies in Scotland: Background, Processes and Procedures* (Edinburgh: Boundary Commission for Scotland).

— (2002b). *Fifth Periodical Review of Parliamentary Constituencies in Scotland: Local Inquiry – Processes and Procedures* (Edinburgh: Boundary Commission for Scotland).

Bourdieu, Pierre (1991). *Language and Symbolic Power* edited and with an introduction by J. B. Thompson (Cambridge: Polity Press).

— (1998). 'Rethinking the State: Genesis and Structure of the Bureaucratic Field' in P. Bourdieu *Practical Reason: On the Theory of Action* (Cambridge: Polity Press).

Boyarin, Jonathan (ed.) (1992). *The Ethnography of Reading* (Berkeley, CA: University of California Press).

Brand, Gerd (1979). *The Central Texts of Ludwig Wittgenstein*, translated and with an introduction by Robert E. Innis (Oxford: Basil Blackwell).

Brand, Jack (1990). 'Scotland' in Michael Watson (ed.) *Contemporary Minority Nationalism* (London: Routledge), pp. 24–37.

Burnside, Ross, Stephen Herbert and Stephen Curtis (2003). *Election 2003* (Edinburgh: The Scottish Parliament).

Butler, David, and Dennis Kavanagh (eds) (2001). *The British General Election of 2001* (Basingstoke: Palgrave).

Byron, Reginald (1980). 'Buying a share: State institutions and local communities on the periphery – a case from Scotland' in R. D. Grillo (ed.) *'Nation' and 'State' in Europe: Anthropological Perspectives* (New York, NY: Academic Press), pp. 137–150.

Callander, Robin, and Andy Wightman (1997). *Understanding Land Reform in Scotland* Proceedings of a conference organised by the Unit for the Study of Government in Scotland, University of Edinburgh.

Campbell, Roy (1991). *Owners and Occupiers: Changes in Rural Society in South-West Scotland Before 1914* (Edinburgh: Edinburgh University Press).

Charsley, Simon (1986). 'Glasgow's miles better: The symbolism of community and identity in the city' in A. P. Cohen (ed.) *Symbolising Boundaries: Identity and Diversity in British Cultures* (Manchester: Manchester University Press), pp. 171–186.

Church, Jonathan (1990). 'Confabulations of community: The Hamefarins and political discourse on Shetland' *Anthropological Quarterly* 63: 31–42.

Clifford, James, and George Marcus (eds) (1986). *Writing Culture: The Poetics and Politics of Ethnography* (Berkeley, CA: University of California Press).

Clifford, James (1988). *The Predicament of Culture: Twentieth Century Ethnography, Literature, and Art* (Cambridge, MA: Harvard University Press).

Cohen, Anthony P. (1987). *Whalsay: Symbol, Segment and Boundary in a Shetland Island Community* (Manchester: Manchester University Press).

— (1996). 'Personal nationalism: A Scottish view of some rites, rights, and wrongs' *American Ethnologist* 23(4): 802–815.

— (1997). 'Nationalism and social identity: Who owns the interest of Scotland?' *Scottish Affairs* 18: 95–107.

— (1999). 'Peripheral vision: Nationalism, national identity and the objective correlative in Scotland' in Anthony P. Cohen (ed.) *Signifying Identities: Anthropological Perspectives on Boundaries and Contested Values* (London: Routledge), pp. 145–169.

Cohen, Anthony P. (ed.) (1982). *Belonging: Identity and Social Organisation in British Rural Cultures* (Manchester: Manchester University Press).

Cohn, Bernard S. (1987). 'The census, social structure and objectification in South Asia' in Bernard S. Cohn *An Anthropologist Among the Historians and Other Essays* (New Delhi: Oxford University Press).

— (1996). *Colonialism and Its Forms of Knowledge: The British in India* (Princeton, NJ: Princeton University Press).

Coleman, Simon, and Pauline von Hellermann (2009) *Multi-Sited Ethnography: Problems and Possibilities in the Translocation of Research Methods* (London: Routledge).

Coles, Kimberley (2007). *Democratic Designs: International Intervention and Electoral Practices in Postwar Bosnia-Herzegovina* (Ann Arbor, MI: University of Michigan Press).

Collins, Peter, and Simon Coleman (2007) *Locating the Field: Space, Place and Context in Anthropology* (Oxford: Berg).

Comaroff, John, and Jean Comaroff (eds) (1999). *Civil Society and the Political Imagination in Africa: Critical Perspectives* (Chicago, IL: University of Chicago Press).

Coombe, Rosemary (1997). 'Identifying and engendering the forms of emergent civil societies: New directions in Political Anthropology' in *The Forms of Civil Society in Postcolonial Contexts*, Special issue of *Political and Legal Anthropology Review* 20(1): 1–12.

Coutin, Susan Bibler (2005). 'Being en route' *American Anthropologist* 107(2): 195–206.

Darian-Smith, Eve (1999). *Bridging Divides: The Channel Tunnel and English Legal Identity* (Berkeley, CA: University of California Press).

— (2002). 'Beating the bounds: Law, identity, and territory in the new Europe' in Carol Greenhouse, Elizabeth Mertz and Kay Warren (eds) *Ethnography in Unstable Place: Everyday Lives in Contexts of Dramatic Political Change* (London: Duke University Press), pp. 249–275.

Das, Veena (1995). *Critical events: An Anthropological Perspective on Contemporary India* (Oxford: Oxford University Press).

— (1998). 'Wittgenstein and anthropology' *Annual Review of Anthropology* 27:

171–195.

Devine, Tom (1999). *The Scottish Nation 1700–2000* (Harmondsworth: Penguin Books).

Dewar, Donald (1998). 'The Scottish Parliament' in David McCrone (ed.) *Understanding Constitutional Change*, Special issue of *Scottish Affairs* (Edinburgh: Unit for the Study of Government in Scotland, Edinburgh University), pp. 4–12.

Dominy, Michele D. (2001). *Calling the Station Home: Place and Identity in New Zealand's High Country* (Lanham, MD: Rowman and Littlefield Publishers).

Duranti, Alessandro (ed.) (2001). *Linguistic Anthropology: A Reader* (Oxford: Blackwell Publishing).

Edwards, Jeanette (1993). 'Explicit connections: Ethnographic enquiry in north-west England' in J. Edwards, E. Hirsch, S, Franklin, F. Price and M. Strathern (eds) *Technologies of Procreation: Kinship in the Age of Assisted Conception* (Manchester: Manchester University Press), pp. 42–66.

— (1994). 'Idioms of bureaucracy and informality in a local housing aid office' in S. Wright (ed.) *The Anthropology of Organisations* (London: Routledge).

— (2000). *Born and Bred: Idioms of Kinship and New Reproductive Technologies in England* (Oxford: Oxford University Press).

Edwards, Jeanette, and Marilyn Strathern (1999). 'Including our own' in J. Carsten (ed.) *Cultures of Relatedness: New Directions in Kinship* (Cambridge: Cambridge University Press), pp. 149–166.

Edwards, Wesley (1998). 'Fixing the terms of statelessness – again' *Scottish Affairs* 23: 27–40.

Emmet, I. (1964). *A North Wales Village: A Social Anthropological Study* (London: Routledge and Kegan Paul).

Ennew, J. (1980). *The Western Isles Today* (Cambridge: Cambridge University Press).

Fabian, Johannes (1983). *Time and the Other: How Anthropology Makes its Object* (New York, NY: Columbia University Press).

— (2001). 'Keep listening: Ethnography and reading' in Johannes Fabian *Anthropology With an Attitude: Critical Essays* (Stanford, CA: Stanford University Press), pp. 53–69.

Fairclough, Norman (2000). *New Labour, New Language?* (London: Routledge).

Falzon, Mark-Anthony (2009) *Multi-Sited Ethnography* (Aldershot: Ashgate).

Fardon, Richard (ed.) (1990). *Localizing Strategies: The Regionalization of Ethnographic Accounts* (Washington, DC: Smithsonian Institution Press).

Faucher-King, Florence (2005). *Changing Parties: An Anthropology of British Political Conferences* (Basingstoke: Palgrave).

Feld, Steven, and Keith Basso (eds) (1996). *Senses of Place* (Santa Fe, NM: School of American Research Press).

Ferguson, James (1990). *The Anti-Politics Machine: 'Development', Depoliticization, and Bureaucratic Power in Lesotho* (Cambridge: Cambridge University Press).

Ford, Richard T. (2001) 'Law's territory (a history of jurisdiction)'. In Nicholas Blomley, David Delaney and Richard T. Ford, (eds) *The Legal Geographies*

Reader: Law, Power, and Space (Oxford: Blackwell Publishers) pp. 200–217.

Forrester, Andrew (2004). *The Man Who Saw The Future: William Paterson's Vision of Free Trade* (London: Texere Publishing).

Fortune, Pete, and Hugh McMillan (2005). *Dumfries: A History and Celebration* (Salisbury: Francis Frith Collection).

Foucault, Michel (1977). *Discipline and Punish: The Birth of the Prison* (New York, NY: Pantheon).

Frankenberg, R. (1957). *Village on the Border: A Social Study of Religion, Politics and Football in a North Wales Community* (Prospect Heights, IL: Waveland).

— (1966). *Communities in Britain: Social Life in Town and Country* (Harmondsworth: Penguin).

Franklin, Sarah (1993). 'Making representations: The parliamentary debate on the Human Fertilisation and Embryology Act' in Jeanette Edwards (ed.) *Technologies of Procreation* (Manchester: Manchester University Press), pp. 96–131.

— (1997). *Embodied Progress: A Cultural Account of Assisted Conception* (London: Routledge).

— (2001). 'Sheepwatching' *Anthropology Today* 17(3): 3–9.

Franklin, Sarah, and H. R. Agone (1998). *Reproducing Reproduction* (Philadelphia, PA: University of Pennsylvania Press).

Geertz, Clifford (1973). *The Interpretation of Cultures* (New York: Basic Books).

Gell, Alfred (1992) 'The Technology of enchantment and the enchantment of technology', in Jeremy Coote and Anthony Shelton (eds) *Anthropology, Art and Aesthetics*, (Oxford: Clarendon Press), pp. 40–63.

Gellner, David N., and Eric Hirsch (eds) (2001). *Inside Organizations: Anthropologists at Work* (Oxford: Berg).

Gellner, Ernest (1983). *Nations and Nationalism* (Oxford: Blackwell).

Ginsburg, Faye D., Lila Abu-Lughod and Brian Larkin (eds) (2002). *Media Worlds: Anthropology on New Terrain* (Berkeley, CA: University of California Press).

Ginzburg, Carlo (1990) *Myths, Emblems, Clues*, translated by John and Anne C. Tedeschi (London: Hutchinson Radius).

Ginzburg, Carlo (1999) *The Judge and the Historian: Marginal Notes on a Late-Twentieth-Century Miscarriage of Justice*, translated by Antony Shugaar (London: Verso).

Glendinning, Miles (1999). 'Rebuilding a nation? The architectural challenge of home rule' *Reconstructions: New Writing for the New Parliament (Edinburgh Review)* 100: 132–140.

Goody, Jack (1986). *The Logic of Writing and the Organization of Society* (Cambridge: Cambridge University Press).

Goody, Jack (ed.) (1968). *Literacy in Traditional Societies* (Cambridge: Cambridge University Press).

Graham, Fiona (2005). *Playing at Politics: An Ethnography of the Oxford Union* (Edinburgh: Dunedin Academic Press).

Gray, John (1999). 'Open spaces and dwelling places: Being at home on hill farms in the Scottish borders' *American Ethnologist* 26(2): 440–460.

— (2000). *At Home in the Hills: Sense of Place in the Scottish Borders* (New York, NY: Berghahn Books).

Green, Sarah F. (2005). *Notes from the Balkans: Relocating Marginality and Ambiguity on the Greek–Albanian Border* (Princeton, NJ: Princeton University Press).

Greenhouse, Carol (2002). 'Introduction: Altered states, altered lives' in Carol Greenhouse, Elizabeth Mertz and Kay Warren (eds) *Ethnography in Unstable Place: Everyday Lives in Contexts of Dramatic Political Change* (Durham, NC: Duke University Press), pp. 1–36.

Greenhouse, Carol J (ed.) with Roshanak Kheshti (1998). *Democracy and Ethnography: Constructing Identities in Multicultural Liberal States* (Albany, NY: State University of New York Press).

Guibernau, Montserrat (1996). *Nationalisms: The Nation-State and Nationalism in the Twentieth Century* (Cambridge: Polity Press).

Gupta, Akhil (1995). 'Blurred boundaries: The discourse of corruption, the culture of politics, and the imagined state' *American Ethnologist* 22(2): 375–402.

Gupta, Akhil and James Ferguson (1997a). 'Discipline and practice: 'The field' as site, method, and location in anthropology' in Akhil Gupta and James Ferguson (eds) *Anthropological Locations: Boundaries and Grounds of a Field Science* (Berkeley, CA: University of California Press), pp. 1–46.

— (1997b). 'Culture, power, place: Ethnography at the end of an era' in Akhil Gupta and James Ferguson (eds) *Culture Power Place: Explorations in Critical Anthropology* (Durham, NC: Duke University Press), pp. 1–29.

Handler, Richard (1988). *Nationalism and the Politics of Culture in Quebec* (Madison, WI: University of Wisconsin Press).

Hanks, William F. (1989). 'Text and textuality' *Annual Review of Anthropology* 18: 95–127.

Hann, Chris, and Elizabeth Dunn (eds) (1996). *Civil Society: Challenging Western Models* (London: Routledge).

Hansen, Thomas Blom (2001). *Wages of Violence: Naming and Identity in Postcolonial Bombay* (Princeton, NJ: Princeton University Press).

Harper, Richard (1997) *Inside the IMF: An Ethnography of Documents, Technology and Organizational Action* (San Diego, CA: Academic Press).

Hassan, Gerry, and Peter Lynch (2001). *The Almanac of Scottish Politics* (London: Politico's Publishing).

Hassan, Gerry and Chris Warhurst (2002). *Anatomy of the New Scotland: Power, Influence and Change* (Edinburgh: Mainstream Publishing).

Hearn, Jonathan (1996). 'The colony at the core: Scottish nationalism and the rhetoric of colonialism' in A. Marcus (ed.) *Anthropology for a Small Planet: Culture and Community in a Global Environment* (St James, NY: Brandywine Press), pp. 50–63.

— (1997). 'Scottish nationalism and the civil society concept: Should auld acquaintance be forgot?' in *The Forms of Civil Society in Postcolonial Contexts*, Special issue of *Political and Legal Anthropology Review* 20(1): 32–39.

— (1998). 'The social contract: Re-framing Scottish nationalism' *Scottish Affairs*

23: 14–25.

— (2000). *Claiming Scotland: National Identity and Liberal Culture* (Edinburgh: Polygon at Edinburgh).

— (2001). 'Taking liberties: Contesting visions of the Civil Society Project' *Critique of Anthropology* 21(4): 339–360.

— (2002). 'Narrative, agency, and mood: On the social construction of national history in Scotland' *Comparative Study of Society and History*, 44(4): 745–769.

Henderson, Ailsa (1999). 'Political constructions of national identity in Scotland and Quebec' *Scottish Affairs* 29: 121–138.

Hetherington, Kregg (2008). 'Populist transparency: the documentation of reality in rural Paraguay' *Journal of Legal Anthropology*, 1(1): 45–69.

Hirsch, Eric, and Michael O'Hanlon (eds) (1997). *The Anthropology of Landscape: Perspectives on Place and Space* (Oxford: Clarendon Press).

Hobsbawm, Eric, and Terence Ranger (eds) (1983). *The Invention of Tradition* (Cambridge: Cambridge University Press).

Holmes, Douglas R. (2000). *Integral Europe: Fast-Capitalism, Multiculturalism, Neofascism* (Princeton, NJ: Princeton University Press).

Hunter, James (1976). *The Making of the Crofting Community* (Edinburgh: John Donald Publishers).

— (1991). *The Claim of Crofting: The Scottish Highlands and Islands, 1930–1990* (Edinburgh: Mainstream Publishing).

— (1995). *On the Other Side of Sorrow: Nature and People in the Scottish Highlands* (Edinburgh: Mainstream Publishing).

Hutchison, Iain G. C. (2001). *Scottish Politics in the Twentieth Century* (Basingstoke: Palgrave).

Hutchinson, John (1994). *Modern Nationalism* (London: Fontana Press).

Jackson, Andrew (1987). *Anthropology at Home* (London: Tavistock).

Jackson, Michael (1989). *Paths Toward a Clearing: Radical Empiricism and Ethnographic Inquiry* (Bloomington, IN: Indiana University Press).

James, Alison, Jenny Hockey and Andrew Dawson (eds) (1997). *After Writing Culture: Epistemology and Praxis in Contemporary Anthropology* (London: Routledge).

Jean-Klein, Iris (2000). 'Mothercraft, statecraft, and subjectivity in the Palestinian intifada' *American Ethnologist* 27(1): 100–127.

— (2002). 'Alternative modernities, or accountable modernities? The Palestinian movement(s) and political (audit) tourism during the first intifada' *Journal of Mediterranean Studies* 12(1): 43–79.

Jedrej, Charles, and Mark Nuttall (1996). *White Settlers: The Impact of Rural Repopulation in Scotland* (London: Harwood Academic Publishers).

Jones, Peter (1999). 'The 1999 Scottish Parliament elections: From anti-Tory to anti-Nationalist politics' *Scottish Affairs* 28: 1–9.

Kellas, James (1992). 'The social origins of nationalism in Great Britain: The case of Scotland' in John Coakley (ed.) *The Social Origins Of Nationalist Movements: The Contemporary West European Experience* SAGE Modern Politics Series vol. 31 (London: SAGE Publications), pp. 165–186.

Kertzer, David I (1996). *Politics and Symbols: The Italian Communist Party and the Fall of Communism* (New Haven , CT: Yale University Press).

Kuhn, Thomas (1962). *The Structure of Scientific Revolutions* (Chicago, IL: University of Chicago Press).

— (1977). *The Essential Tension: Selected Studies in Scientific Tradition and Change* (Chicago, IL: University of Chicago Press), pp. 225–240.

Kus, Susan, and Victor Raharijaona (2000). 'House to palace, village to state: Scaling up architecture and ideology' *American Anthropologist* 102(1): 98–113.

Lang, Ian (2002). *Blue Remembered Years* (London: Politico's Publishing).

Latour, Bruno (1987). *Science in Action: How to Follow Scientists and Engineers Through Society* (Cambridge, MA: Harvard University Press).

— (1993). *We Have Never Been Modern*, translated by Catherine Porter (London: Harvester Wheatsheaf).

— (1996). *Aramis or The Love of Technology*, translated by Catherine Porter (Cambridge, MA: Harvard University Press).

Levine, Amy (2004). 'The transparent case of virtuality' *Political and Legal Anthropology Review* 27(1): 90–113.

Lindsay, Isobel (1997). 'The uses and abuses of national stereotypes' *Scottish Affairs* 20: 133–148.

Littlejohn, James (1963). *Westrigg: The Sociology of a Cheviot Parish* (London: Routledge).

Lovell, Nadia (ed.) (1998). *Locality and Belonging* (London: Routledge).

Lundberg, Thomas Carl (2007). *Proportional Representation and the Constituency Role in Britain* (Basingstoke: Palgrave).

Lynch, Peter (1996). *Minority Nationalism and European Integration* (Cardiff: University of Wales Press).

Macdonald, Sharon (1997). *Reimagining Culture: Histories and Identities in the Gallic Renaissance* (Oxford: Berg).

McConnell, Allan (2004). *Scottish Local Government* (Edinburgh, Scotland: Edinburgh University Press).

McCrone, David (1992). *Understanding Scotland: The Sociology of a Stateless Nation* (London: Routledge).

— (1998). 'Land, democracy and culture in Scotland' *Scottish Affairs* 23: 73–92.

McCrone, David, Robert Stewart, Richard Kiely and Frank Bechhofer (1998). 'Who are we? Problematising national identity' *Sociological Review* 46(4): 629–652.

McCulloch, Andrew (2000). *Galloway: A Land Apart* (Edinburgh: Birlinn Ltd).

McEwen, John (1976). *Who Owns Scotland? A Study in Land Ownership* (Edinburgh: EUSPB).

McKean, Charles (1999). 'Theatres of pusillanimity and power in Holyrood' *Scottish Affairs* 27: 1–22.

Malkki, Liisa (1997). 'News and culture: Transitory phenomena and the fieldwork tradition' in Akhil Gupta and James Ferguson (eds) *Anthropological Locations: Boundaries and Grounds of a Field Science* (Berkeley, CA: University of California Press) pp. 86–101.

Marcus, George (2002). *The Sentimental Citizen: Emotion in Democratic Politics* (Pennsylvania, PA: Pennsylvania State University Press).

Marcus, George E. and Michael M. J. Fischer (1986) *Anthropology as Cultural Critique: An Experimental Moment in the Human Sciences* (Chicago, IL: University of Chicago Press).

Maurer, Bill (2002). 'Anthropological and accounting knowledge in Islamic banking and finance: Rethinking critical accounts' *Journal of Royal Anthropological Institute* 8: 645–667.

Mewett, Peter G. (1982). 'Associational categories and the social location of relationships in a Lewis crofting community' in Anthony P. Cohen (ed.) *Belonging: Identity and Social Organisation in British Rural Cultures* (Manchester: Manchester University Press), pp. 101–130.

Mitchell, James (1999). 'Consensus: Whose Consensus?' in Gerry Hassan and Chris Warhurst (eds) *A Different Future: A Modernisers' Guide To Scotland* (Glasgow: The Big Issue in Scotland and The Centre for Scottish Public Policy), pp. 28–33.

Mitchell, James, David Denver, Charles Pattie and Hugh Bochel (1998). 'The 1997 devolution referendum in Scotland' *Parliamentary Affairs* 51(2): 166–181.

Mitchell, Timothy (1990). 'The limits of the state: Beyond statist approaches and their critics' *American Political Science Review* 85(1): 77–96.

Miyazaki, Hirokazu (2003). 'The temporalities of the market' *American Anthropologist* 105(2): 255–265.

— (2004). *The Method of Hope: Anthropology, Philosophy, and Fijian Knowledge* (Stanford, CA: Stanford University Press).

Moore, Sally Falk (2005). *Law and Anthropology: A Reader* (Oxford: Blackwell Publishing).

Morgan, Bryn (1999). *Scottish Parliament Elections: 6 May 1999* (House of Commons Library Research Paper 99/50).

Nadel-Klein, Jane (1986). 'Burning with the fire of God: Calvinism and community in a Scottish fishing village' *Ethnology* 25(1): 49–60.

— (1995). 'Occidentalism as a cottage industry: Representing the autochthonous "other" in British and Irish rural studies' in James G. Carrier (ed.) *Occidentalism* (Oxford: Oxford University Press), pp. 109–134.

— (1997). 'Crossing a representational divide: From west to east in Scottish ethnography' in Alison James, Jenny Hockey and Andrew Dawson (eds) *After Writing Culture: Epistemology and Praxis in Contemporary Anthropology* (London: Routledge), pp. 86–102.

Nairn, Tom (1997). *Faces of Nationalism: Janus Revisited* (London: Verso).

Navaro-Yashin, Yael (2002). *Faces of the State: Secularism and Public Life in Turkey* (Princeton, NJ: Princeton University Press).

Neville, Cynthia J. (1998). *Violence, Custom and Law: The Anglo-Scottish Border Lands in the Later Middle Ages* (Edinburgh: Edinburgh University Press).

Neville, Gwen Kennedy (1979). 'Community form and ceremonial life in three regions in Scotland' *American Ethnologist* 6(1): 93–109.

— (1987). 'The sacred and the civic: Representations of death in the town ceremony of Scotland' *Anthropological Quarterly* 62(4): 163–173.

Oakeshott, Michael (1962). *Rationalism in Politics and other essays* (London: Methuen and Co.).

Ong, Walter (1982). *Orality and Literacy* (London: Routledge).

Paley, Julia (2001). *Marketing Democracy: Power and Social Movements in Post-Dictatorship Chile* (Berkeley, CA: University of California Press).

Parman, Susan (1990a). *Scottish Crofters: A Historical Ethnography of a Celtic Village* (Fort Worth, TX: Holt, Rinehart and Winston).

— (1990b). 'Orduighean: A dominant symbol in the Free Church of the Scottish Highlands' *American Anthropologist* 92(2): 295–305.

Parry, Richard (1999). 'Quangos and the structure of the public sector in Scotland' *Scottish Affairs* 29: 12–27.

Paterson, Lindsay (1994). *The Autonomy of Modern Scotland* (Edinburgh: Edinburgh University Press).

— (1999). 'Why should we respect civic Scotland?' in Gerry Hassan and Chris Warhurst (eds) *A Different Future: A Modernisers' Guide to Scotland* (Glasgow: The Big Issue in Scotland and The Centre for Scottish Public Policy), pp. 34–42.

Rabinow, Paul (ed.) (1984). *The Foucault Reader* (New York, NY: Pantheon).

Rapport, Nigel (1993). *Diverse World-Views in an English Village* (Edinburgh: Edinburgh University Press).

Rapport, Nigel (ed.) (2002). *British Subjects: An Anthropology of Britain* (Oxford: Berg).

Reed, Adam (2002). 'Henry and I: An ethnographic account of men's fiction reading' *Ethnos* 67(2): 181–200.

Riles, Annelise (1996). 'Division within the boundaries' *Journal of the Royal Anthropological Institute* 4(3): 409–424.

— (1998). 'Infinity within the brackets' *American Ethnologist* 25(3): 378–398.

— (2001). *The Network Inside Out* (Ann Arbor, MI: University of Michigan Press).

— (2003). 'Law as Object' in Sally Engle Merry and Donald Brenneis (eds) *Law and Empire in the Pacific: Fiji and Hawaii* (Santa Fe, NM: School of American Research Press), pp. 187–212.

Riles, Annelise, ed. (2006). *Documents: artifacts of modern knowledge* (Ann Arbor: University of Michigan Press).

Rossiter, D. J., R. J. Johnston and C. J. Pattie (1999). *The Boundary Commissions: Redrawing the UK's map of Parliamentary constituencies* (Manchester: Manchester University Press).

Royal Society of Edinburgh (2002). *Inquiry into Foot and Mouth Disease in Scotland* (Edinburgh: The Royal Society of Edinburgh).

Schofield, R. S. (1968). 'The measurement of literacy in pre-industrial England' in Jack Goody (ed.) *Literacy in Traditional Societies* (Cambridge: Cambridge University Press), pp. 311–325.

Scott, James C. (1998). *Seeing Like a State: How Certain Schemes to Improve the Human Condition Have Failed* (New Haven, CT: Yale University Press).

Seawright, David (1996). 'The Scottish Unionist party: What's in a name?' *Scottish Affairs* 14: 90–102.

— (1998). 'Scottish unionism: An east west divide?' *Scottish Affairs* 23: 54–71.

— (1999). *An Important Matter of Principle: The Decline of the Scottish Conservative and Unionist Party* (Aldershot: Ashgate).

— (2002). 'The Scottish Conservative and Unionist party: "The lesser spotted Tory"?' in G. Hassan and C. Warhurst (eds) *Tomorrow's Scotland* (London: Lawrence and Wishart).

Seidel, Gill (1975). 'Ambiguity in political discourse: A sociolinguistic investigation into a corpus of French political tracts of May '68' in M. Bloch (ed.) *Political Oratory in Traditional Society* (London: Academic Press), pp. 205–226.

Sellen, Abigail J. and Richard H. R. Harper (2003) *The Myth of the Paperless Office* (Cambridge, MA: MIT Press).

Shore, Cris, and Susan Wright (eds) (1997). *Anthropology of Policy: Critical Perspectives on Governance and Power* (London: Routledge).

Smith, Alexander Thomas T. (2008). 'Disaggregating the electoral roll: Electioneering and the politics of self knowledge' *Journal of Legal Anthropology* 1(1): 28–47.

— (2006). 'Dispelling doonhamers: Naming and the numbers game' *Political and Legal Anthropology Review* 29(2): 208–227.

Solway Firth Partnership (2001). *Proceedings of The Solway Firth Partnership Annual Standing Conference* (Dumfries: Scottish Natural Heritage).

Somers, Margaret (1992). 'Narrativity, narrative identity, and social action – Rethinking English working-class formation' *Social Science History* 16(4): 591.

— (1994). 'The narrative constitution of identity: A relational and network approach' *Theory and Society* 23: 605–649.

— (1995). 'Narrating and naturalizing civil society and citizenship theory: The place of political culture in the public sphere' *Sociological Theory* 13(3): 229–274.

Strathern, Andrew, and Pamela J. Stewart (2001). *Minorities and Memories: Survivals and Extinctions in Scotland and Western Europe* (Durham, NC: Carolina Academic Press).

Strathern, Marilyn (1981). *Kinship at the Core: An Anthropology of Elmdon, a Village in North-West Essex in the Nineteen Sixties* (Cambridge: Cambridge University Press).

— (1988). *The Gender of the Gift* (Berkeley, CA: University of California Press).

— (1991). *Partial Connections* (Savage, MD: Rowman and Littlefield) ASAO Special Publications no. 3.

— (1992a). 'Parts and wholes: Refiguring relationships' in Adam Kuper (ed.) *Conceptualizing Society* (New York, NY: Routledge, Chapman and Hall), pp. 204–217.

— (1992b). *Reproducing the Future: Essays on Anthropology, Kinship and the New Reproductive Technologies* (Manchester: Manchester University Press).

— (1992c). *After Nature: English Kinship in the Late Twentieth Century* (Cambridge: Cambridge University Press).

— (1995). 'Foreword: Shifting contexts' in Marilyn Strathern (ed.) *Shifting Contexts: Transformations in Anthropological Knowledge* (London: Routledge), pp. 1–11.

— (1996) 'Cutting the network'. *Journal of the Royal Anthropological Institute* 2(3): 517–535.

— (1999). *Property, Substance and Effect: Anthropological Essays on Persons and Things* (London: Athlone Press).

Strathern, Marilyn (ed.) (2000). *Audit Cultures: Anthropological Studies in Accountability, Ethics and the Academy* (London: Routledge).

Street, Brian (ed.) (1993). *Cross-Cultural Approaches to Literacy* (Cambridge: Cambridge University Press).

Tambiah, Stanley J. (1968a). 'Literacy in a Buddhist village in north-east Thailand' in Jack Goody (ed.) *Literacy in Traditional Societies* (Cambridge: Cambridge University Press), pp. 86–131.

— (1968b). 'The magical power of words' *Man (Lond.)* 3: 175–208.

Taussig, Michael (1997). *The Magic of the State* (New York, NY: Routledge).

Taylor, Brian (1999). *The Scottish Parliament* (Edinburgh: Polygon).

Thompson, Hunter S. (1973). *Fear and Loathing on the Campaign Trail '72* (San Francisco, CA: Straight Arrow Books).

Trevor-Roper, Hugh (1983). 'The invention of tradition: The Highland tradition of Scotland' in Eric Hobsbawm and Terence Ranger (eds) *The Invention of Tradition* (Cambridge: Cambridge University Press).

Tyler, Katharine (2003). 'The racialised and classed constitution of English village life' *Ethnos* 68(3): 391–412.

— (2004). 'Reflexivity, tradition and racism in a former mining town' *Ethnic and Racial Studies* 27(2): 290–309.

Vincent, Joan (ed.) (2002). *The Anthropology of Politics: A Reader in Ethnography, Theory, and Critique* (Oxford: Blackwell Publishing).

Verdery, Katherine (1993). 'Ethnic relations, economics of shortage, and the transition in Eastern Europe' in Chris Hann (ed.) *Socialism: Ideals, ideologies, and local practice* (London: Routledge).

Watson, Rubie S. (1986). 'The named and the nameless: Gender and person in Chinese society' *American Ethnologist* 13(4): 619–631.

Wedeen, Lisa (1999). *Ambiguities of Domination: Politics, Rhetoric and Symbols in Contemporary Syria* (Chicago, IL: University of Chicago Press).

— (2003). 'Seeing like a citizen, acting like a state: Exemplary events in unified Yemen' *Comparative Studies in Society and History* 45(4): 680–713.

— (2004). 'Concepts and commitments in the study of democracy' in Ian Shapiro, Rogers Smith and Tarek Masoud (eds) *Problems and Methods in the Study of Politics* (Cambridge: Cambridge University Press).

Wightman, Andy (1997). *Who Owns Scotland* 2nd edn (Edinburgh: Canongate Books).

— (1999a). *Scotland: Land and Power* (Edinburgh: Luath Press).

— (1999b). 'Land reform: A lever for economic and social renewal' in Gerry Hassan and Chris Warhurst (eds) *A Different Future: A Modernisers' Guide to Scotland* (Edinburgh: Centre for Scottish Public Policy and The Big Issue in Scotland), pp. 147–154.

Williams, Raymond (1975). *The Country and the City* (London: Verso).

Wilson, Richard Ashby (2001). *The Politics or Truth and Reconciliation in South Africa: Legitimizing the Post-Apartheid State* (Cambridge: Cambridge University Press).

— (2003). 'Anthropological studies of national reconciliation processes' *Anthropological Theory* 3(3): 367–387 (Special issue on Political Violence and Language).

Wolf, Eric (1990). *Envisioning Power: Ideologies of Dominance and Crisis* (Berkeley, CA: University of California Press).

Wright, Kenyon (1997). *The People Say Yes: The Making of Scotland's Parliament* (Argyll: Argyll Publishing).

Wright, Patrick (1985). *On Living in an Old Country: The National Past in Contemporary Britain* (London: Verso).

Wright, Susan (ed.) (1994). *Anthropology of Organizations* (London: Routledge).

Index

Lightning Source UK Ltd.
Milton Keynes UK
UKOW04f0719180314

228307UK00001B/31/P